THE ART OF ENGLISH COSTUME

By the same author

THE PERFECT LADY

WHY WOMEN WEAR CLOTHES

ENGLISH WOMEN'S CLOTHING IN THE NINETEENTH CENTURY

FEMININE ATTITUDES IN THE NINETEENTH CENTURY

FEMININE FIGLEAVES

GROUP OF EARLY XVth CENTURY FIGURES

Though executed in France the scene fairly represents
the corresponding English costume. The King's robes are
conventionalised. Note, on the principal standing figure,
the huge hanging sleeves of the green houppelande, with
red linings ; the parti-coloured trunk hose, the high
collar and flat hat.

From La Grande Bible Historiale, Royal MS., British Museum.

THE ART OF
ENGLISH COSTUME

by
C. WILLETT CUNNINGTON

Honorary Adviser to the Gallery of
English Costume, Manchester

'In æsthetics . . . those disclosures which
seem fatal to the dignity of art seem so
perhaps only in the proportion of our
ignorance.'   R. L. STEVENSON

COLLINS ST. JAMES'S PLACE LONDON

FIRST PUBLISHED IN 1948

CONTENTS

PREFACE   1

I   COSTUME—AN ART   3

II   THE USE OF SYMBOLISM   17

III   SOURCES OF INFORMATION   31

IV   ÆSTHETIC ASPECTS OF COSTUME   37

V   THE PRINCIPLES OF FORM   46

VI   FORM IN MAN'S COSTUME   55

VII   HEADGEAR IN MAN'S COSTUME   70

VIII   FORM IN WOMAN'S COSTUME   79

IX   WOMAN'S SLEEVE AND GLOVE   94

X   WOMAN'S HEADGEAR AND HAIR   105

XI   OTHER FACTORS AFFECTING FORM   120

XII   THE PRINCIPLES OF COLOUR   133

XIII   THE USE OF COLOUR   147

XIV   TEXTURE AND MATERIALS   163

XV   MOBILITY IN COSTUME   176

XVI   PRINCIPLES OF SEX-ATTRACTION   192

XVII   SEX-ATTRACTION IN MAN'S COSTUME   206

XVIII   SEX-ATTRACTION IN WOMAN'S COSTUME   218

APPENDIX A   233

APPENDIX B   235

INDEX   237

COLOURED ILLUSTRATIONS

GROUP OF EARLY XV CENTURY FIGURES, FROM
LA GRANDE BIBLE HISTORIALE, ROYAL MS., BRITISH
MUSEUM   *Frontispiece*

PORTRAIT OF ANNE VAVASOUR BY MARC GHEER-   *facing page*
AERTS, 1605   36

PORTRAIT OF LOUISE RENEE DE PENENCOUET DE
QUEROUAILLE,   DUCHESS   OF   PORTSMOUTH,
PAINTED IN 1682 (AGED 35) BY MIGNARD   100

COLOURED DRAWING OF FLORENCE NIGHTINGALE
(SEATED) AND HER SISTER, BY WILLIAM WHITE, 1839   164

MONOCHROME ILLUSTRATIONS

Plates 1-16 *follow text page* 68

1. Group of figures from the tomb of Sir Roger de Kerdeston, 1340
2. Effigy of Beatrice, Countess of Arundel, 1439
3. Effigy of Joan, Countess of Arundel, 1487
4a. Brass of Alice, wife of Sir J. Hanley, 1403
4b. Brass of Elizabeth Clere, 1488
5. Brass of man and wife, Norwich, 1430
6. Urswyk brass, Dagenham, 1479
7a. Brass of Elizabeth Perepoynt, 1543
7b. Brass of G. Coles and wives, 1640
8a. Effigy of Lady Fitzherbert of Norbury, 1483
8b. Effigy of wife and daughters of Sir J. Suckling, 1629
9. Portrait of a Gentleman in Red, 1548
10. Portrait of the Princess Elizabeth, 1540-50
11. Men's headgear, *circa* 1600
12. Miniature of the Earl of Dorset, 1616
13. Effigy of the daughters of Lord Teynham, 1620
14. Caricature of a Cavalier, 1646
15. Portrait of a Lady, 1635
16. Women on horseback, a. 15th and b. 17th centuries

Plates 17-32 *follow text page* 132

17. Portrait of Mary Pettus, 1740
18. Portrait of Charles Tottenham, *circa* 1745
19. Portrait of the Vanneck family, by Devis, 1752
20. Portrait group of gentlemen, by Batoni, *circa* 1760
21. The Polonaise of 1777
22. Westminster Election, by Dighton, 1788
23. Fashion plate. Evening dress, 1807

x

24a. Brass of Lady Sacheverell, 1558
24b. Fashion plate, 1822
25. " Bond Street Loungers," 1820
26. Caricature of 1827
27. Line drawing of Alfred D'Orsay, 1828
28. Portrait of Alderman Watkins, 1845
29. Two carte de visites, 1860, 1862
30. Two carte de visites, 1865, 1872
31a. Hyde Park costume, 1885
31b. Golfing costumes, 1894
32. Gentlemen's walking costumes, 1865 and 1870

Plates 33-48 *follow text page* 196

33. Fashion plate, 1874
34. Fashion plate, 1878
35. Photograph of archery group, 1862
36. Group photograph, 1866
37. Photograph of ladies' tennis costumes, 1884
38. Fashion plate of evening dresses, 1878
39. Photograph of bathing costume, 1886
40. Fashion plate of garden party dress, 1895
41. Fashion plate of man's lounge suit, 1906
42. Photograph of dress of black face cloth, 1908
43. Fashion plate of " Hobble-skirt " costume, 1912
44. Photograph of Ascot dress, 1923
45. Photograph of backless evening frock, 1930
46a. " The New Look "
46b. Dress of spotted red sateen, 1886.
47. Photograph of tailored afternoon dress, 1947
48. Photograph of evening gown, 1947

ACKNOWLEDGMENTS FOR ILLUSTRATIONS

Reproduced by gracious permission of His Majesty the King

plate 9

Hardy Amies Ltd. *plate* 47

The British Museum *Frontispiece and plate* 14

The Corporation of Manchester *plate* 28

The Daily Mail *plate* 39

Messrs. Debenham & Freebody *plate* 48

Mr. Arthur Gardner *plate* 8a

Mr. Francis Howard
Portrait of Anne Vavasour by MARC GHEERAERTS

Messrs. Jacqmar Ltd., London *plate* 46a

Messrs. M. Knoedler & Co. *plates* 19 *and* 20

Mr. Le Grice *plate* 8b

Manchester City Art Galleries *plate* 15

The National Buildings Record *plate* 13

The Board of Governors, National Gallery of Ireland *plate* 18

The National Portrait Gallery
Portrait of the Duchess of Portsmouth by MIGNARD
Portrait of Florence Nightingale and her sister by WILLIAM WHITE

Norwich Museums Committee *plate* 17

The Oxford University Press *plate* 21
(From *English Women in Life and Letters* by M. PHILLIPS and
W. S. TOMKINSON)

Planet News Ltd. *plate* 45

Messrs. Spink & Son Ltd. *plate* 22

The Tailor and Cutter *plates* 41 *and* 43

The Victoria and Albert Museum
plates 6, 7a *and* 7b, 12, *and* 24a

Mr. Victor Stiebel 46a

PREFACE

THE aim of this book is to present the continuity of a living art ; to indicate how it has grown from those early expressions of it, some six centuries ago, in which we are just able to trace the origins of our own styles arising from human desires which we share with our ancestors.

I have tried to emphasise that the Art of English Costume does not exhibit merely a series of disconnected historical episodes in pictorial guise. Passing events have left finger-prints but the stuff and substance of the Art continues ; there have been no abrupt gaps ; the overlapping of styles has never been absent. Beneath the upper layers of the fashionable world always there has been a stratum of tradition blending the present with the past. Marks of the middle ages still survive.

And there has always been an undercurrent—the English artistic impulse—flowing quietly through the centuries in spite of twists and turns and obstructions, sometimes coming to the surface, sometimes hidden under the froth of Fashion. There is, and always has been, the natural desire to beautify in a characteristic English way : to arouse agreeable emotional reactions and, in the wearer of costumes, to enjoy the effect they produce on others.

Mankind has seized with avidity on this ingenious way of expressing ideas and provoking feelings.

Unlike most forms of Art, that of Costume requires more than a passive audience ; it needs the active co-operation of artist, client and spectators together, and it is that which gives it its human quality, to be seen at its best not in the austerity of museums, but in the bustle of life. It reminds us that we have not really changed much in essentials these six hundred years ; we have the same impulses though we express them differently, perhaps, and find other means of satisfying them.

Such a book as this, then, attempts to exemplify a thesis by selecting from a mass of material sufficient to illustrate the conception of Costume as a living Art. Details which do not clarify the purpose, or might obscure it, are omitted.

I

The causes of the innumerable changes of expression, which we call " Fashions," have been traced in general terms. It has always seemed to me to be quite insufficient to " explain " a fashion, or indeed any art form, by stating that it came from France or Italy or Spain, just because that particular country happened at the moment to be a dominating influence. We do not borrow an artistic impulse ; what we often do borrow is the technical method of expressing it, and that only if it happens to be an improvement on our own. When it suits us we borrow technique, but not otherwise. The underlying ideas which we try to express in our art forms are a native product.

The distinction becomes clear if we compare the English fashions of any period with contemporaries of some other country. Those are seen, no doubt, to have points in common ; much more significant, of course, is the fact that they differ.

It is that distinction which reveals the true national art sense. As Costume is an Art, it follows that when we wear clothing of our own choice we all become artists. We are trying, not always with success, to paint a picture that tells a story. It is this picture, composed by a whole nation during six centuries, and still being added to, that this book tries to describe.

The illustrations have been selected, as far as is practicable, from those not too familiar to readers of books on this subject, in the belief that fresh faces reveal more than those we know too well.

In the appreciation of Costume it is not the meticulous detail, but the general impression that matters, and I have therefore omitted reference to technical methods of construction. We are viewing a comedy from the front of the house, not exploring the dressing-rooms. We don't need to know the tricks of make-up ; we don't need to peep at the back of the scenery. We are content to sit in the stalls and watch the curtain go up.

I am greatly indebted to my friend, J. L. Nevinson, for suggestions and criticism, especially for Costume details of the sixteenth and seventeenth centuries, periods which he has made his own. I have also received great kindness from those in charge of museums, libraries and art galleries, in allowing me to examine the contents, and, in some cases, reproduce them as illustrations.

2

CHAPTER I

COSTUME—AN ART

VISUAL ART is the arrangement of materials so as to express Ideas. The nature of the materials determines the kind of Art ; the nature of the arrangement determines its Style ; the nature of the ideas determines its Theme.

Each of these elements can vary in quality, so that " good art " and " bad art " are equivocal terms unless we know to which element they apply ; the relative attention paid to each element varies at different times, so that in one epoch it may be the novelty of materials, in another the ingenuity of arrangement or the loftiness of the theme which appeals most to the artistic instincts of a community.

It follows that in comparing art forms of one epoch with those of another we must be sure that we are, in reality, comparing like with like, and not two different categories, when we are tempted to describe one as " good art " and the other as " bad."

These considerations apply to the oldest of the arts, Costume. Primitive man very early in his career came to realise that clothing, in addition to its utility function, could be used to express ideas ; indeed, this may well have been its primary purpose. At any rate, he discovered that a distinctive garb would denote the tribal chief, the witch-doctor, and also distinguish one sex from the other. The primitive ideas thus expressed were those of social rank, occupation, and sex attraction.

Clothing, by expressing ideas, had become the art we call *Costume* ; an art which has been pre-occupied with those three fundamental ideas ever since.

It is convenient to preserve the word *Clothing* to

denote garb which is functional only, its purpose being to protect the body from the forces of nature ; Costume, on the other hand, as an expression of ideas, must necessarily recognise the presence of other human beings, to whom its significance is mutely directed. In a word, Costume is an Art which implies spectators, without whom it would have no meaning.

The clothing of people who have adopted solitary life rapidly loses its quality of " costume "—that is, it ceases to express ideas though it may express habits. It becomes incongruous with odds and ends borrowed perhaps from the other sex, if such happen to be convenient. Utility becomes the only desideratum. In fact, Costume is seen to be an art which cannot survive for long in solitude.

From its primitive beginnings this art expanded its range of Ideas so as to express not merely objective notions, but also subjective, such as states of feeling, joy, grief and the like, especially by the differential use of colours.

It was further realised that Costume could not only express the emotions of the wearer, but that it could induce emotions in the spectator, such as fear or admiration, and, of course, arouse sexual interest. Thus, unlike other arts, the aim of Costume can be both subjective and objective, and its psychological effects on the wearer are apt to be overlooked when costumes of a remote period are being considered. The question should, in fact, occur to us, was that particular mode intended primarily to express the wearer's mind, or to impress the spectator's ? Is the idea represented an exposure or an imposure ? As civilisation has advanced man's Costume has become more and more a part of himself, so that it has acquired some of the properties of an outer skin—almost an artificial organ of expression. We look at his face (the principal part of his body still left naked) in order to judge of his character, his feelings, and even his breeding ; but in many cases we could learn more from his costume ; the apparel oft betrays the man.

We no longer regard Costume as only a disguise ; in fact it may well be the opposite, exposing all manner of thoughts and desires of which the wearer is scarcely conscious. Costume is far more revealing than nudity ; hence, no doubt, its greater attraction. We cannot therefore fully appreciate this art unless we always remember that here is something highly significant, whether we have sufficient historical knowledge for its interpretation or not.

Costume presents the resultant of forces which may be opposed ; there is the normal human impulse to beautify the body, and there are impulses which may be sufficiently strong to overcome that inclination, for the time being. Thus, the desire to inspire fear may outweigh the desire for admiration, appearing hostile rather than friendly, repelling rather than attract-ing, and there are moments when a cloak of ugliness signifies a desolate spirit that would shun the world. Ugliness, indeed, may be the most suitable medium for expressing ideas which cannot be implied in forms of beauty.

In fact, when we examine the innumerable modes which Costume has assumed at different times—and we marvel at some of the more astonishing—we are surprised only because we have failed to understand their real significance. There was always a motive inspiring them, an imperative need to express an idea, and human beings will go to any length to accomplish that end, checked only by the normal preference for the beautiful, and, in the case of costumes, by the practical limits of what can be worn. However extravagant and awkward those fashions may be—and they may have to be so in order to express corresponding ideas—yet in the long run beauty and utility will restore law and order, and a wave of hysteria may be followed by one of austerity.

The point that is often overlooked is that hysterical fashions will, of themselves, relieve an emotional tension, and so lead the way to sobriety.

Elsewhere I have defined Fashion as " a taste shared by a large number of people for a short space of time." It tells us of some pervasive influence temporarily distorting the sense of beauty ; the two are, in fact, antagonistic. How paradoxical, then, to speak of a " beautiful fashion ! "

The Art of Costume displays a continuous oscillation, the desire for beauty, never wholly in abeyance, acting like gravity on the swing of the pendulum. Consequently in most fashions we can detect elements of unsophisticated beauty blended with features which are the product of other impulses.

This compromise is, and generally has been, a distinctive quality in English Costume. We do not love extremes. We seldom favour the heights reached by other nations, nor do we sink to their depths. Perhaps we are restrained by our innate sense of beauty, or is it only our sense of humour ? At any rate, we do not encourage hysterical displays, and extreme forms of fashion must usually be searched for elsewhere than in England.

The Art of Costume is intimately associated with morals, an important aspect of which it represents, as it were, pictorially.

At the same time its excursions as a form of art exploring new modes of expression are limited by the moral conventions of the day ; not, be it observed, of yesterday.

It is, in fact, a moral art, and, as we criticise the costumes of some past epoch, we cannot judge them fairly as works of art unless we realise what were the conventions of their time.

6

We see this art sometimes tugging at a moral leash, as though eager to scamper ahead, sometimes in chastened mood, following at the heels of propriety.

Without some acquaintance with the habits of an epoch we may easily draw false conclusions from its costumes. Often, of course, the evidence is convincing enough. Our early sixteenth century, for example, employed styles massive in strength of design, with men clothed in almost brutal masculinity. We may safely deduce from them that an exuberant vitality was in the air, and that vigour rather than grace was the ideal (*Plate* 9)

Similarly the modes of the eighteenth century suggest from their complicated elegance that it was scarcely an age of spiritual austerity.

On the other hand, while we may draw moral deductions from widespread fashions, such as followed the first Great War, it would be dangerous to conclude from the fashions worn after the Restoration of 1660, by ladies of that court, that licentious conduct was then the general habit of English women. The fashionable portrait painter is seldom a safe guide to current morality.

Costume tells us, in dumb show, a good deal about standards of what we call " decency." The term is, of course, only a relative one, for what is considered " decent " in one age may be thought " indecent " in another. Everyone is aware that many of the costumes worn to-day would have horrified our grandparents. But we must not assume that the change has always been in one direction, nor conclude that it will continue so. If, for example, a modern girl in tennis costume were to meet across the net a man of A.D. 1500 also in his tennis costume it would be hard to say which would be the more shocked at the sight.

It is singular that while the frank display of sexual features has been for some six centuries accepted as

7

" decent " in female costume, a corresponding exhibition in male costume has been limited to less than two, say from Agincourt to the Armada, with a modified revival in the tight buck-skin breeches of the Regency ; from which we may conclude that a fashion which the modern mind would reject as " indecent " was then accepted without apparent protest.

We might suppose, if we were to rely wholly on their respective costumes, that a portrait of Henry VIII must have offended the chaster mind of Charles II.

Evidently it is not safe to assume that anatomical display is necessarily " indecent " or even provocative. It may be by our standards, but not considered so by another generation, past or future.

The influence of religion, as exerted by the Church on the art of Costume, cannot be ignored. It has usually been directed against the very human inclination to use that art to increase the interest of the sexes in each other. The records of the middle ages abound in fulminations against fashions that, to the theological eye, appeared inflammatory. Sometimes one must suppose that one needed a long course of monastic training to be able to detect, in the shape of a shoe or a hat, or the cut of a sleeve, this Satanic influence ; even to-day there are divines so gifted that a mere trifle, such as the modern bathing costume, will cause them to boil over ; for it happens in all forms of art that if the technique is unfamiliar the idea expressed by it is often misunderstood. The cure, obviously, is greater familiarity.

But apart from these curiosities, the restraint exercised by the Church has been, on the whole, for the ultimate benefit of the Art of Costume. It has tended to control the range of ideas which that art has, from time to time, tried to express. The Church has stamped with its approval those fashions which benefit the community as a whole, while disapproving of those which might give the individual a fictitious advantage. It has always thrown its weight in the scale of modesty ; and in the Art of Costume modesty usually means, in effect, a preference for a simple technique as against an extravagant one, though sometimes modesty may itself be lavishly proclaimed by devices which are in themselves extravagant.

In all arts over-emphasis is condemned as bad technique, and in Costume especially so, whether we are supported in our condemnation by reasons theological or æsthetic.

The history of this art tells us that the Church, in its long contest with human instincts, has not been without its victories ; at least, the enemy has sometimes been driven underground. One of the most remarkable phases of apparently effective suppression was in the long period before the fourteenth century when for centuries the costume of the sexes was not markedly differentiated, at least to the extent we have become accustomed to, and that of women was almost entirely lacking those features which the modern eye regards as " sex-attractive."

A kind of nun-like garb, century after century, concealed the physical contours, and supplied an attitude of serene passionless dignity to the female figure. The hand of the Church, it seems, lay heavy on her. In outward appearance almost a nun, but what was beneath ? We cannot tell. History tells us that she had little or no choice in the selection of a mate ; the arts of allurement would therefore have been superfluous.

At any rate, with singular abruptness, early in the fourteenth century, the Englishwoman of the superior classes began to discard that conventional garb (*Plate* 1), and she and the man of her day soon after burst out into a riot of costume designs in which " sex attraction," as we understand it, formed a very obvious motif.[1]

[1] 1347. The trousseau of Princess Joan, aged 14, included a " double cotehardie for riding," a forerunner of the riding habit, and also corsets.

9

From that date, too, the respective costumes of the sexes have preserved a distinction which is in itself an attraction. We know that the change, the most marked that has ever taken place in the history of English costume, occurred at a time when the domination of the Church had greatly relaxed. We may suppose— but it is only a supposition—that the two were related as cause and effect ; a more weighty cause, in all probability, was the fact that women were no longer being regarded as mere chattels to be bought and sold. They were, in fact, beginning to select their mates instead of these being chosen for them, and the costumes of both sexes suggest very strongly that social life, at least for those classes, was becoming tinctured with a new interest.

Chaucer, writing towards the end of the century, ascribed the change of costume which had occurred about 1327 to the " coming of the Hainaulters." He referred to the followers of Queen Isabella and Mortimer when they returned from Flanders, dethroned Edward II, and put the youthful Edward III on the throne: " They ordeyned and changed every year divers shapes of disguisings of clothing of long large and wide clothes, destitute and desert from all old honeste and good usage ; and another time short clothes and tight-waisted, dragged and cut on every side slashed and loose with sleeves and tippets of surcoats and hoods over long and large and overmuch hanging ; that they were more like to tormentors and devils than common men ; and the women more foolishly surpassed the men in array . . . the which peradventure afterward brought forth and encaused many mishaps and mischiefs in the realm of England." In short, it was all the fault of " those foreigners."

There is another effect traceable to Christian morality as expounded by the Church, which the Art of Costume has often betrayed in its fashions when the expression of natural instincts has been forbidden, namely the excessive use of erotic symbols ; so that the Church's teaching may be in part responsible for the very thing it so strongly condemns.

The influence of religious beliefs on this art is seldom entirely absent, for habits once established linger long after those beliefs have lost their original vitality. Even to-day the " Sunday best " is not quite extinct from the wardrobe of many. During the Victorian age the bonnet, and not the hat, was for some reason considered proper for women to wear in a sacred edifice, where, of course, the ungloved naked hands should never be exposed to the eyes of their Maker.

Some, at least, of the vicissitudes which the art of English Costume has experienced since the earliest times may be attributed to such moral influences ; we have had phases of apparent " repression," and phases of " exhibitionism," and we might ape the scientists in constructing a graph showing on a curve the effect of these and similar causal agents. The result would be curious but unconvincing, for Art defies the groping fingers of Science striving to explain human nature.

It has been mentioned that ideas of social distinction and occupation are among the principal ones which the Art of Costume attempts to indicate. Here, too, it tends to fall back on the use of symbols as the most obvious way of doing so ; expensive materials and jewellery were always the hallmark of a special class. Frequently the single and the married woman have had distinctive dress, and in the middle ages sumptuary laws attempted, though usually in vain, to confine the use of particular styles to certain ranks. Perhaps less obvious but more interesting are those features in Costume which appear to be positively awkward to wear, and to serve no practical purpose. We might instance the lace collars and ruffles of the seventeenth century cavalier—or equally the starched collar still in use (*Plates* 11, 14, 25). Inconvenient to wear, no doubt, but very convenient as indicating that the proud owner did not earn his living by heavy manual work : ergo, that he belonged to a superior social level. So, too, the trailing skirts of the Victorian lady signified that she did not belong to the walking classes.

We see, in fact, all through the centuries forms of costume which were, one supposes, intentionally uncomfortable or inconvenient. Their purpose was doubtless to indicate a social habit or distinction, which, at this distance of time, we can only guess at. After all, human beings don't make themselves uncomfortable unless for a reason which, in their judgment, outweighs the physical discomfort ; but mental discomfort is the more intolerable, as most of us discover if we find ourselves in the wrong sort of attire at some social function.

When the modern spectator, oblivious of his or her own unreasonable fashions, ridicules those of the past, it only means that their purpose is not understood. The fault lies with the spectator. So, too, when a past fashion does not obey the laws which we are pleased to lay down as governing beauty, to dismiss it as " bad taste " is to ignore the primary object of this art. People have never made themselves needlessly ugly except for some strong inducement, though we may be unable to discover what that was. And we must always recollect that Costume is never concerned with the verdict of posterity. From time to time enthusiasts attempt to " reform " this art, and invent styles divorced from tradition, in designs that shall be not only supremely comfortable, but also conforming to whatever rules govern good art at the moment. But as such designs express no ideas, the rest of humanity will have none of them.

The Art of Costume, then, is seen to be a curious blend of the obvious and the subtle ; it presents a picture and also a puzzle. Always there is something to tempt the speculative observer to ask : why this, thus ? For nothing is worn by men and women without a purpose, though that may be hidden even from the wearer.

If we examine the costume of the individual, we find that it deviates, if ever so slightly, from the standard pattern of the epoch or social set. Touches of individuality are apparent. The wearer selects details that, in his judgment, become his personality, for no one is so humble that he is willing to abandon his individuality. He assumes a costume that will express the characteristics which he wishes to display, and conceal those he does not care to reveal. (Most of us are more successful in the former than in the latter, for our efforts to conceal are often traitors.)

How much of man's dignity is due to his tailor, and woman's charm to her dressmaker, can be judged if, by some mischance, we are seen in wholly inappropriate clothing ; so, too, the individual's personality almost vanishes when it is garbed in uniform, which, in fact, is the purpose of uniforms.

A costume freely chosen is rich in information, though we may not be able to say, of specimens in the past, how much was individual taste and how much was the taste of the day, unless, of course, we have a large number of contemporary costumes from which to judge.

So, too, the fact that a particular style known to have been common in one country appears to have left no trace in another, becomes significant only if our search has been exhaustive. Its absence, if sufficiently established, then indicates that some influence was strong enough to prevent the art of that country from employing the feature in question. The history of English Costume affords many such examples ; the high " steeple " headgear, known as the " hennin," was commonly worn in the fifteenth century by women in Burgundy, and has, in fact, survived in Normandy and Brittany as part of peasant dress. It was assumed by English authorities

13

until comparatively lately that this fashion had doubtless
been adopted in this country ; but, as pointed out by
the late Francis Kelly, modern research has failed to
discover a single example in the brasses and similar
records of English origin, and therefore we are now
entitled to conclude from such negative evidence that
the extreme form of the " steeple " hennin was never an
English fashion.[1]

Thomas Walsingham (d. 1422) in his *Hist. Angl.*
stated : " About the middle of the fourteenth century
there was hardly a female, who could be styled a gentle-
woman, that had not in her house some portion of the
spoils . . . from Caen, Calais or the cities beyond the
seas." Many of such purely " Continental " extrava-
gances seem to have revolted our English common sense ;
some were perhaps regarded as " bad art ; " others
were too explanatory of hidden thoughts and feelings ;
but whatever the restraint was due to, we have to reckon
it an important factor controlling the art of Costume,
and indeed other forms of art as well, in this country.
Polydore Vergil, writing *circa* 1520, remarked : " The
English ladies wore habits made according to the French
mode, whereby they lost on the side of modesty more
than they gained in point of grace." Moderation is
our national characteristic.

In Costume we may have borrowed largely from
abroad, but almost always with an inclination to modify
what we borrow, and thus to stamp it with an English
touch.

It remains to consider briefly some other factors

[1] While the " steeple " hennin has never appeared in this country
—except in theatrical productions—modifications or substitutes in
headdresses shaped like flower-pots or domed liked brimless bowlers
are not infrequently found. Of the former sort examples may be seen
in the wall paintings in Eton College, in the effigy of the Countess of
Westmorland at Brancepeth church, Durham (1485), or in the
Urswyk brass (*Plate* 6) at Dagenham, Essex (1479). Examples of the
domed variety appear in the effigy of Lady Crosby, Great St. Helen's
church, London (1480), and in the brass of Elizabeth Clere (*Plate* 4b)
at Stokesby church, Norfolk (1488).

affecting the development of the art in this country. In general terms we may say that the range and quality of the materials used have, of course, progressively improved, together with the technical skill of those working with them ; we have, as against this, to recognise that, especially in the last hundred years, the art has appealed to a much wider and less cultured class, whose tastes are necessarily less exacting, and for whom quality has had to be subservient to cost. The ideas expressed by an art under such circumstances tend to be trite ; mass-produced work can hardly be otherwise. So that the advance in the art of Costume must at some point in its career have received a check from these conditions, in spite of progress in invention.

If we were to attempt to decide at what period the art of Costume reached its acme in this country, it would be difficult to resist the claim of the years about 1870. And for these reasons. The nation's prosperity at that moment allowed the numerous—but not too numerous—patrons of the art full scope. Materials were abundant, and still of a high quality, though the first signs of adulteration were starting. The tailor and the dressmaker were extraordinarily skilful, and still individual in their work.

In particular, the period was distinguished by the introduction of highly important new ideas into the realm of Costume. The novelty of the walking dress, the sports costume, and the " tailor-made," then appearing as a distinctive style for the first time in the history of women's dress, marked a profound change in their social status, and were, in fact, the only really original ideas contributed to feminine costume since the fourteenth century.[1] In addition, men's clothing had begun to shake itself free from the last vestiges of the

---

[1] Until the eighteenth century, women's dresses were made by men tailors. See the account books of Joyce Jeffreys (end of seventeenth century).

old " peacock " tradition, and was acquiring the wholly new notion of physical comfort—a homely but significant innovation.

It is worth noting that all these new ideas were contributed by this country which, as we are so often told, always lags behind others in the art of Costume.

Measured by its technique and its ideas—the only proper test—the epoch of 1870 stands out above its rivals. The fact that in its range of ideas some, then novel, have now become commonplace, while others, then vital, are now obsolete, should not affect our judgment.

This preliminary survey of the principle factors affecting the Art of English Costume is intended to remind the reader of the essential meaning of that art. To appreciate it we may sometimes have to put aside prejudices of our own day, and we must have sympathetic understanding of the ideals of former times.

We must avoid the vulgar error of *looking down* on our ancestors, and on the kind of ideas which engrossed their attention. Is our own superiority sufficiently established to permit of that?

In criticising the technique of this art we can hardly fail to be struck by its fondness for the use of *symbols*, and it will be convenient to discuss this artistic mannerism in a separate chapter.

CHAPTER II

THE USE OF SYMBOLISM

A SYMBOL is a sign associated with an Idea, and, as we might expect, has always been a device commonly used in the Art of Costume. If its meaning is well understood it can convey a great deal to the spectator ; thus, a cross, a crown, or a broad arrow worn by a person would express very distinct ideas about the wearer.

The design of a garment or the pattern of a textile may be more or less reminiscent or suggestive of ideas which convention does not permit to be plainly stated. Such are the many erotic and the occasional religious symbols appearing in Costume (apart from the ecclesiastical vestments which are so largely symbolic in origin).

Symbols may also be used to indicate in the wearer, or to induce in the spectator, a variety of emotional states, and this is particularly so with colours, some of which have acquired a specific significance, such as black for mourning, white for purity.

A further group of symbols, often used to indicate occupation or social rank, are, in fact, vestiges of some item of Costume which once had a recognised function associated with them, such as the scholastic gown, or the " gentleman's " dress suit.

The list might be extended indefinitely, but for our purpose it is sufficient if we bear in mind that some symbols indicate a function, past or present, while others are purely arbitrary in origin and have obtained their special significance only from custom (and when we say custom we probably mean a long-standing association of ideas). At this point the question may be asked, why do we employ symbols in Costume at all ?

Why, especially, should they gratify the wearer or impress the spectator more, in fact, than a plain statement of the idea implied by them ? Instead of costly raiment to indicate wealth, a necklace of banknotes would surely be even more convincing, or, in place of strawberry leaves on a coronet, why not a plain label, " I am a duke ? "[1]

Our interest is not aroused by the obvious, and symbols please better than realities just because they excite the imagination to interpret them, and this is conspicuously the case with erotic symbols which gratify by subtle allusion. These whisper what must not be spoken aloud. The original meaning of such symbols may have been forgotten, and all that remains is a tradition that in some peculiar way they have agreeable associations. We may choose to explain this survival of flavour as a stirring of the unconscious memory or, more simply, by the fact that it was liked by our predecessors and we accept their tastes without question. Force of habit is, after all, as good an explanation as one more recondite and Freudian.

We know that habits persist but also that they may fade, and a good example of this is our use of black. A sad colour ? Only from centuries of association with the idea of mourning, originally used to render the grief-stricken less conspicuous, hence a symbol of grief : hence a " sad colour." But some races have used other colours, such as red which the Romans wore for mourning ; and as mourning itself is rapidly disappearing and black is being used more and more as a convenient colour for daily work, its old associations

---

[1] It has been observed that in the Balkans, now that gold coins have disappeared, women will sometimes adorn themselves with paper money wrapped up in cellophane, in place of the old necklace of coins. It would answer the purpose of displaying evidence of wealth if we were to wear our income-tax receipts in some conspicuous place.

are fading, and it is even being employed as a decorative tint. Losing its symbolic value it is acquiring an æsthetic one.

So, too, symbols formerly charged with feeling may lose their " emotional tone " and become inert, a fate which has overtaken woman's glove, once a trophy over which poets sang and lovers wept ; and also her shoe, a peep at which was once a cherished privilege, but having lost its emotional tone it has also lost its graceful design.

On the other hand the emotional tone of a symbol may increase until it outstrips that of the idea it represents ; thus, the eroticism of woman's underclothing (suggestive, of course, of undressing) may be more " attractive " than actual nudity which leaves nothing to excite the imagination. (It is significant that man's underclothing has never possessed a similar charm.)

It may be noted that the emotional tone of a symbol tends to fade with too frequent display ; feminine underclothing was most effective in the days when it was least visible ; royal purple no longer arouses a sense of awe, just as the coachman's cockade and the gentleman's top hat have ceased to inspire respect.

Nevertheless we cling to symbols which have vague historical associations, especially in ceremonial costume ; they add a picturesque touch without which the occasion would lose its impressiveness. We would not be without our beefeaters in their Tudor costume, or our lifeguards arrayed in relics of the seventeenth, eighteenth and nineteenth centuries, with a bit of fifteenth century plate armour thrown in.

Even our postmen, though they no longer ride about the country from one post to another, retain in their uniform traces of the coaching days. Indeed, the insignia of office, such as a mayor's chain, and the various kinds of uniform, both civil and military, are useful symbols to remind spectators that the wearers are not merely individuals but are representatives of law and order.

While most of the depressing symbolism that used to accompany funerals has now happily disappeared, we are generally reluctant to abandon the symbols without which a wedding would seem, in the eyes of many, to be scarcely " proper ; " the bride still insists on being married in white, the symbol of purity, with a veil, the symbol of virginity, to a bridegroom in " morning suit," the symbol of gentility, and she wears a ring, the symbol of union, is married in church, the symbol of respectability, and departs under a shower of confetti, the symbol of fertility, for what is symbolically described as a " honeymoon."

But in addition to these types, of which a moment's consideration will recall innumerable petty examples, the Art of Costume uses features which are less readily recognised as symbols.

Mere exaggeration of size is a case in point, giving a fictitious air of grandeur and importance ; the Court train and indeed all large trailing garments seem to magnify the wearer's personality. This device may be applied to some particular region of the body, and it is significant that the ceremonial costume of the learned professions draws special attention to the head, the centre of learning, by various kinds of striking headgear such as the legal wig, larger on the (presumably) more learned judge than on the (presumably) less learned barrister : the bishop's mitre, larger than the curate's wide-awake, and the Tudor cap of the University " doctor," more impressive than the undergraduate's mortar-board. Similarly when women wish to add to their dignity they enlarge their distinctive garment, the skirt, which on special occasions may trail for yards behind them. It is said that Empress Catherine of Russia's coronation robe had a train of a hundred and twenty feet.

So, too, the use of the hoop, as worn by women in the sixteenth, eighteenth and nineteenth centuries, by keeping bystanders at arm's length, was clearly a symbol intended to give an air of mystery to the unattainable. The huge hanging sleeve which we see in the fifteenth century houppelande (and *Frontispiece Plate* 5), and which has survived in the master of arts' gown, was originally a device whereby the civilian demonstrated his growing importance in the state, and that his was not a profession of " arms." A more peaceful symbol could scarcely be devised, with sleeves encumbering every movement but at the same time magnifying his appearance. A queer form of local enlargement is the exaggeration in the apparent size of the feet, as in the fifteenth century, by extending the length of the shoe, and in the sixteenth by expanding its breadth. The extravagant length of the pointed shoe of the fifteenth century does not seem to have been so marked in this country as elsewhere. But Holinshed's Chronicle of 1586, writing on 5. Ed. IV of 1465, states : " This year it was proclaimed in England that the beakes or pikes of shooes and boots should not pass two inches, upon paine of cursing by the cleargie. . . . Before this and since the yeare of our Lord 1382 the pikes of shooes and boots were of such length that they were fain to be tied up to the knees with chaines of silver and gilt, or at least with silken laces."

The first paragraph is in the Statute. The second is unsupported by evidence.

The pointed toe served to draw attention to the lower limb then displayed in tights. " The men wore shoes with a point before, half a foot long ; the richer and more eminent personages wore them a foot, and princes two feet long, which was the most ridiculous thing that ever was seen." (Paradin, Histoire de Lyons.)

In the sixteenth century, in the reign of Queen Mary, " square toes were grown into fashion insomuch that men wore shoes of so prodigious a breadth that there was a proclamation that no man should wear his shoes above six inches square at the toe." (Bulver, 1653.)

We may suppose this fashion added to the " he-man " appearance and helped to balance the otherwise top-heaviness of the costume.

Similarly all manner of symbols to emphasise, usually by exaggeration of size, the secondary sexual character-istics have been frequently employed ; to increase the breadth of men's shoulders by padding, as in the fifteenth century, when the practice was condemned as " a thing exceedingly vain and displeasing in the sight of God," is a familiar example seen to-day.

Although woman's costume has often expanded the shoulders in order to diminish the apparent size of the waist by contrast, the curved outline of the female shoulder has usually been carefully preserved, although the modern woman in imitation of masculine habits has borrowed man's square shoulder line.

A survey of the Art of Costume reveals that while the face has always been a principal point of interest, the degree of attention drawn to it has varied enormously. In women especially it has been at times almost in-significant, as though the feelings it might display were unimportant or—shall we say ?—too private for publica-tion. At least, we get that impression from the thirteenth century wimple and veil as equally as from the early Victorian bonnet. The Victorian hat, aggressively appearing in the 1860's as a symbol of emancipation, released the face from its prison house, and from that day it has never " looked back."

It is notorious that woman has, from time immemorial, used a host of devices to make her face either more " beautiful " (that is, more attractive) or more inscrut-able ; the first category of fashions men have accepted with complacence but have disapproved of the second. Thus at the end of the Fourteenth Century : " Fair daughters, see that you pluck not away the hairs from your eyebrows, nor from your temples nor from your foreheads, to make them appear higher than Nature has ordained." But, as some of the contemporary brasses show (*Plate* 3), the exhortation was often ignored.[1]

The effect of such devices together with painting, patches and the like, is to produce an expressionless mask, a Sphinx-like symbol of inscrutability very baffling to the male eye which therefore resents it. On the other hand, the face both of men and women has had phases of extraordinary exploitation when it has been surrounded by a halo, crowned with enormous and fantastic coverings, festooned with artificial locks, and these aided in their object by marked lines in the costume pointing like advertising fingers in the direction of the head. We may instance the butterfly headdress of 1460-80 as one of the most inconvenient ever worn by Englishwomen (*Plate* 6), or for that matter, the vast wigs worn by men at the end of the seventeenth century.

A very peculiar effect was obtained by the sixteenth century ruff worn by both sexes (*Plates* 8*b*, 11 and 13). It appeared to cut off the head from the body, curiously reminiscent of the contemporary method of execution and thus resembling the French Directoire fashion of wearing a scarlet neck band " à la guillotine." The ruff marked the head as a separate exhibit.

" Ruffs stand a full quarter of a yard and more from their necks," an Elizabethan writer comments, " but if it happens that a shower of rain catch them then their great ruffs strike sail and down they fall as dishclouts fluttering in the wind. There is a certain liquid they call starch wherein the devil has learned to wash and dive their ruffs which, being dry, will then stand stiff and inflexible about their necks. A more monstrous

---

[1] Eyebrow plucking is strongly suggested in many of the brasses of the " butterfly headdress " period (1460-85) when apparently the hair was also shaved off the front of the forehead. For example, see the brass of the wife of R. St. Leger, Ulcombe, Kent (1470).

23

kind of ruff set three or four times double is fitly called 'three steps and a half to the gallows.'"

Certainly there is no sign in Elizabethan costume that either sex suffered from shy self-effacement. Indeed a "superiority complex" is demonstrated in the women with their enormous farthingales, and the men with their huge trunks ballooned in doublets of which it was said : "there never was any kind of apparel invented that could more disproportion the body of man than these doublets with great bellies do, hanging down beneath the groin and stuffed with four, five or six pounds of bombast at the least" (*Plate* 12.) The symbol has even entered into our language in the word "bombastic." [1]

In our search for symbols in the costumes of our ancestors it would no doubt be possible to multiply these examples, as indeed would be the case with more recent modes, if we had the eyes to see them in our own clothing, but those mentioned will suffice for the purpose of indicating that when we are faced with some feature which appears to have served no useful purpose, we should suspect either that it is a survival of something or that it is a symbol of something. It has, or has had, a meaning, whether it signifies a social distinction, occupation, sex appeal, or simply a prevailing attitude of mind ; or, alternatively, a relic of such.

We have, in fact, always to bear in mind that nothing in the Art of Costume is meaningless, and that it is one of the most conservative of the arts, being reluctant to abandon its inheritance. On the other hand there is always a childish love of change. The two inclinations sound incompatible, but in practice they produce a

[1] The Spanish type of farthingale came in about 1550, and was composed of a series of graduated hoops like a crinoline ; the French type, fashionable from 1570, was in the nature of a bolster tied round the waist, so that the skirt presented the shape of a drum. From about 1590, a stiff flounce, pleated, surrounded the edge at hip level (*Plate* 8b).

compromise and so we wear the oddest mixture of old and new.

Till quite recently mounted soldiers wore bits of mediæval chain mail on their shoulders ; the civilian wears a useless necktie as a remnant of a gentleman's neckcloth ; his coat, with its futile collar which is never turned up, is still buttoned left over right so that he can easily reach the sword which is no longer on his left hip ; his waistcoat, which is no longer a coat, is called a " vest " by his tailor though it has long ceased to be one, and he blows his nose in a head-covering or " couvrechef " which is often carried, not in the pocket, but up the sleeve, but is still a pocket-handkerchief.

A sex garbed in such relics should not be surprised that women, more conservative still, have clung for so many centuries to their prehistoric skirt as a symbol of their sex.

With what reluctance do they exchange it for the more convenient slacks on those rare occasions when they are willing for their costume to look—slack.

It is no doubt because symbols become so familiar that we are reluctant to discard them, even though their meaning is lost ; in their costume, women seem much more conservative than men, for though they may appear to be perpetually changing their fashions yet these are but variations of modes long established. To-day a woman, scorning, perhaps, the fashions of yester-day, will wear a fifteenth century cotehardie (which she calls a " housecoat "), ties a mediæval kerchief over her head, and uses shoes that were discarded by the Normans.

The popular saying that " fashions repeat themselves " is applied mainly to the Art of Costume. It would be more accurate to say that the symbols used in this art are repeated over and over again. Naturally this applies in particular to erotic symbols, of which men and women never tire. Some of these are sufficiently obvious, drawing attention to the anatomical differences of sex by exaggeration, special colouring and design, while others have become so stylised that their origin may now be unrecognisable ; yet they are accepted as " attractive " —meaning that subconsciously they stir agreeable memories, or are as shadows of erotic images only dimly perceived.

Such symbols are the more " attractive " just because they trespass on forbidden ground.

Designs of textiles are sometimes described as " very chaste," an expression as suggestive as its opposite number, " sensual."

That curious dread, so marked in many English people, of symbols which might be accused of being erotic, can only be explained on the supposition that human beings dislike being reminded of an instinct which is the chief source of their happiness. Fortunately in this country a sublime ignorance of their true implication allows a wide range of erotic symbols to be employed in this art, to everybody's satisfaction ; for instance, a cotton frock printed with alternate rows of heart and buttock symbols (the former being, of course, merely the latter modestly turned upside down) was recently voted " most attractive." The student of Freud, in his search for phallic emblems, must not neglect this promising field. . . .

It is sufficient to say that so long as reticence is the convention, the use of such symbols, decently disguised, is likely to continue. It may be noted that their use in women's costume began to become noticeable in the fourteenth century, when a certain degree of choice of husband was permitted ; prior to that time the only " attractive " symbol employed was evidence of the parents' wealth as displayed by the richness of the daughter's attire.

That the use of such symbols has diminished in the costume of the modern woman (though far from disappearing) as compared to their prevalence in the days of Victorian respectability, may be attributed to several causes.[1] Their significance, in some cases, is better understood, and when they are recognised for what they are much of their fascination vanishes ; a franker outlook does not require those furtive allusions ; but above all, other less erotic modes of attraction are beginning to take their place. Thus, signs of good physical health (" sunburn," real or artificial, is surely a symbol of this) is a modern form, together with an air of competence which is the note of the present day costume ; an appearance of intelligence may be, in our circumstances, more attractive than mere physical glamour, though glamour is still regarded by many as a promising substitute.

All those conventions which form sartorial " etiquette" are, in a sense, arbitrary symbols used to distinguish, by different kinds of apparel, various social occasions. They range from the garments in which we " dress for dinner " to those shades of variation which mark the " town " costume from the " country."

There is no rational explanation why the City man does not wear shorts and a pullover nor why a woman's dress may be more *décolletée* in the evening than in the day ; nevertheless we insist that symbolism shall be preserved. Few of us would care to imitate Balzac who, if he had an evening engagement, would put on his dress clothes when he rose in the morning. From moral courage or indolence ? Probably the latter, for on one occasion he forgot to put on his trousers, and appeared at the evening party without them.

But for most of us, to be incorrectly garbed at a social function causes one of the most exquisite forms of mental agony that civilisation has invented, and it needs a

[1] Some of the most blatantly erotic symbols can be found in modern costume designs ; but it is significant that these soon vanish from the market. Presumably the symbolism is too obvious for popular taste to stomach them.

tough hide to dispense with the requisite symbols which convention demands. In the palmy days of Ascot, the late Lord Harris once appeared in the Royal Enclosure dressed in a lounge suit of a loud check pattern, and a bowler hat. King Edward's withering greeting : " Mornin', Harris ; goin' rattin' ? " was the penalty for wearing inappropriate symbols.

It is significant that from time immemorial those who aspire to rise in the social scale will display their ambition by adopting—not always with success—the symbols of the costume worn by the rank just above them. The elaborate Sumptuary Laws of 37. Ed. III endeavoured to restrain this ; the wives of gentlemen under the estate of knighthood might not wear jewellery, while the wives of esquires owning £200 in land might use edgings of miniver, but not ermine, on their garments. We might discover in the length of the mortar-board tassel allowed to University graduates and denied to undergraduates, a faint relationship to those mediæval distinctions ; just as the outdoor shoe has become socially " superior " to the boot, implying less trudging occupations.

We still recognise, in a general sense, that certain materials, on account of their cost, have their social significance, although silk, once an exclusive material of the wealthy, is now in its artificial imitation so universally worn that its symbolism is, in effect, worn out.

It is a sign of the times that costumes which formerly denoted humble or subordinate occupations are now shunned by those so engaged. The countryman's smock, the domestic cap and apron, as well as similar liveries of service, have given place to costumes which may even be less suitable for the work in question, but which have the social advantage of not being " symbolic." The less obvious drawback of this levelling up in costume is indicated in Gilbert's lines :

" When you have nothing else to wear
But cloth of gold and satins rare,
For cloth of gold you cease to care
. . . .
When everyone is somebodee
Then no one's anybody ! "

We learn, or should learn, from such instances that when a costume symbol is rejected, it implies a rejection of the idea it represents, and a desire to get rid of a badge of servitude implies a demand for greater freedom.

So, too, the persistence of a functionless symbol in Costume suggests a wish, recognised or only dimly felt, to preserve the idea represented by it.

In addition to the types of symbols already mentioned there is a group which might be described as " trophies," insignia captured or borrowed from other countries as mementoes of wars, victories, and notable events and persons admired. As such, we have employed Scottish tartans, the pine pattern in textiles taken from our Indian possessions, to say nothing of the Prince of Wales' feathers which we (incorrectly) regard as a trophy of Crecy six centuries ago. We have at times worn actual garments of foreign extraction, such as the Garibaldi as a compliment to that hero, and many events of passing interest have had a momentary reflection in our clothing and headgear ; but though it is customary to attribute so many of our fashions, especially women's, to " foreign influence " which we have meekly accepted as such, it would be more correct to say that many have been, in a sense, trophies, representing not gifts but loot ; so that they signify not seldom triumphs rather than tributes. We have worn mementoes from head to foot of victories from Crecy to Waterloo, but none recalling defeats.

We may say, in fact, that while we have often and willingly learnt new technical methods in this art from foreign sources, the ideas expressed in English Costume have been essentially native and our own.

It has seemed desirable to emphasise the points mentioned in this chapter, before passing on to the consideration of the purely æsthetic aspects of the art, because we cannot properly understand it unless we are alive to the significance of the many symbols which have always formed its notable feature. If, for example, we were going to study the art of church architecture, it would be essential to have some preliminary knowledge of the symbolism in which it abounds, and without which, much of the buildings would be meaningless.

So, too, in the Art of Costume. Here in its symbols— if we can interpret them correctly—is displayed a pictorial history of the progress of social ideas in our country, which may illustrate or even, in some instances, correct preconceived notions about our ancestors. We see that they must have had much the same sort of impulses which we possess (for they, too, were human beings), but that they often expressed them in manners very different from ours. Their costumes tell us that they attached different values to some ideas which we hold precious ; they would have thought it strange that Costume should primarily be designed for comfort and utility ; they might have thought it more strange that we attach so little importance to magnificence, as some future generation may marvel that we accepted so much ugliness. But in all ages it has been an art speaking in the language of signs ; is that not in itself a symbol of civilisation, signifying that we have eaten of the tree of knowledge ?

CHAPTER III

SOURCES OF INFORMATION

THE costume itself, worn on the living model, obviously
supplies a kind of information which we cannot get
by other means. But this requires that the model shall
fit the costume mentally as well as physically ; the
costume and the personality of the wearer must
harmonise with each other, and this means much more
than a mere physical fit. On this account we find that
costumes of the past are not easy to " fit " on to living
models of to-day ; some types of personality seem to
have become rare.

Nevertheless, if we are so fortunate as to be able to
examine such costumes on appropriate living models,
we are then in a position to criticise them with a certain
measure of confidence, but this applies, of course, only
to those of the last two hundred years ; costumes earlier
than that are practically not available for the purpose.

From that date back to about A.D. 1500 we have to
rely on pictures and drawings. Here, at once, we are
faced with difficulties. We have to allow for the
idiosyncracies of the artist, and those slight distortions
which he is inclined to make. He will bring out some
features and minimise others ; or he may paint costumes
which were not the current modes.

Reynolds, for example, seems to have employed for
his women sitters a kind of fancy dress of his own
invention. Gainsborough, in his later period, seems to
have disliked depicting the hooped skirt.

Moreover, it may be a fashion to be painted in the
costume of a former period, perhaps an ancestor's dress,
or, as in the early eighteenth century, in the " Ruben's
style," just as, some fifty years ago, it was not uncommon

for women to be painted in " Empire dress," revealing to the critical eye that neither sitter nor painter were quite at home with that epoch. The " Rubens " dress, as shown in the well-known portrait of Helène Fourment by that artist, reappears again about the middle of the eighteenth century in portraits by Hudson, Allan Ramsay and others, with slight variations. It supplied the lady of fashion with an attractive " fancy dress " in which to be painted, but it has also set a pitfall for the student of period costumes.

By comparing with genuine examples we come to realise that it is almost impossible for an artist to reproduce the costume of a period not his own without betraying signs that it is only a " reproduction ; " the stage and the films are generous in supplying evidence of this inability.

When for our knowledge of mediæval Costume we have to rely on such sources as illuminated manuscripts, wall-paintings, brasses and tapestries, our difficulties are greatly increased. The exact dates of exhibits may be uncertain ; we cannot be sure that the costumes depicted were really contemporary or whether they were not partly guess work. If we choose to assume that a monk labouring at illuminating manuscripts in a monastery was a reliable guide to the fashions of the day, it is, after all, only an assumption.

Before accepting evidence as to English costumes from illuminated MSS., we have to be sure that they *were* English. Too often French sources have been used, on the assumption that the modes of the two countries were identical, which they never were. We learn from contemporary household accounts and wills, what garments and materials were usual.

Effigies enable us to see figures and their costumes in the round, and give details not visible in brasses ; the latter, however, being more abundant, especially in the fifteenth century, inform us what types of garment were the more commonly worn, and give negative evidence as to what was *not* worn. But, as Mr. Kelly pointed out, it is necessary to check dates. A brass may have been made some years after the death of the deceased, or even before ! Thus, that of Julia Yelverton, Rougham church, Norfolk, has a pediment head dress, though dated 1481, while the brass of Sir Henry Grey and wife at Kelteringham church, Norfolk, shows costumes at least thirty years earlier than the date of death.

The same applies to tapestries. And there is this further difficulty : are we looking at English modes, or was the artist a foreigner imbued with the styles of his own people which unconsciously he has engrafted on to English figures ? We know, of course, that foreign modes were borrowed by English people, but we cannot be sure to what extent, and on this the illustrator may be deceiving us.

All this means that an atmosphere of uncertainty obscures our knowledge of mediæval costume, which comments by contemporary English writers are not sufficient to dispel. Their note of disapproval of " fashions " carries an exaggeration which has to be discounted. We are often compelled, for want of better, to accept foreign sources of information—and misinformation.

In the last hundred and fifty years of this art we have the assistance of Fashion Plates. Although there are available for that period the actual costumes themselves which give information obtainable from no other source, yet the fashion plate is of great assistance if used with understanding. It is essentially not a portrait of a costume, but only a guide, and it is because we lack such guides to remoter epochs that their costumes are often baffling.

The fashion plate tells us, not what the costume will look like when worn, but what is the idea it attempts to express ; in other words, what the designer—and wearer—would like it to look like. It represents a chart to guide us to that idea, and so, to make the path clear, the fashion plate exaggerates the track which the wearer is to follow.

Therefore it emphasises the salient features, especially those that are novel. These indicate the nature of those social aspirations prevalent at the moment. And we are shown not merely the ideal Form but also the ideal Pose. The " psychology " of the fashion plate portrait has yet to be studied as a guide to the types of men and women who, in their day, were supposed to be ideally attractive. We may smile at the doll-like charms of a hundred years ago ; what will be said of ours, a hundred years hence ?

A gallery of these idealised figures would portray the eternal triumph of Hope over Experience, for too often they dangle before us pictures of the unattainable. Here is a degree of languid grace seldom seen in real life ; there, in all its naïvety, is the " pretty doll." At one time Venus appears in the ascendant, at another, chaste Aphrodite.

We watch the Junoesque creature of Edwardian days presently transfigured into a flattened schoolboy (after the first Great War), and to-day, seven feet high, she stalks across the pages of the fashion journal with slinky legs, bony hips and a hawk-like physiognomy.

It would be unwise for some future historian of our social era, poring over such records, to conclude that the Englishwoman of to-day always resembled a starved bird of prey.

It is equally unwise for us to accept fashion plates of the past at their face value as accurate evidence of former generations, an error which writers who derive their knowledge of the subject mainly from that source are prone to commit.

In a word, the fashion plate gives us the basic formula of construction, while the actual costume gives the composition built upon that foundation.

34

For costumes of the last hundred years we have also the assistance supplied by photographs, and these can be invaluable, for they tell us, if sufficient numbers are available, what a particular style of costume actually looked like as worn by different people ; we discover, for instance, how seldom English women, at any rate, could wear their crinolines as the fashion plate depicts. We also see the variations worn on different occasions and by different social classes. From a large collection of photographs we can also deduce what styles were actually popular and what were confined to a small group of fashionables, or even confined to the pages of the fashion journal.

The amateur " snap-shot " is not to be neglected, for it gives us revealing incidents of social behaviour. How did costumes look when the wearers stood, walked, or sat ? We note, for example, how women in crinolines seemed to prefer to be photographed when standing, even when the husband by the side is seated ; we conclude that the crinoline was apt to reveal too much in a sitting posture.

And photographs also inform us how long a particular fashion remained in being, and what sort of costume was often worn by those who refused to accept the dictates of fashion. Thus we find a number of women who evidently were not wearing crinolines in the Sixties, or bustles in the Seventies and Eighties, in spite of the fashion.

There remains to mention as another source of information, the written accounts taken, of course, from contemporary sources.

The fashion journal hardly began to appear before the beginning of last century, and then with much unreliable information culled very often from foreign sources. By the middle of that century it was well established, but it still to-day retains the misleading tendency to advertise modes as " accepted," when, in fact, they are only " acceptable." The future historian will have to do a good deal of " checking up " from more prosaic sources if he wishes to reconstruct a reliable picture.

For remoter times we have to search memoirs, novels, plays and diaries for chance descriptions and comments on the costumes of their day. And the further we go backwards in time, the denser becomes the obscurity surrounding the subject ; about certain garments of the Middle Ages we are very much in the dark, and especially how far foreign modes were actually adopted in this country, beyond, perhaps, the limits of the Court circle.

Our climate is not likely to have preserved actual specimens of garments such as were unearthed, some twenty-five years ago, in a frozen state in Greenland, and dating from the fourteenth and fifteenth centuries. These astonishing relics of the middle ages, now in the Copenhagen museum, reveal the actual cut and construction of garments we had only read about or seen illustrated ; one can detect gores and godet pleats, not therefore very modern inventions.

From such faint gleams, as we peer into the darkness of the past, we get a glimpse of an Art striving to express something beyond mere utility.

PORTRAIT OF ANNE VAVASOUR

Note the French farthingale, open type of ruff with deep décolletage, hair piled high (over pads), glove carried in hand. The colour scheme is polychromatic, the principal colours—grey, salmon in two shades and green—being very much what might have been worn in the 1880's, but softer and distributed more uniformly. We do not, of course, know how much these colours have softened by age.

After the painting by Marc Gheeraerts, 1605, in the possession of Francis Howard Esquire.

CHAPTER IV

ÆSTHETIC ASPECTS OF COSTUME

THE principal aspects of Costume are Form, Colour, Texture and Mobility, but the trained observer looks for various subtle qualities—derived from those features —in estimating the æsthetic merits of a costume. Some of these qualities will be discussed in this chapter.

One cannot approach the subject without immediately recognising how much in common the art of Costume has with the art of Acting. Both attempt to express mental as well as physical attitudes ; Costume is the scenery in which the comedy of " civilisation " is played, and the love of " dressing up," universal in one sex and not uncommon in the other, is a recognition of this.

To regard this popular taste merely as an expression of exhibitionism is to miss its more profound significance; surely it indicates a desire to discover in " fancy dress " or in the modes of forgotten ancestors, a style of costume which shall illuminate the personality more than does the garb of the day. The popularity of " dressing up " tells of a daydream of unsatisfied longings, and a yearning for a means of expressing the personality. Hence the perennial attraction of " Fashion," especially for women, whose scope for self-expression was, until modern times, more limited than men's.

From this it follows that there is—or should be—an æsthetic relationship, recognisable by an observer, between the costume and the personality of the wearer. We may go even further and say that such relationship should be not merely physical but almost psychological. These meanings are implied, in fact, by conventional terms, such as " stylish " and " becoming."

It is necessary to insist that these are much more than

mere trade terms ; they have their subjective meaning, and refer as much to the wearer as to the costume worn.

Of the expressions " fashionable " or " modish," it is sufficient to say that they merely imply that a costume is in the manner of the day ; not, be it observed, necessarily of the present day, for a costume of a former epoch may have all the appearance of having been " fashionable " in its time. All that these terms mean is that the details of the costume are so precise and consistent with each other that we can ascribe an exact date to the whole ; and it is certainly possible to do this with all " fashionable " costumes of the past couple of centuries. Where the date cannot be determined precisely, it is safe to say that the specimen was never really " fashionable."

The terms " stylish " and "smart " are practically synonymous, and have no reference to the date of the costume in question. They refer, not to its history, but to its quality of construction. For a costume may be exactly in " the fashion," yet not " smart." In the eighteenth century, " smart " referred to the wearer and not to the costume. Thus in *Joseph Andrews* (1742), " All the smarts were eclipsed in a moment ; " and in *The London Chronicle* of 1762, " Very spruce smarts have no buttons nor holes upon their surtouts."

To-day the word has been transferred to the costume, but what exactly does it mean ?

It certainly does not refer simply to the quality of the materials, though it is sometimes confused with this ; and as we may be able to say of a specimen from the past that it looks " smart," even though we are ignorant of the fashions of that time, there must be some quality which does not depend for recognition on familiarity with those fashions. By that quality of " smartness " we mean, in fact, that it possesses what is called a " good line."

The term implies an æsthetic element which needs

training as well as natural good taste to appreciate ;
the term itself is, perhaps, ill-chosen, for it is often
misunderstood and more often misused.

It has no reference to Hogarth's " line of beauty." It
was introduced into the Art of Costume in the 1870's as
dressmaker's jargon, when it was known as " *la ligne*."
In this relation, the " line " of a costume may be
defined as that imaginary axis round which the design
has been constructed. Though it has no actual existence,
the trained observer instinctively perceives it in imagination when he inspects the costume worn on a suitable
model ; it is, of course, less easily recognised when the
costume is inspected off the model.

As the word " line " has its general meaning as well
as this specific one, it will be convenient to distinguish
the latter by the word " axis." The axis of a costume
may be resolved into types : the straight, the angular
and the curved.

Each of these types appears in twofold forms : the
straight, as vertical or horizontal ; the angular, as
obtuse or acute ; the curved, as circular or elliptical.
(How logical it would be if costumes were described in
geometrical instead of pseudo-historical terms !)

Further, we may note that the axis of a costume may
be simple or compound—that is, either of a single type
or of a mixture of types. Take for example a Victorian
crinoline costume (*Plates* 29, 35, 36). Its axis would be
represented by an inverted " Y " ; that is, a combination of a vertical, above an angular axis, the angle being
sometimes obtuse (greater than a right angle). A dress
of 1895, with huge gigot sleeves above a gored skirt,
would present a combined axis, the upper part being
semi-circular and the lower being an acute angle
(*Plate* 40).

What constitutes a " good line " in a costume ?

Although fashions are perpetually varying, there
persists almost unchanged the inclination among discrim-

inating people for a " good line," though perhaps they may not be able to explain what precisely it is that their judgment demands.

We can, however, extract from the customs which have governed the Art of Costume for centuries, rules which we may almost call " laws " dealing with the nature of the axis. For behind the ephemeral tastes of the moment there lies an instinctive inclination towards æsthetic correctness—we call it " beauty "—which asserts itself in spite of the frantic efforts of Fashion to offer substitutes.

We may formulate these laws thus, always bearing in mind that they represent the accumulated experience of generations as to what produced results æsthetically satisfying :

1. The axis should be consistent in its nature throughout a costume. If the axis is compound, straight lines may be united to angles (these being themselves straight lines meeting at a point) ; but neither should be linked on to curves. The former have the quality of hardness and the latter of softness, and to join two such incongruous types jars. On the other hand, the semicircular and the elliptical curves blend admirably together, as seen, for example, in the flowing Edwardian dresses (*Plate* 42).

2. The sex of the wearer can be emphasised by the nature of the axis of a costume. Thus, a strongly marked vertical plus horizontal axis gives a masculine appearance, even to a woman's dress. Her dress of 1923 (*Plate* 44) had an axis resembling the masculine " H ", and many tailored costumes of to-day present the same formula.

On the other hand, an axis composed entirely of combined curves gives a feminine appearance, even to a man's costume, as, for example, in that of the Dandy of 1830. If we analyse the portrait of D'Orsay, we find the costume composed almost wholly of curves (*Plate* 27).

3. Each type of axis (straight, angular and curved) should exhibit in a costume *both* of its two opposites : vertical-horizontal ; acute-obtuse ; circular-elliptical. This is because a costume requires to present height and breadth in due proportion, and vertical lines, acute angles and elliptical curves emphasise height, while their respective opposites emphasise breadth.

4. Whatever may be the type on which the design is based, it should be echoed elsewhere in the costume, either in the trimmings or surface details, so that the observer cannot fail to sense it ; for the design should announce the type of axis on which it is composed just as a musician announces his theme. If the axis is vague or confused, the eye is irritated ; if it is over-stated, the observer is bored. The subtle costume is one in which the axis compels attention and rewards it.

(In this relation I have used the word " type " in place of " style," because the latter word is so often given, in popular speech, a meaning associated with smartness.)

Needless to say one does not criticise a costume with a set-square and theodolite. It is the general impression which the trained eye obtains from looking at it that counts. In practice the analysis of its line is felt rather than measured. Nevertheless it is well to bear in mind that the recognition of a good " line " is not a mere whim of the expert, but is based on the above-mentioned " laws."

It is possible, of course, to conceal—at least from uncritical eyes—poverty of " line " in a costume, by the richness of the material and the wealth of accessories. Yet at some later date, when the glamour of that particular mode has vanished, a cool observer will have no difficulty in detecting it. And this applies to men's costume as well as to women's, especially in those epochs when men over-dressed.

On the other hand, we may discover the true tests of " smartness " in costumes, men's and women's, of remote periods, just as we may be able to detect in some ruined building evidence of a fine design. A costume once truly " smart " can never lose that quality ; as, too, a costume with a bad " line " can never acquire that quality. The point deserves to be stressed because a natural gift for detecting " line " in costume is not an English characteristic. Too often— at displays of new models, for example—the word is lavishly applied to subsidiary details ignoring the fundamental axis of design.

The quality of " smartness " is sometimes attributed to " cut," but this is to confuse the work of the designer with that of the builder. With this distinction in mind we are entitled to criticise the costumes of the past, even though we may be ignorant of the technique by which the cut of those garments was effected. We judge simply by the results as they appear to the eye.

We have, of course, to allow for the practical limitations of that time, the less efficient implements, paucity in the range of colours and materials, but even so we cannot but be struck, when examining actual garments, by the steady improvement of tailoring and dressmaking skill revealed up to about some seventy years ago. In other words, the art of " cutting " reached its height at that time.

It is remarkable what poor workmanship is to be found in the gorgeous suits and dresses of the eighteenth century, for example, and as we have hardly any ordinary costumes available for examination earlier than that date we can only guess about the " cut " of more remote epochs. Of them, though pictures may enable us to judge of materials, colour and design, we cannot be so sure of the " line," and we know still less of the skill in " cut."

We find that in men's costume good cutting began to

42

appear in the eighteenth century, and in women's not until about a hundred years ago. If we wonder why this was so, the answer seems clear ; it was not till then that clothing was made to fit—perhaps because they had not got the requisite skill.

The appearance of what we call " a good fit " gives us an æsthetic satisfaction for which our ancestors found a substitute in lavish decoration, often concealing bad workmanship under excess of ornament.

It seems, then, that æsthetic standards have changed fundamentally ; we have only gradually learnt to demand of the designer a " good line," and of the tailor or dressmaker a " good cut." It is not without significance that our meaning of the word " smart " is less than two hundred years old. When we speak of a " smart costume " we—unconsciously—attribute some of that quality to the personality of the wearer ; for there are certainly some people who seem able to transfer, as it were, an appearance of smartness from themselves to their clothes.

Here is an æsthetic aspect peculiar to the Art of Costume which we call " becomingness," a harmony established between an inanimate thing and a person, so that we hardly know whether it is that the costume suits the wearer or the wearer suits the costume.

A becoming costume seems like a translation of the wearer's personality into the language of clothes. Not only must the two, if they are to become each other, have a kindred spirit, but they must be modelled on the same line, and the same laws of construction and design should apply to both. For it seems that the human body may or may not have its own good line, and to be becoming, the costume must have one of the same type. If the human line is vague and indefinite, breaking all the rules of design, why then, the line of the costume must follow suit, for it has to form a sort of exterior portrait. I have seen a dress of plain black silk mounted on a stand, which was so charged with the personality of its original owner that observers immediately recognised it as having been a dress of Queen Victoria's.

The æsthetic effect on the wearer, of knowing that a costume is becoming, is one which cannot be ignored in considering this art, for immediately that costume is seen at its best. Its subjective influence can be very great ; the wearer derives from it a peculiar confidence, rising to the occasion and setting off the costume to its maximum advantage. In doing so both become " better looking."

The very human desire to " look one's best " is not only a source of inspiration to the designer but serves also to sustain the wearer ; that old lady who, on her death-bed, called for her best cap, without which, she declared, she could not face the Almighty, was surely paying the highest possible compliment to her Maker— of caps. . . .

Æsthetic requirements are not satisfied with the choosing of a becoming costume. It must not only become the wearer but also the circumstances in which it is to be worn. In other words, we cannot properly appreciate or even understand ancestral costumes unless we can picture both the appropriate wearers and the appropriate surroundings. The margin between the sublime and the ridiculous is very narrow ; a gentleman in full evening dress, seen in broad daylight hardly escapes looking comic. The eye is struck by the incongruity. It is the situation which is unbecoming to the costume.

So far as the surroundings are concerned, an important æsthetic aspect is the illumination by which the costumes of former ages were intended to be viewed. In the day-time the size of the windows, and at night the kind of artificial lighting, would obviously have affected the appearance of costumes worn, especially as regards their colour.

44

In a broad sense, then, the æsthetic aspect of the
Art of Costume is affected by a great many attendant
circumstances. Specimens exhibited in showcases have
but a faint resemblance to the living art, and reproductions, in modern materials, are seldom more than
approximate. In a word, it is exceedingly difficult to
see the costumes of former generations exactly as they
looked to the original wearers, and so, in criticising
those works of art, we have always to recollect our
limited vision. That this applies almost as much to the
future as to the past is suggested by a passage in Oscar
Wilde's lecture on the Æsthetics of Costume in 1884.
Having declared that the costume of the Cavalier
period was man's supreme effort towards attaining a
beautiful design, he added this forecast : " The costume
of the future in England, if it is founded on the true
laws of freedom, comfort and adaptability to circumstances, cannot fail to be most beautiful because beauty
is the sign always of the rightness of principles."

CHAPTER V

PRINCIPLES OF FORM

IN its relation to the human body the Art of Costume
has been governed by one of two principles which are
fundamentally opposed to each other. In the one the
costume is designed to display the human shape, to
which, therefore, the covering plays a secondary part.
In the other the body is used to display the costume,
which then plays the principal part.

The former may be called the " Classical " principle,
and it is one which has only very rarely and in a
modified degree been employed in this country. The
latter, which I have called the " Gothic " principle, has
governed the costumes of both sexes with hardly a break
since remote times. It is, in varying degrees, the art of
concealing the body.

In extreme forms it may even so distort the human
shape that the outlines of the costume have hardly any
relation to the shape of the contents. As distortion is
the essence of this " Gothic " art, it is curious how
violent have been, from time to time, the protests against
it. Whenever the costume of either sex has exceeded
some purely arbitrary limit of distortion, a clamour is
heard in favour of the superior beauty of the human
body. When the body is allowed to become too
apparent, it is greeted with an even louder chorus of
disapproval.

Of the former sort, a typical snarl came from Alexander Barkley, in *The Ship of Fooles of the World* (1508) :

" Ye counterfeit catiffs, that are not content
As God hath you made ; His work is dispised ;
Ye think you more wise than God omnipotent ;
Unstable is your ways, that shewes by your garment."

46

While Philip Stubs, in *The Anatomy of Abuses* (1595), lamented the men of fashion of his day : " Their curiosity and niceness in apparel transnatureth them, as it were, and maketh them weak, tender and infirm." (This of the Elizabethans !)

The same cry has echoed down the centuries, and seventy years ago, in the heyday of the bustle, Mrs. Haweis was urging a style of dress for her sex that should conform more—but not too much more—to the shape of their bodies, while the Æsthetic Movement demanded a return to flowing drapery, wanly picturesque.

On the other hand, in 1653 Bulver was condemning the excessive decolletage of fashionable ladies as " an exorbitant and shameful enormity," while at the end of the fourteenth century Chaucer was criticising masculine fashions and their " horrible disordinate scantinesse of clothing as ben their cut sloppes or hanseleynes, that thurgh thir shortenesse cover not the shameful membres of man." Perhaps the English genius for compromise could not, in this respect, be more happily expressed than in Chaucer's own words : " I say that honestee in clothing of man or woman is uncovenable; but certes the superfluitee or disordinate scarcitee of clothing is reprevable."

Nevertheless, the " Gothic " principle has enormously enriched the Art of Costume. By comparison, the human body, seldom a thing of beauty, and with a very limited career as such, cannot so easily be changed in appearance nor can it be used as a medium for expressing ideas. Costume, on the other hand, affords a limitless canvas for that purpose in which originality can be expressed in a thousand ways. Age itself offers the designer material almost as rich as does youth, and, while the human body presents a monotonous repetition of design, Costume is an Art which can, if it chooses, benefit by experience.

For such reasons as these the Gothic mode so far

surpasses the Classical that attempts to revive the latter have never captured more than the briefest attention in this country. We sometimes see costumes which attempt to combine the two incompatible principles ; the results are seldom happy, for each form of art has its distinct laws.

The Gothic (with which alone this country is concerned) has its own laws and also limitations. It is an Art hampered by the requirements of utility, function and economics. It may also seek to express ideas which jar on the æsthetic sensibilities ; there may be a popular urge which for a time overwhelms æsthetic " good taste," though eventually the normal instinct for beauty will reassert itself.

Whereas the Classical forms of costume are essentially fixed, the Gothic are perpetually moving towards some goal dimly perceived, governed in their progress by certain laws of which the chief is the *law of balance*. Instinctively we demand of any upright structure that it shall not look top-heavy ; and yet by that very quality such objects may seem endowed with the magical power of being able to defy the laws of gravity.

Though the Art of Costume has usually observed the law of balance, it may, exceptionally, deliberately break it with success. The unbalanced costume, in either sex, wears an audacious air, even defiant, and to be effectively consistent this challenging spirit has to be sustained throughout the design. In faltering hands it may easily be a dismal failure and the top-heavy structure appear a veritable burden of Atlas ; with the requisite assurance, however, even the laws of gravity can be defied.

We judge of the balance of a costume by the position of what appears to be the greatest diameter ; if this is above the mid level the costume is unbalanced (*Plate* 43), but a spurious appearance of balance can be given by various devices such as a transverse line across the upper half, or by adding heavy-looking features near the foot ;

and an exaggerated balance by widening the base line (*Plate* 40) is commonly used to add stability and even dignity to ceremonial costumes of both sexes, or merely to counterbalance some wide feature near the top, such as excessive breadth of shoulder line or broad headgear.

More subtle methods of suggesting balance may be in the details of the costume itself, such as lines sloping upwards and inwards, or by devices which draw attention solely to the upper part of it, so that any lack of balance below passes unnoticed, and by the skilful distribution of colours, dark masses in the lower half suggesting "weight."

A problem which the Art of Costume has taken centuries to solve—and of which even now the solution is far from satisfactory—is whether the design should treat the body as a single structure or whether the limbs should be regarded as distinct from it.

Until the fourteenth century there was a curious reluctance, in both sexes, to divide the body into its components ; men, except labourers at work, wore long gowns, and women, of course, had no legs until quite modern times. Even the arm was frequently smothered in sleeves which merged into the rest of the costume. For centuries men and women had worn costumes which closely resembled each other, and traces of this survive in the gown of the monk and the nun.

As Mr. Kelly expressed it in his *History of Costume and Armour* : " During the eleventh, twelfth and thirteenth centuries the costume of both sexes, broadly speaking, retained something of the simplicity and flowing lines of the antique." The skirt had not become exclusively a feminine garment.

It was about the middle of the fourteenth century that English costume became, almost abruptly, alive to the possibilities of this art, and the first step was taken towards breaking up the uniformity of the whole by defining the waist. From that momentous decision we trace revolutionary changes ; the costumes of the two sexes parted company and presently men's legs emerged as separate attachments to the trunk. And as woman's waist became at the same time markedly defined, the costume of both acquired a novel change.

This fundamental change introduced, of course, a number of new problems ; should the two portions thus separated present harmony or contrast in respect of colour, material and closeness of fit ? At what level should the transverse line be placed in each sex ? How would this affect the appearance of balance ?

These æsthetic problems the Art attempted to solve in ways different in the costume of each sex. Thus the male costume used as a basis of construction the transverse horizontal line with two lateral uprights ; the female costume cultivated the angle and the curve, though each sex would frequently borrow from the other ; but while men have often used angles, they have generally eschewed curves as being too feminine in their implications.

The new positions had become stabilised, so to speak, by the end of the fifteenth century, and just as historians regard that as the beginning of Modern History, so, too, it may be considered as marking the beginning of the modern Art of Costume. A new constructional formula had been worked out and henceforth Man's costume was to be based on the shape of the letter " H " (*Plate* 9) ; Woman's on the letter " X " (*Plate* 10). It was as though He—was faced by X, the Unknown Quantity ; and we are still under the spell of this magical formula.

For nearly six centuries these two basic formulæ have governed the structure of men's and women's costume supplying each sex with its distinctive form. Whenever one has adopted, if ever so slightly, the symbol of the other, the effect is very recognisable, and the costume is described as " effeminate " or " mannish " if on analysis we detect signs of the feminine " X " used by man, or of the masculine " H " used by woman. And this does not depend on borrowing the distinctive garments of the other sex so much as on borrowing the basic formula.

We are inclined to say that a " natural instinct " persuades us that it is in better taste for the costumes of the sexes to be clearly differentiated from each other, forgetting that this custom is, after all, barely six centuries old, and certainly not " instinctive." The deep-rooted horror with which our European civilisation has regarded any inclination towards homo-sexuality is no doubt responsible for the marked distinction between the costumes of the sexes. In the Victorian era the borrowing by women of a masculine fashion or garment was sternly condemned as " fast," " indelicate," " unwomanly " and even " immoral." Modern conditions have forced that barrier but we have to admit that hetero-sexual attractions are largely sustained by the Art of Costume ; if both sexes wear the same kind of costume we must expect a psychological result in course of time.

We see to-day that for a great many purposes women are abandoning that distinction, and are wearing clothes indistinguishable from men's, especially when their occupation is similar to men's. We are, in fact, seeing a curious change taking place ; the form of costume is being dictated by the nature of the occupation (work or pastime) with a lessening distinction between that worn by each sex. In other words, for such occasions costume is becoming a sort of civilian " uniform " which is both classless and sexless. Its form becomes more and more modified to give greater efficiency until at last it will express nothing else.

We saw interesting experimental forms in the uniforms of the women's services in the recent war ; the attempt to make them " classless " was successful, but the attempt to eliminate " sex attraction " and the basic formula of design, the feminine " X," was defeated by the paramount claims of sex instinct. And if we examine the early efforts, towards the end of last century, to devise " sports costumes " suitable for women, we see how reluctant those pioneers were to abandon completely the claims of that instinct, even though the nature of the sport required it (*Plate* 37).

The change in the form of costume which is going on at present, for certain occupations of work or play, illustrates a struggle between the need for efficiency and the urge of sex ; and this results in the evolving of a costume whose form is used by both sexes indifferently, for all sorts of purposes and occasions.

We must expect that such a costume will gradually lose sex-characteristics and develop a " neuter " form, a change which must surely have a profound effect on the Art of Costume as a whole.

For six centuries the desire to stamp the costume of each sex with distinctive features has been very largely responsible for the resulting forms, in the male by overloading the upper half of the body with clothing, in the female by overloading the lower. The former effectively suggested the solidity of great muscular strength, the latter suggested the solidity of an immobile sedentary life ; but as those distinctions of function are rapidly disappearing we must expect that their costume symbols will also disappear—as, indeed, is beginning to happen.

It seems therefore that when we criticise the efforts of our ancestors to devise the ideal form of costume for those epochs and conditions, we are apt to forget that Form has been affected and even controlled by all sorts of conflicting principles. Broadly speaking we may say these have been æsthetic, moral and functional, and of these, " moral " principles have been much the most powerful. The segregation of the sexes, emphasised by the marked difference of form in their respective costumes, with a judicious but restrained measure of "sex attraction" permissible in them, the curbing of extravagant display—once regarded as "sinful," then as "vulgar," and now as "ridiculous"—these are some of the moral principles which have materially affected the Form of Costume.

These moral influences have fluctuated over a much wider range than have the æsthetic tastes which tend to vary more in the choice of colours than in the choice of form.

Although Form of Costume is, of course, affected by other influences, such as the economic—there are times when we have to cut our coat according to our cloth—it is singular how reluctant both men and women have been, and still are, to allow the form of their costumes to be dictated solely or even principally by function. We insist on introducing features inspired by morals or æsthetics.

The Form of Costume is, then, the resultant of a combination of forces, sometimes antagonistic, which may present to the observer at a later date an insoluble problem. It may be noted here that there is often a striking resemblance between forms used in the Art of Costume and those used in other contemporary arts. Mr. Laver has pointed out the similarity in design of the blouse of the end of last century and of the lamp-shade of that date. It is noticeable that the outline of the Elizabethan farthingale skirt, with its clumsy combination of vertical line merging into a curve as it descends, had a curious replica in the bowl of the contemporary chalice (when inverted). Similarly the narrow tubular skirt of the Regency period resembled the bowl of its contemporary champagne glass which, by 1830, expanded in keeping with the expanding skirt. Many other such resemblances can be detected in the Art of Costume, going to show that such shapes happen at a particular time to be "popular" and so are widely used for very different objects. This supplies (if it were needed) a further argument against the popular notion that "dress designers create the fashions." They can hardly be held responsible for the form of lampshades, champagne glasses and Elizabethan chalices.

When we are tempted to exclaim of our ancestors, " Why on earth did they wear that extraordinary form of clothing ? " it is because we don't know all the factors in the case.

Or it may present the appearance of a patchwork of motives which we can patiently disintegrate and apportion to their respective causes. We pick out components obviously denoting class distinction and sex attraction, features indicating some kinds of occupation, we detect the restraining influence of contemporary morals and we see evidence, perhaps, of racial æsthetic taste.

All that we might expect to find. What is surprising is the small part which utility seems to have played in the form of design. In the case of many garments or costumes it is as though they had been given those singular shapes in spite of, rather than because of, the function they were meant to perform ; all of which goes to indicate that the forms which the Art of Costume take may be derived from impulses which are entirely unrecognised by the generation wearing them, and may prove even more enigmatic to their successors.

CHAPTER VI

FORM IN MAN'S COSTUME

THE form of male costume has evolved from that of an upright oblong, solid from shoulder to ankle, as at the beginning of the fourteenth century, into a segmented structure resembling in outline the letter " H ", a process effected by the liberation of the lower limbs from the rest of the costume above (*Plates* 1, 9, 20, 22, 28, 31, etc.).

For the last six hundred years this has been the feature distinguishing man's costume from woman's. His trunk, almost always over-clothed, has presented a solid, apparently inflexible, rectangular block supported on a pair of tapering flexible cylindrical limbs, with a dividing line usually horizontal and at a variable level.

It was easy to design a costume which treated the whole body as a single uniform object capable of being concealed under a long gown ; but with a body divided into two such different parts—differing in structure, shape and function—an entirely new conception of costume was called for. The long descending lines as seen in the gown were now broken in two. But at what level ?

Is this to be determined on æsthetic, utilitarian or " moral " grounds ? The correct proportions between the upper and the lower segments produced by the transverse division, the level of flexibility at the hip joints, and considerations of decency, these are conflicting, and it is not to be wondered at that for at least two hundred years various levels were tried ; in fact, we might say that solely on this account man's costume was experimental until the eighteenth century when, by the process of " trial and error," something like the correct level for the division of his costume was discovered.

The fifteenth century produced some very maladroit experiments with a full upper garment reaching to the hips above legs in tights, and a second transverse line formed by the girdle some few inches above the first line (*Plate* 1). Shortening the upper garment still more, put the principal line above the buttocks, much as is still seen in the Eton jacket, not, however, a very elegant level for the rotundities of later years, and it is not surprising that contemporary writers fulminated at the spectacle thus revealed.

It is true that the long form of Houppelande[1] concealed much of the lower limb (*Plate* 5), but the more daring wore it hip-length (*Frontispiece*) or dispensed with its protection altogether, displaying the whole length of the limbs in tights.

During the sixteenth and seventeenth centuries a much lower level for the principal transverse line was employed. Thus, either the doublet was skirted (so as to resemble the Scottish kilt) thereby causing the upper half of the thighs to be absorbed into the trunk and making the lower limbs correspondingly shortened (and this gives the familiar portraits of Henry VIII that peculiarly burly appearance), or by expanding the " trunk hose " or short breeches so that they disguised the natural shape of the thighs and extended the breadth of the trunk down over them (*Plates* 7b, 12).

We see the cavalier of Charles the First's day in recognisable though loose-fitting knee breeches (*Plate* 14),

---

[1] The Houppelande was a high-necked gown, fitting the bust and shoulders and descending in heavy folds sometimes to the ground, sometimes—in men—only to the knee. It had vast funnel-shaped sleeves, and a high collar often rising up behind the neck. In women the collar was not infrequently flat across the shoulders. The waist was short, and defined by a belt.

This garment began to be worn by Englishmen about 1380, and by Englishwomen about 1400, the fashion lasting till the middle of that century.

and a temporary return, after the Restoration, to greater disguise in the so-called "petticoat-breeches" or Rhinegrave. The legs of these were so wide that they sometimes led to odd accidents. Thus Pepys reports (1661) meeting a friend who "told of his mistake the other day to put both his legs through one of the knees of his breeches, and went so all day." The appearance of petticoat-breeches is indicated in Wycherley's *The Dancing Master* : "While you wear pantaloons they make thee look and waddle (with all those gewgaw ribbons) like a great old fat slovenly water dog." [1]

It is not till the next century, however, that the problem of proportion and the treatment of the leg was really mastered. In fact, it was not until the tailor learnt to cut that the designer could "compose" a costume. Even so, the old custom of concealing the thighs was continued by the length of the waistcoat until 1760, and by the length of the coat which reached the knee (*Plates* 18, 19).

All such fashions had the effect of lowering the centre of gravity of the whole figure, adding to the massiveness of the male trunk, but, on the other hand, they diminished the apparent length of lower limb and so made it look less agile.

During the first half of the sixteenth century the trunk was not only extended in depth, but also in breadth, by expanding the shoulder line so that its shape became almost square. With its massive surface elaborately decorated by patterns and slashing so as to compel attention to that region, and with only the lower half of the leg left to represent the natural man, an impressive but top-heavy disguise was the result.

---

[1] A curious resemblance to the petticoat-breeches of the Restoration may be seen in the Hastings brass at Elsing church, Norfolk (1347), and still better in the effigy of Sir J. Blanchfront, at Alvechurch, Worcs., (1346), where the lower part of the surcoat is pleated as it covers the upper half of the thighs. Earlier the surcoat hung loose to the knee, over the armour.

It presented a number of transverse lines well marked, and the angle was hardly used to lighten the weighty appearance, the natural angles at the armpit and fork being concealed. An exaggerated masculinity verging on the brutal was the effect produced.

In the second half of that century, however, the angle, with the assistance of modified curves, became the constructional figure. For some eighty years, from 1550 to 1630, the prominent feature was the markedly pointed waist. This, with the hugely inflated trunk hose, was almost a caricature of the female shape (*Plate* 12), which at that time was wholly distorted and unrecognisable in the farthingale. And as the front aspect of the trunk was stiff and shield-like, with a pinched-in waist as though in stays, and the head was framed in a ruff very similar to a woman's, the mimicry was grotesque.

Similarly the Cavalier with his " love locks " falling on the shoulder, the lace collar and ruffles, and ribbons at the knee, and pointed waist, was gracefully effeminate in appearance

From the Restoration, and for about a hundred years after, the thigh was concealed by the skirts of the closed coat so that, in effect, the solidity of the trunk seemed to extend down almost to the level of the knees. The division was certainly not æsthetically well chosen, for the proportions were always bad, the figure being top-heavy. But this exaggeration of the size of the trunk was suggestive of muscular strength with a substantial sturdiness of frame. No doubt this was impressive on spectators and very probably appealing to women.

With growing refinement of manners this insistence on physical burliness ceased to be in good taste, and in consequence the transverse line, demarking the trunk from the lower limbs, became raised by shortening the waistcoat and reducing the skirts of the coat.

It is from that time, about 1760, that the modern

conception of masculine costume should, properly speaking, be dated. The change, by reducing the bulk of the trunk and lengthening the amount of limb exposed, imparted greater flexibility to the whole and added a more youthful grace. The new style favoured youth, and therefore had more sex appeal (*Plate* 20).

From the middle of the fourteenth to the middle of the eighteenth centuries the lower limbs were struggling for freedom, but as we watch them slowly emerging we may easily mistake the motive ; this, it seems, was quite as much the desire to attract as the desire for greater liberty. This is suggested by that chorus of moral disapproval which greeted each stage of liberation, from the shortening of the cotehardie in the fourteenth century exposing the whole lower limbs in tights—a chorus echoed in the days of the Regency tight buckskin breeches—to the Victorian trouser-taboo as mentioned in a subsequent chapter.

We may compare the disapproval which greeted man's legs as they emerged with the still noisier vociferation provoked in modern times by women's, as they, too, sought greater physical freedom. Each sex, in fact, has been reluctant to regard legs simply as a means of movement ; their element of sex appeal is always retained.

Such influences naturally affect the design of man's costume, and so, for the lower limbs, we find a variety of forms have been tried. These may be classified as :

1. Complete concealment, as by the ankle-length gown. This adds an air of dignity just because it eliminates the suggestion of sex attraction. It therefore becomes the elderly and is appropriate for the clergy and learned professions generally, and on ceremonial occasions when anything in the nature of sex appeal would be out of place.

2. A partial exposure of the shape of the lower limb

from below the knee, the shape of the thigh being concealed or distorted.

3. A disguised shape of the whole limb, as in modern trousers, thereby depriving it of its natural attraction.

4. Exposing the shape of the limb modified by change of material and colour at the knee, as in knee breeches and stockings.

5. Exploiting the shape of the limb in either tights or close-fitting long breeches.

Each of these variants affects the design of the whole costume, and especially its balance, because it affects the level at which the costume is transversely divided.

I have suggested that up to the middle of the eighteenth century this level demarking the trunk was generally low so as to exaggerate its dimensions. Costume assumed forms differing, no doubt, in method of execution, but all tending to magnify muscular strength.

Precisely the same spirit dictated the design of the sleeves during the whole of that period ; they never betrayed the real shape of the arm but always exaggerated its musculature, and very frequently the sleeve was little more than an additional fold of the body garment, as is still the case in a number of official and ceremonial robes worn to-day.

During the sixteenth century sleeves were frequently detachable, as though they did not really belong to the costume but were a sort of extended glove, and when presently the sleeve became a permanent attachment, the æsthetic problem arose—whether the arm-covering should be designed as a subsidiary part of the trunk-covering, which it becomes whenever the arm hangs down by the side, or whether it should be treated as an independent feature, which it becomes whenever it is in movement. And further, there was the technical problem how to attach the sleeve at the shoulder and how to allow for flexibility at the joints.

Some of these points are further discussed in the chapter on " Mobility." It is sufficient here to state that sleeves tended to be loose-fitting and, in fact, badly designed until the middle of the eighteenth century, when the huge reversed cuff (*Plate* 18), the last surviving feature of the voluminous sleeve, shrivelled up and has to-day left as a fossilised remnant a couple of buttons and false buttonholes at the wrist, which the recent war has now condemned as a futile extravagance.

For some two hundred years now man's arm has been a comparatively free agent, and the design of the sleeve has more or less corresponded to the shape of the arm, though always, of course, flattering its musculature.

We may attribute the change of design to the improved tailoring which began in the eighteenth century, but this only arose from an increasing demand for better cut. It would be more correct to say that both the upper and the lower limbs were being freed from the rest of the figure and allowed a greater degree of flexibility. It was no longer essential for a man to look burly ; it was more important to look graceful.

A small but significant feature may be detected in the manner of attaching the sleeve at the shoulder ; no longer did a poor technique compel the covering up of the joint by such devices as the Elizabethan " wing " (*Plates* 11, 12), or concealing it under ribbon bows or falling collar. It had acquired a new degree of flexibility which persisted for about a hundred years until, in the 1860's, the forerunner of the " lounge suit," with its much looser cut, gave the arm still wider powers of movement (*Plate* 36).

We may say that the need for flexibility has jogged the elbow of fashion and so produced the modern sleeve ; but æsthetically the breadth of the trunk has been diminished, and its proportions thereby improved, by reducing the bulk of the sleeves. We still shrink, however, from revealing the true dimensions of the arm muscles. Man likes to pretend that his arms are substantial right down to the wrists.

It is perhaps permissible to suggest that the sleeve is the weakest part in the design of man's costume. This view is certainly supported by the many efforts made at different epochs to overcome its defects. It is as though man was still in doubt whether his arms were weapons or ornaments. We have only to watch a public speaker trying to disembarrass himself of those awkward encumbrances ; they stick out like signposts or hang limply, until in despair the owner hides them behind his back. How much more fortunate is the clergyman in his mediæval robes !

The essential form of man's costume had been, until the middle of the eighteenth century, one in which the dimensions and importance of the trunk had been stressed either by increasing its breadth or its length, and always by making its surface highly decorated. We may say, too, that when the emphasis was on breadth, headgear likewise was broad, and when the emphasis was on length of trunk, headgear tended to be tall and striking, thereby extending its effect upwards. And in the former case the sleeves would be very capacious to add to the effect of breadth.

After 1760 a profound change took place.

Slimness of the trunk with exaggerated vertical lines and growing importance of the limbs characterised the new mode, which—as all profound fashion-changes tend to do—soon proceeded to go to extremes. But before that happened the style of dress worn by men from, say, 1760 to 1770, is generally regarded as combining dignity and grace to a high degree, and it is worth analysing such a composition to discover what are the elements giving it those characteristics (*Plate* 20).

We find that the transverse line is now represented only in minor details, such as the line of the coat pockets and the top of the stockings. The division between the trunk and the lower limbs is indicated by an angle formed where the bottom button of the waistcoat is fastened. In fact, angles have become a feature in such a costume, as are seen in the slope of the coat from the neck downwards, the waistcoat openings above and below, and the natural fork of the knee breeches, while the symbol is ingeniously echoed in the three-cornered hat.

But more important in its general effect on the costume is the flare which is given to the skirts of the coat by the stiffening of the lining. This causes there to be a slight break of the descending line at the level of the waist, at which point the flare begins.

We have only to compare the shape of an eighteenth century coat with that of a Victorian frock coat ; the flared skirts of the former impart an air of lightness and movement as the lines of the coat " go off at a tangent." There is, on the other hand, a deadly gravity about the frock coat which becomes a notorious laughing-stock when displayed in statuary. The eye positively wearies of those tedious perpendiculars which frame the trunk and thighs, and resents the apparent absence of flexibility at what is presumably the hip level.

The flared skirts of the former century, however, suggest the mannered gentleman " with fascination in his very bow."

It is worth noting, in that costume, that the waistcoat flaps themselves flare apart, forming an obtuse angle, while the waistcoat opening above is an acute angle. It is the property of obtuse angles to give a sense of strength to a design, while acute angles give height and grace. Where both are employed in a costume, with the acute at a higher level than the obtuse, these features give the effect of " graceful strength."

It was by such niceties of design that men's costumes about the middle of the eighteenth century obtained an artistic eminence which has probably not been rivalled.

We recognise the consistency of their aim to express refined masculinity. The angle is employed with discretion, and there is an absence of confusion and irrelevant details, features which at that time were novelties indeed. Incidentally, sex appeal seems to be implied rather than proclaimed.

Perhaps for that very reason it was not a style likely to hold the approval of the fashionable world for long. At any rate, by 1770 it had degenerated, the fronts of the coat being cut away into long elliptical curves with shortened skirts ; the flaps of the waistcoat became curved and the cuffs much diminished. With a cravat tied in a bow, and the breeches at the knee fastened by ribbons instead of buttons, it had become the costume favoured by the " Maccaroni," and as such presented a picture of effeminate glamour. The costume of the Maccaroni was described by one who knew him as being " a coat of light green, with sleeves too small for the arms, and buttons too big for the sleeves ; a pair of Manchester fine stuff breeches without money in the pockets ; clouded silk stockings but no legs ; a club of hair behind larger than the head that carries it ; a hat the size of sixpence on a block not worth a farthing." From *The Maccaroni Magazine* for 1772 we learn on the best authority that " the late stunting of coats having promoted the growth of skirts, the pockets are capable of holding conveniently a tolerable sized muslin handkerchief and smelling-bottle. Shoes are decreased in heel two inches and cut like a butter-boat to show the clock of the stockings . . . the head is dressed rather lower with one slanting side-curl *en deshabille*."

The exquisites were leading the way towards a more obvious mode of sex appeal, as exhibited later by the bucks of the Regency (*Plates* 22, 23). By the close of that century the whole composition of the costume had changed, in order to glorify the shape of the lower limbs. These were exhibited in the tightest of breeches reaching up to the midriff, with the coat cut well away at the sides so as to expose the moulding of leg and thigh, while the waistcoat was shortened as much as possible, and now cut square below.[1]

This gave a singularly "high waist" effect, with a transverse line across at a level which had not been used by man since the fifteenth century.

The general effect of this change of design was to remove any suggestion of top-heaviness, the weight being far more evenly distributed. The whole figure being slimmer, such a fashion naturally favoured youth. If we look at portraits of the period 1790 to 1830 we get the impression of a slender, long-legged, youthful man, capable of great agility ; one sees the legs of a dancer at a period when, in fact, dancing of a much more active sort, especially the Valse, had been recently introduced.

Such modes seem, in portraits, singularly unsuitable to portly elders, but in those war years from 1793 to 1815 it was natural that the Art of Costume should have concerned itself mainly with the youthful hero exploiting his physical charm.

This phase of " leg-worship "—which, as an expression of sex attraction, has been practised in the male costume of this country in various forms for six hundred years—declined into effeminacy about 1830. The exquisites of those days, Bulwer Lytton, " the padded man who wears the stays," and above all, Count D'Orsay, " the last of the Dandies," indicate in their

---

[1] From *The Times* of September 20th, 1799, we read : " If ever, in some centuries to come, the little hat, stuffed coat and long-toed shoe of a modern fine Gentleman should be discovered in some Museum of Antiquities they would no doubt give birth to many learned doubts and speculations. By the size of a pair of modern Leather Breeches it will naturally be inferred that the present race of men were of a Colossal form " (*Plate* 22).

portraits a design of costume composed almost wholly of curves, both elliptical and semi-circular. If it were not for a masculine breadth of shoulder one might even suppose those shapes were women in masculine garb (*Plate* 27).

We speak of " the last of the Dandies." It would be more appropriate to call that chapter " the last of the male leg," for it was followed by that extraordinary era of leg-taboo, when the limb itself could not be mentioned, nor even its covering ; trousers became " inexpressibles " or " unmentionables," and presently, when suits of one material appeared, the trouser portion was alluded to as " a pair of dittoes."

Although in modern times we profess to have got rid of such taboos, it is noticeable that the shape of the male leg—which was revealed in the peg-top trousers of early Victorian days (*Plate* 28), and to some extent in the close-fitting trousers of the late nineteenth and early twentieth centuries—is now more than ever disguised in the loose-fitting trousers of to-day.

I have suggested that the form of man's costume began to take modern shape about 1760, and if we contrast the treatment of the trunk since that time with its previous designs, we find that the former pictorial treatment then became architectural in character. In the main, the older method was to decorate the surface of the trunk as one might paint a canvas, giving a wealth of detail scattered over its surface ; there was a marked disinclination to leave large areas plain and unadorned, and there was a free use of functionless ornamentation.

Since the date I have suggested, 1760, the architect rather than the painter has inspired the composition. One sees the greater use of significant lines, often to suggest height, angles to suggest slimness, and an increasing use of plain untreated surfaces with patterns so subdued that they merely give a background. Further, there has been an inclination to break up the trunk surface into compartments, by the use of descending lines ; for example, in the modern suit the edges of the coat and the central line of waistcoat buttons divide up the front of the trunk into four sections. These may be so designed as to have a proportional relationship to each other.

During the nineteenth century the proportion of the whole figure occupied by the solid looking trunk, varied in a remarkable manner. For the first third of that century the lower limbs, as previously mentioned, were the principal feature. They were then eclipsed by the trunk, the outline of which was greatly extended downwards, at the expense of the unmentionable legs, by such buttoned-up garments as the surtout and the paletot, together with the frock coat.

The surtout was perhaps the most characteristic of that somewhat prosaic period, and especially popular with the middle-class man ; it figures in the illustrations of Dickens's early novels. It resembled a much shortened frock coat, often double-breasted, and with wide, short lapels. The paletot was a fitted garment, slightly waisted, and nearer to the frock coat in style (*Plate* 30*b*). But both imparted a curious " cylindrical " effect to the whole figure, causing the trunk portion to be extended downwards almost to the knees. This tubular shape was echoed in the " chimney pot " hat, and became, in fact, the distinguishing outline of the gentleman.

When, however, in the 1860's, for informal occasions the prototype of the lounge suit was introduced, with its short coat buttoned at or to the neck (*Plates* 35, 36), and cut comfortably loose over a short waistcoat, this marked a profound change in the whole conception of man's costume. Henceforth there were to be, for the gentleman at least, two styles running concurrently : one for " smart " occasions, tubular in outline with " extended trunk," the other designed mainly for comfort, in which " cut " and good proportion were the essential features.

The bad proportions of the frock coat, when buttoned up, encouraged the development of the " morning coat," in which the skirts are cut away at the sides, exposing the whole length of the lower limbs, and thus diminishing the apparent length of the trunk (*Plate* 34).

Its long sloping lines tend to add to the height of the whole figure, and diminish its breadth. It is therefore a " smarter " style than the round jacket of the lounge suit. It is also more " pictorial," in that it presents a contrast of colours, the upper part being different from the lower in that respect.

The suit, on the other hand, being composed of a single material throughout, and that of a subdued pattern as a rule, is distinctly more architectural in its nature. Its merits depend entirely on design and cut, together with material ; it is devoid of ornament, and colour is only a subsidiary feature (*Plate* 41).

It seems that the Art of Costume has been steadily changing its nature during the last couple of centuries, gradually discarding inspiration drawn from the painter, and accepting more and more the influence of the architect. It is noteworthy that while this change began first in man's costume, it has in recent years become noticeable in women's, at least in their day costume.

Colour tends to fade out of a classless commercial world, and costume becomes less " picturesque." Not necessarily less artistic, however, for those who can appreciate the subtleties of Form. The comment is often made that in the last hundred years the Englishman's costume has become " dull." It has certainly discarded to a great extent the use of colour, but in so doing it has, in reality, become more subtle. Although there may seem a superficial resemblance between the well-cut and the makeshift suit, no one sensitive to the niceties of

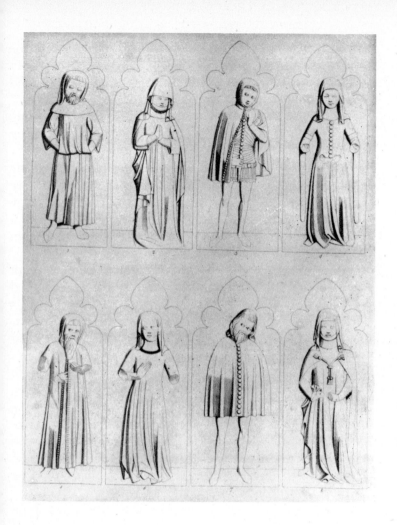

1. *Group of eight figures from the tomb of Sir Roger de Kerdeston, Reepham
Church, Norfolk, 1340.* The elders show the modes of " yesterday " while
the younger are in the fashions of " to-day."

Top row, left to right. (i) Tight-sleeved tunic, surcoat with loose sleeves.
(ii) Kirtle with buttoned tight sleeves under surcoat ; wimple and hood.
(iii) Short buttoned cotehardie. (iv) Kirtle under buttoned cotehardie
with hanging tippets.

Lower row, left to right. (v) Long loose cotehardie, buttoned. (vi) Plain
cotehardie. (vii) Short buttoned mantle. (viii) Loose gown with mantle
and wimple.

(From Stothard's Monumental Effigies).

2. *Effigy of Beatrice, Countess of Arundel, at Arundel, 1439.*
Horned reticulated head-dress 22 ins. wide. Sideless
surcoat over kirtle ; voluminous skirt. Sleeves of kirtle
buttoned to the wrist. Mantle on the shoulders.

(From Stothard's *Monumental Effigies*).

3. *Effigy of Joan, Countess of Arundel, at Arundel, 1487.*
Note extreme décolletage of the sideless surcoat, its
voluminous skirt held up revealing the ornamental kirtle,
the sleeves of which are turned back at the wrists. The
girdle is just visible through the gap in the surcoat and there
is a decided suggestion of tight-lacing. The face indicates
eyebrow plucking and the forehead shaving. The side
view of the head is almost " Egyptian " in character.

(From Stothard's *Monumental Effigies*).

4a. (left). *Brass of Alice, wife of Sir J. Hanley, at Dartmouth Church, 1403.* Shows reticulated head-dress, sideless cotehardie with buttoned front ; tight buttoned sleeves of kirtle.

(From Boutell's *Monumental Brasses*).

4b. *Brass of Elizabeth Clere, at Stokesby Church, Norfolk, 1488.* Shows domed head-dress, a transitional form later developing into the pediment head-dress. Note furred " bertha " and cuffs.

(From Cotman's *Norfolk Brasses*).

5. *Brass, formerly at St. Mary in Costany Church, Norwich, of a man and wife. c. 1430.* Both wearing houppelands. Note the woman's high waist and form of horned head-dress.

(From Cotman's *Norfolk Brasses*).

6. *Brass of the family of Sir T. Urswyck, at Dagenham, 1479.* The widow wears a wimple and veil; the two married daughters next to her have butterfly head-dresses, while the other daughters have truncated cone head-dresses with flowing hair, indicative of virginity.

7a. (top on opposite page). *Brass of Elizabeth Perepoynt, West Malling, 1543.* Shows late form of pediment head-dress; hanging sleeves with embroidered and cuffed under-sleeves.

7b. (bottom on opposite page). *Brass of G. Coles and his wives, St. Sepulchre Church, Northampton, 1640.* Note the women's hats; their costumes and ruffs are decidedly " old-fashioned " for the date. The man's costume is that of a respectable bourgeois. Contrast his costume with that shown in plate 14.

7a, b. For captions see facing page.

8a. *Effigy of Lady Fitzherbert of Norbury, Derby, 1483.* Note the mitred head-dress, sideless surcoat over fitting kirtle. Mantle of rank attached to the shoulders.

8b. *Effigy of wife and daughters of Robert Suckling at St. Andrew's Church, Norwich, 1611.* The wife is wearing the Spanish form of farthingale, while the daughters are wearing the later (French) type. The ruff, worn by the former is "old-fashioned" by this date, and the daughters have discarded it. But both mother and daughters are wearing fashionable head-dresses.

9. *Portrait of a Gentleman in Red*, *1548*. The immense breadth of
shoulder line is accentuated by horizontal emphasis. Balance
obtained by the feet being wide apart.

10. *The Princess Elizabeth, 1540–50.* Heavily embroidered gown, the skirt open over embroidered petticoat. Hanging over-sleeves with slashed under-sleeves. Head-dress approaching the " French hood " in design. The emphasis of the costume is on angles.

11a. *Earl of Northampton*

11b. *Sir Walter Raleigh*

EN'S HEADGEAR, circa 1600.
(From Lodge's *Portraits*).

11c. *Earl of Exeter*

12. *Miniature of the Earl of Dorset by Isaac Oliver, 1616.* Bombasted trunk-hose ; emphasis on angles. The pointed waist of the doublet, the shoes and embroidered stockings are noticeably " feminine " in feeling.

13. *Sepulchral effigy of the daughters of Lord Teynham, Lynsted, Kent, 1620.*
The marked décolletage of the left-hand figure indicated she was unmarried. Note sleeves, different forms of ruffs and head-dresses.

14. *Caricature of a Cavalier, 1646.* All the details in his costume which offended Puritan taste are carefully exaggerated.

15. *Portrait of a Lady, 1635.* Note the sleeve, paned and puffed, with ribbon bows at elbow. The square-cut corsage is filled in with lace. The style may have been a "revival" of the mode of 100 years earlier.

16a. *Two figures of women on horseback*, one sitting aside, the other astride, both from the Ellesmere Chaucer of the 15th century.

16b. *Woman riding side-saddle*, from a contemporary woodcut of the early 17th century.

Form (which depend, of course, on design and cut) can fail to distinguish between the two.

Failure cannot be concealed by added decorations, or poverty of design and bad proportion distorted by flamboyant colouring. The Art of Costume is becoming more austere ; it has been forced, as it were against its will, to adapt itself to modern conditions, and is slowly becoming " practical " in its designs. In this sense its scope is expanding, while the range of design is contracting. If all classes dress alike, the discriminating man will demand the highest possible skill from his tailor, so that his costume may bear marks of distinction.

An art attempting to express itself under such conditions, and deprived of such easy means as richness of materials and colouring, will be driven to depend more and more on refinements of Form.

CHAPTER VII

HEADGEAR IN MAN'S COSTUME

THE supreme importance of his head, in man's estimation, has always called for special attention to be paid to what is worn upon it. This, in turn, will affect or be affected by the arrangement of his hair. The two have generally combined to magnify some aspect of his appearance, sometimes by adding to his height, sometimes by increasing the breadth or indeed the whole size of the head. It is noticeable that the learned professions have been accustomed to wear headgear having this enlarging property, such as the legal wig, the scholastic mortar-board, the episcopal mitre.

It is equally noticeable that, unlike woman, man avoids headgear which might provoke ridicule or amused comment ; he has always refused to wear anything resembling in shape a dunce's cap tapering off to a point. The male costume never jests. Man's head is a serious matter. We have always to bear in mind that formerly his headgear was far more an integral part of his costume than it is to-day. Men wore their hats indoors as well as out until the eighteenth century, and therefore the cut of their hair has always to be reckoned with the hat on, and not bareheaded, at least in day costume. In criticising the artistry of such costume, the headgear cannot be ignored.

To-day, when the lounge suit style is almost universally worn, the hat is optional ; indeed, the modern suit appears better proportioned when worn without a hat, and headgear of all kinds is losing its vitality and meaning.

Formerly the headgear and the cut of the hair conformed in spirit to the style of costume, and the function of the headgear was to accentuate the theme announced by it, as a cadenza attached to the body of the work. As such, the headgear was allowed a degree of license which might not be permitted elsewhere ; in the great age of audacious headgear, the Elizabethan and Jacobean period, with those astonishing displays of bravura, though one might see defiance challenging all-comers, and even rashness, the comic is wanting.

Madcaps there were, perhaps, but never fool's caps.

In the eighteenth century the management of the hat itself was a searching test of manners ;[1] and even in the nineteenth it still served a useful purpose—its shape distinguished class from class. In general terms headgear may be said to fulfil its function of emphasising the message of the costume, by utilising height, breadth, shape and posture.

Of height it is enough to say that when the costume is designed to indicate this quality, the headgear, too, will aim high, but always with this precaution : though the costume may lavishly employ acute angles, as in the period about 1600, the headgear will hardly go beyond the obtuse angle, or else avoid that symbol altogether by using the truncated cone or the sugar loaf. One can collect many instances of these from portraits of that date, while the truncated cone reappeared in the Regency period, and the sugar loaf as the Victorian " bowler " (*Plates* 25, 30, 36).

On æsthetic grounds the truncated cone is a singularly unfortunate shape to select, for, placed on the crown, it gives the wearer the shape of an imbecile's head, and

[1] The cocked hat was a mark of gentility, and the art of cocking it correctly had to be learnt. Moreover, different forms of cocking had different implications. Thus *The London Chronicle* for May, 1762, informs us : " Hats are now worn upon an average six inches and three-fifths broad in the brim and cocked between Quaker and Kevenhuller . . . there is a military cock and the mercantile cock ; and while the beaux of St. James' wear theirs diagonally over their left or right eye, sailors wear the sides of their hats tucked down to the crown." At the end of the century the cocked hat, much enlarged, and folded flat, was carried under the arm as a *chapeau bras*.

explains the mentally defective appearance of so many of the Regency rakes.

When women have ventured to wear this shape, as during the last part of the fifteenth century, they took care to tilt it so far back that the unlucky resemblance was absent.

From those experimental shapes of the Regency period, with the cone squat or extended, the brim flat or pointed or absent, there finally arose the " stove pipe " or " chimney pot " hat of the Early Victorians. There could scarcely have been a more convincing symbol of lofty aspiration and evidence of the superior class wearing it. It put the Upper Classes a foot taller than ordinary mortals.

With the levelling influence of democracy, that altitude has sunk ; the social guillotine has cut off the gentleman's topper and hurled it into the basket. Those high hats enabled the gentleman to wear those ankle-length overcoats without looking overwhelmed by them, for it was the aim as well as the privilege of the gentleman to look distinguished.

Breadth of headgear should be in proportion to the degree of emphasis which the costume lays on that feature, and the flatter the headgear the more its breadth has to be accentuated to escape a loss of dignity. For if the brim scarcely extends beyond the ears, as in some of the straw hats worn between 1860 and '70, the head appears shrunken ; the same effect is seen in the narrow-brimmed bowlers of the '70's and early '80's. They suggest a small-headed race.

The flat caps and hats of the first half of the sixteenth century (*Plate* 9), in keeping with the breadth of shoulder line in the costume and the square cut hair, were generally wide enough to avoid the suggestion of puny insignificance which the narrow flat headgear is apt to give. We may explain this because we expect the breadth of headgear to have some affinity to the breadth of the shoulders ; if the two are in strong contrast the effect is ridiculous.

The shape of headgear varies between the round circumference and the angular, with the crown flat or domed. The domed crown is a natural concession to the shape of the head ; it was used in the fifteenth and late sixteenth centuries, and again in the Victorian bowler. Its fatal defect, æsthetically, is the resemblance in shape to that of a bald head. Consequently some additional feature has to be given to detract from the resemblance, extra height added to the dome, a curly or ornamental brim, or a jaunty feather at the side ; or the hat may be worn at a rakish angle. (The point, though a small one, is a good illustration of how the Art of Costume eschews mimicry of physical blemishes or defects, or even of anything which might perhaps recall such misfortunes. Costume is, above all things, always optimistic, hoping for the best.)

Occasionally the circumference of man's headgear has been markedly angular, the bicorne and tricorne hats of the eighteenth century being the most conspicuous examples (*Plates* 20, 22). They became a style of costume in which angles were conspicuous ; it is noteworthy how rapidly the hat lost that angularity as soon as the costume of the early Regency began to extol height and slimness ; whereupon the hat shot up in sympathy. And later, when the Dandy of 1830 cultivated a measure of effeminacy, his hat acquired feminine curves (*Plate* 27).

The first tall silk hat was invented by John Hetherington, a haberdasher of the Strand, and was worn by him for the first time on January 15, 1797, thereby provoking a riot. The *St. James' Gazette* of January 16 reported that he was charged with a breach of the peace for having appeared on the public highway wearing upon his head a tall structure having a shining lustre and calculated to frighten timid people. Several women had fainted at

73

the sight, children screamed, dogs yelped and a small boy had had his arm broken. *The Times* remarked : " In these days of enlightenment it must be considered an advance in dress reform, and one which is bound, sooner or later, to stamp its character upon the entire community. The new hat is destined to work a revolution in headgear."

In fact, if we want to realise how well, on the whole, the headgear of an epoch became its costume, we have only to transpose a sketch of such a hat on to the costume of a different date. Thus a Tudor flat cap worn with a Regency costume, or an Early Victorian " stove pipe " above to-day's lounge suit, would look strangely disproportionate. A close examination shows that headgear has, like costume, its " line " or imaginary axis of construction ; and this should have some harmonic relationship to that of the costume.

Moreover, the hat itself has its own proportions, and in this respect the headgear worn by men during the first quarter of last century was remarkable ; the proportions were often bad, sometimes grotesquely so, while at the same time the variety of shapes was extensive. There were, for example, the sporting " Turf " shape, the driving " Tilbury," the " Oxonian " and "Collegian" as imparting a studious air, with the " Aylesbury " and the " Anglesea " for general tastes, each with its distinctive height of crown and slope of sides (*Plate* 25).

It was an age of experiment and change ; for the first time men were wearing hats with flat crowns raised well above the head ; their height and breadth as well as the proportions and shape of the brim had all to be tested by " trial and error."[1]

The effect of posture—that is, the position of the headgear relative to the head—is extremely important

---

[1] The beaver hat was becoming displaced, among fashionable folk, by the silk hat about the time of Waterloo.

During the war hats were taxed, a stamp having to be affixed to the lining.

(*Plate* 31*a*). As every one knows, the wrong tilt gives a totally wrong impression. A hat placed squarely on the crown suggests stability ; a backward tilt gives it a childish look, while a forward tilt makes it appear demure. Neither of these last two impressions has man ever sought to convey in his headgear.

But he has often combined a slight backward with a sly sideways tilt, and this combination has a range of its own significance : smart, gay dog, reckless, vulgar . . . becoming intoxicated even, as the side lurch grows more and more pronounced. A mere suspicion of insouciance, however, reinforced by a sweeping plume on a curving hat sufficiently large, and the composition recalls the Cavaliers' romantic poise.

It seems the sideways tilt is a privilege of youth, and that the elderly adopt it at their peril. . . .

If we compare the headgear of the two sexes we are struck by the fact that men have tended to use its variations in shape, etc., at any epoch mainly to denote differences in social class and occupation, while women have used them mainly to denote differences of person-ality. Consequently a man's headgear will indicate his group, a woman's her individual characteristics. In modern times, as it is considered bad taste to indicate social class too conspicuously in dress, a man is not unwilling to abandon the wearing of a hat altogether, for its main purpose has gone. A woman, on the other hand, is reluctant to surrender this illuminating medium for self-expression and, when conditions permit, we may expect that her millinery will become once more important.

As man becomes bareheaded out of doors, the practice encourages him to indulge in fancy hair-dressing, and so to-day there are more types of masculine coiffure than there are of hats ; one sees the side-parting, the centre-split, the undulant and the butter-slide. . . .

When we see in pictures the headgear worn by men

of the remote past, we must assume that some of the curious variations had social significances now lost to us ; they are not to be judged solely on æsthetic grounds. The role of the Victorian " top hat " for example, was complex, and the circumstances under which it was to be worn were strict. While in the confines of " the City " it was permissible to wear it with a round jacket ; outside that magic circle the combination would have been unspeakably awful, while a bowler above a frock coat would have been totally inconceivable.

It seems that formerly far more thought was paid to such niceties of costume than is the modern habit, and it is evident that man's headgear was not primarily intended as a means of protection, but as a mark of distinction. And now, since such marks have ceased to be considered in good taste, hats have ceased to be either distinctive or distinguished.

An interesting feature in the Art of Costume is the treatment of the neck—that is to say, the junction of a very flexible to a comparatively inflexible region. We may suppose that formerly there was the traditional disinclination to expose a very vulnerable region to attack, and that therefore it became a custom for the neck to be concealed or actually guarded. At any rate a bare neck was unheard of until Byron chose to shock the world with that display of physical exhibitionism.

The various methods of concealing the neck, some derived from forgotten forms of armour, served either to emphasise social rank or to fill in that æsthetically awkward gap between head and trunk ; all had the practical effect of restricting the movement of the head. And ultimately such restraint came, by the association of ideas, to indicate in itself a kind of social superiority.

Perhaps the most singular example of this was the Elizabethan ruff, although in actual practice the high starched collar of the end of last century was even more inconvenient, seeing that it was worn by men engaged in all sorts of activities, whereas the Elizabethan ruff was mainly ceremonial.

If we consider the sort of articles which have been used at various times for separating the head from the trunk in this way, the ruff, the collar, the stock, the neckbands and cravats (*Plates* 7*b*, 8*b*, 20, 27, 28, 29*a*, etc.) all have this in common, that they tend to be either white in colour or else black ; the colouring of the face is thus kept apart from that of the costume. (The idea of starching the cravat, rendering it stiff, had been introduced by Beau Brummel. The effect of this ingenious device is recorded in *The Mirror* of May 7, 1825, where it was stated that : " Dandies were struck dumb with envy and washerwomen miscarried " at the novel spectacle.) By this means the hue of the skin is not " killed " by the adjoining garment ; a similar device is usually employed at the wrist, and these are the only two places where man exposes his bare skin to view.

In striking contrast to this method of separating the head from the trunk was the wearing of a flowing wig which filled in the neck space, causing the head and trunk to merge into one. This fashion, which lasted from the Restoration until into the reign of George II, had the advantage of making the head appear more than ever important.

Man's dislike of baring his neck, which is in such marked contrast to woman's liking for doing so, was no doubt responsible for the appearance of the coat collar as soon as the wig shrank in size and ceased to cover the neck. By 1760 the coat collar was creeping into fashion, to become by the close of that century extremely heavy and high-standing (*Plate* 22). It is to be noted that, except for sport, man has never ventured to discard the coat collar since. And only with reluctance is he abandoning the privilege of wearing the starched collar which denotes the fact that he is above the manual worker.

It is evident, then, that man's headgear serves a very different purpose from woman's. It is not such an integral part of the costume ; it is less personal ; it announces—or did once announce—the wearer's rank. It has never betrayed the secrets of his mind.

CHAPTER VIII

FORM IN WOMAN'S COSTUME

ALTHOUGH the costumes of the sexes have features in common there is this radical difference in Form, that Man's tends to give a fair notion of the general shape of his body without accentuating its sexual characteristics ; sometimes he has looked hardly human, but he seldom looks merely " male." In modern times, clean shaven and wearing garments which are no longer his exclusive property, the form of his costume has even become ambiguous.

But Woman's has usually tended to conceal the real shape of her body while emphasising its sexual characteristics. A woman dressed in male attire may easily pass for a man ; it is far more difficult for him to look the part dressed as a woman.

The essential feature of her costume, then, has been disguise of shape, partial or complete. For this, art is needed, and so it is on hers rather than on his that the Art of Costume has expended its greatest efforts of imagination. It has usually striven to present pictorially something of the fascination of the inscrutable. To provoke questions she clothes herself in conundrums.

The scaffolding on which the building has been constructed is not too obvious, so that a survey of all the varieties of Form which woman's costume has presented during the last six centuries would at first sight appear bewildering. To the casual glance they might well seem to be too capricious and inconsequent to admit of analysis.

But that appearance of confusion is largely due to the accessory details which overlie and disguise the fundamental Form of the costume they adorn. They may even lead us to forget for a moment that it has a meaning at all ; that here is a symbol indicative of social ideas.

If its Form is an unconscious expression of the prevailing mental attitude, and therefore changeable, it retains a persistent note ; it is never wholly without sex-consciousness.

In a later chapter sex-attraction in Costume will be discussed ; here it is enough to remind the reader that the terms mentioned are by no means synonymous. Her costume, especially in former times, was a constant reminder to a woman of her sex and the physical restrictions enforced on her thereby ; it demonstrated not only her own attitude of mind, but that of the community towards her sex. On that account it was not necessarily " sex-attractive," though obviously that motif was seldom absent, but it could not fail to keep her " sex-conscious." Indeed we may even suspect that the Form of her costume helped to circumscribe the range of her outlook.

We note that in former times of strict conventions the occasional rebel would indicate her independence of mind by refusing to wear conventional costume, as though, by casting it off, she was freeing herself from more than a physical trammel. Do we not see something of the sort to-day in the woman who aspires to lead a " sex-free " life ?

Among the conventional-minded, Costume has sometimes assumed forms apparently designed to imply a high degree of physical helplessness, almost approaching complete incapacity to move : the upper ranks of society would distinguish themselves by forms which were too inconvenient and uncomfortable to be willingly copied by ranks below. The train of the court dress, requiring the assistance of attendants, is a survival of that exclusive attitude. The trailing skirts of the " Perfect Lady " have always been a class-distinction. In fact, we may say that the higher up the social scale the more uncomfortable and inconvenient has been the dress.

Stripped of its inessentials the Form of Woman's Costume is found to be comparatively simple in structure, and its principal variations not as numerous as might, at first sight, be expected.

Taking as the basic symbol of construction the figure represented by a capital " X ", the point of intersection represents the position of the " waist " (actual or artificial). On this basis a number of simple variations can be made, either by varying the position of the intersecting point—thus producing a high or a low waist ; or by varying the angle of intersection, making it more acute or more obtuse. The more obtuse this angle, the wider, naturally, will be the baseline— i.e. the bottom of the skirt ; the more acute the angle, the narrower will be the bottom of the skirt.

Thus there are two variable factors : the position of the intersecting point and the degree of the angle there formed. Usually both vary in combination through a considerable range, which we can classify into definite types.

Thus, high waist and wide angle (e.g. the crinoline dress of 1864).

High waist and narrow angle (e.g. the late Regency dress).

Low waist and wide angle (e.g. Elizabethan dress).

Low waist and narrow angle (e.g. the dress of the early 1880's).

It will be observed that both factors affect the balance of the whole costume ; merely raising the waist appears to increase balance (on the principal of the optical illusion previously mentioned).

Still more is balance given by a wide baseline—i.e. a skirt wide at the bottom, or with the addition of a train. But if the angle is made so narrow that the two lines are nearly parallel, like a closed pair of scissors, one obtains the structural formula of the *tubular* dress (*Plate* 44).

The balance of such a shape is obviously precarious and will be greatly affected by the position given to the waistline, which has now become no longer a point of intersecting angles but a transverse line. It thus approximates to the " H " formula of the male costume, especially if situated at the level of the real waist, as in man's.

This situation will therefore be usually avoided in woman's dress, and the waistline be placed either very high (as in the early Regency dress)—a position which also has the advantage of giving balance, or very low (as in the day dress of 1923-8). Here the disadvantage is the conspicuous absence of balance, especially when the dress is not trained.

Alternatively the tubular-shaped dress can avoid this pitfall by eliminating the transverse line altogether, merely indicating the approximate position of the waist by its natural curve. Such was the method of the dress of 1878-9.

The two parallel lines forming the outlines of the tubular dress can, however, be still further inflected until they positively incline *inwards* as they descend ; the result must necessarily cause a complete lack of balance, as was seen in the " Hobble-skirt " dress of 1910-12, where the greatest breadth was at the shoulders (*Plate* 43).

All those types of Form which are constructed on two lines intersecting or parallel may conveniently be classified as *pure Linear* Costumes. They tend to have a certain character of their own, with outlines that are decisive and clean cut. As a result, " visibility is good." To be effective they require to be made of materials that are not too soft and flimsy. It is a type admirably adapted for the " tailor-made " (*Plate* 47), and appeals to the modern woman for just those qualities which seem to express a directness of approach and certainty of poise. For the coy hesitancy of the Victorian young lady a vaguer outline was eminently suited. It is perhaps significant that the " straight up and down " linear dress became prominent during the Suffragette movement.

The Linear Form becomes markedly modified when the basic lines of construction are no longer straight but curved, either wholly or in part. Thus two new forms are produced, the *Curvilinear* and the *Semi-curvilinear*.

If the upper portion of the " X " symbol is convex on each side, representing the shape of bodice and sleeves as one, the lower portion of the " X " may either remain as two straight lines—the Semi-curvilinear type, as in the blouse and gored skirt of the '90's (*Plate* 40)—or it, too, may be curved ; and this curve may be either convex, producing a dome-shaped skirt as in the 1840-50's, or concave, producing a flared skirt as in Edwardian days (*Plate* 42). Thus there are two curvilinear forms and one semi-curvilinear.

It is evident that the introduction of curves into the basic formula for Costume at once increases the range of possible designs, and this because curves have an infinite variety. We may have curves that are segments of circles, and some of the early " beehive " forms of crinoline skirt have almost the outline of a semi-circle standing on its diameter. Or, at the other extreme, there are those long elliptical outlines which distinguished the late Edwardian costume, and again the evening dresses of the 1930's.

These elliptical curves—the constructing of which is a feature of the present century with materials cut on the cross—are, of course, a replica of the curves of youth, and therefore favour the youthful form, while the semi-circle sort gives an unmistakable matronly appearance to the composition. As such it was very appropriate to the Early Victorian style of dress.

This outline of the principal types of Form is intended

to supply, only diagrammatically, as it were, useful land-marks in the general survey of this extensive field. In-numerable minor varieties and mixtures of types have constantly appeared—and disappeared with changing circumstances—for Form in Costume always moves with the times. But we must also not forget that, to the spectator, a particular Form can be often changed completely by the addition of some outer garment which, in its turn, produces a new Form. However, it is convenient to have in mind some " plan of design " when criticising a costume ; it enables us to test it for any breach of æsthetic laws and thereby discover why a particular costume " looks wrong." Why, in fact, it *is* wrong, in spite, perhaps, of a mass of confusing details intended to cover a defect of that sort.

Analysis may reveal two kinds of fault : defects in the basic design or defects in the subsidiary features. The former will give to a costume a vague inconsequence, and this is the commonest fault in modern dress ; the latter tends to produce " fussiness," the common fault in Victorian dress (*Cf. plates* 38 and 48). An observer who is very sensitive to Form and balance may view that fault with tolerance, while finding it hard to excuse common errors of the present age ; though perhaps the more usual judgment of any epoch is to be very conscious of the fault of ancestors, and blind to its own. The Art of Costume flourishes on that supposition.

Having thus analysed the principles on which the Form of Costume is based, we may now turn to examine the Form of the finished structure. Just as we speak of the " orders of architecture," so, too, it would be logical to speak of the " orders " of Costume, based on some such system as I have indicated ; we might have our " Classical " and " Gothic " with their variations, and I have found the use of such terms very convenient in this art.

In practice, however, styles of Costume have been

quite arbitrarily given names taken from some garment or some noticeable feature in the dress, or even from a person. Thus we meet with " pelisse robe," " redingote," " Watteau sacque " and a host of other terms which convey very little to the uninitiated.

How much more informative a catalogue of costumes would be if descriptions were a little more scientific ! Thus a " medium high-waisted semi-curvilinear dress of 45 degrees basic angle " would at least give the reader some notion of its essential Form, though perhaps not encouraging its sale.

But the Art of Costume clings to its lack of system, and just as pictures are grouped into " the school of " a painter or even a locality, so the Victorians were wont to describe costumes as " à la " some notable mistress of royalty whose style of dress was supposed to be familiar to all. To-day an " Agnes Sorel bodice " or a " Montespan sleeve " would convey very little. We no longer pay these old-world compliments to ladies of easy virtue. Nor are we very consistent in naming the finished article. Do we clearly distinguish a " frock " from a " gown," and what precisely is " an evening inspiration ? " The modern terms of commendation in Fashion journals seem to be " slick," " sophisticated," " amusing " and " husky." Posterity must not confuse these with the old-fashioned words " charming " and " pretty."

By confining ourselves, however, to less rhapsodical terms we can classify the various types of structure according to the formation of the finished article, and we find that during the past five centuries Woman has been satisfied with remarkably few. Only in shape and name has there been much change.

Her costume has been built on one of two Principles : either *closed* or *open* down the front.

Each of these Principles has variations which it may be convenient to designate as Types. Thus, the Closed

Dress presents two Types, according to whether it is made in one piece or in two separate pieces (bodice and skirt).

A. (1) The Closed Dress, one-piece Type.

This is the oldest type of dress used in this country, dating back to the Classical influence. It was the only one used until the close of the fifteenth century. We see about that time an increasing dissatisfaction with its limitations, evidenced partly by the custom of making the upper portion tight enough to reveal the shape of the figure, and partly by the novelty of cutting down the neck so as to expose much of the shoulders and bosom.

We may call such a garment a *Gown*, its features being that the waist is only indicated by a girdle or slight shaping, and that the skirt is full, flowing and reaching to the ground, often with a train (*Plates* 1, 2, 3). It is evident that such a type of garment, if shortened and deprived of its train and fullness, will have changed its character ; from being stately and " immobile " it will have acquired mobility and a more youthful appearance. In this form we call it a *Frock*, a name given when it was first introduced in the Regency period, probably because, being at that time so often of white material, it had a fanciful resemblance to the countryman's " smock-frock " (which, in its turn, had descended from a mediæval garment).

The closed one-piece type of costume has two variations or *Styles* :

(*a*) The Single Dress style.

The practice of wearing a single dress (that is, without an under-dress) does not appear to have become usual until after the Renaissance. Since then, of course, the single dress style has had, in spite of interruptions and occasional rivals, a long reign down to the present day.

Its feature is that it allows freer movement and so is more suited for outdoor activities than

(b) The Double-Dress style. That is, one dress worn over an under-dress.

This was the style habitually used all through the middle ages, both garments reaching to the ground, and both, in effect, *gowns*, of which only parts of the under-dress—such as the longer sleeves—were visible. They were the descendants of the classical tunic and super-tunic, the under-dress or tunic being called the " kirtle," over which was worn in the fourteenth century a gown known as a " cotehardie " (*Plate* 1), and in the fifteenth century one known as a " houppelande ; " the feature of the former being its close fit over the figure, and its decolletage, while the latter was distinguished by its voluminous folds, huge hanging sleeves, and being girdled as high as possible (*Plate* 5). The " sideless coat," sometimes called " sideless cotehardie " or " sideless supertunic," appears in the second half of the fourteenth and during much of the fifteenth centuries. In this a large gap is revealed on each side from the armpit to the waist, often bordered with fur ; through this " window " the tight-fitting kirtle exposes the shape of the figure and usually a part of the girdle is seen (*Plates* 2, 3, 4a, 8a). It corresponds to the sex-attractive device seen in evening dresses some fifteen years ago whereby the shape of the breasts was revealed.

Owing to the lack of perspective in brasses the sideless coat often appears to be a short jacket over the tunic, but this appearance, increased by the edging of fur, is deceptive. The structure is more clearly seen in effigies.

From the Renaissance, the closed double-dress type of costume seems to have almost disappeared until its revival in the Regency period, with, however, this important difference : the name " tunic " was applied to the *outer* of the two garments which was only knee length ; a mode—with its Regency name—which has had occasional revivals since, especially just before the first Great War.

The feature of the Regency style of tunic costume is that the tunic is short and narrow so that a " straight up and down " appearance is given even when the under-dress is trained. The feature of the mediæval style of double-dress (tunic and super-tunic) is that the full flowing lines of the two gowns are preserved in their lower part.

The double-dress style had its greatest revival during the last quarter of the nineteenth and early years of the present centuries (*Plate* 43).

It is essentially a style for immobile attitudes ; in the seated posture, for example, the double thickness of skirt helps to diminish the prominence of knees, and the material can fall into spreading folds.

A. (2) The Closed Dress, two-piece Type.

The notion of dividing the dress into two separate garments appears to have been unknown (in this country) before the Renaissance. The earliest traces of a division may be seen in a few brasses of about 1490 where a transverse line suggests stitching of the bodice to the skirt.[1]

We do not know when the practice of having a dress in two separate parts actually came into use, but it had become common in Elizabethan times, and must have been a necessity with the farthingale.

It is evident that, apart from practical convenience, the separation into two parts brought some æsthetic advantages. It became easy to use two entirely different materials and colours for each, and this would draw attention to the line of juncture—namely, the waist. I

[1] The brass to the wife of W. Berdewell at West Harling church, Norfolk (1490), shows a distinct line of seam between the bodice and skirt. This is the earliest English evidence I know that indicates the division of the one-piece dress into two separate garments. The Italians were nearly a hundred years in advance of us in this.

have little doubt that originally such was the motive leading to this structural novelty. The sixteenth century waist was anything but insignificant.

As a separate garment the advantage could be taken by the skirt to develop a number of new shapes, and the range expanded by pleats and gathers ; while the bodice was set free to venture untrammelled into designs hither-to unexplored, in partnership with the sleeve. The Art of Costume was being wafted by the breezes of the Renaissance into a New World.

The possibilities which this type gives to the use of colours will be discussed in a separate chapter ; here we have to note how this horizontal division, far more decisive than the old style of girdle, at once affects the general appearance of the whole costume ; it has become a " two storey building ; " and this introduces fresh æsthetic problems. No longer can the costume present long descending and unbroken lines from neck to feet ; and when an outdoor garment such as a short coat is worn, is it to be made in correct proportion to the bodice or to the whole costume ? Take, for example, the jacket or cape such as were worn in the middle of the eighteenth and a great deal in the latter part of the nineteenth centuries : these give at the back a transverse line which does not correspond in position with that formed by the waistband in front.

Or those still shorter garments, like the bolero, which barely reach to the waist and so often reveal an awkward gap behind. Sometimes the junction of bodice and skirt is concealed by an elaborate " Swiss belt " or similar device, or, quite frankly, a masculine waistcoat is worn with a jacket, but the results are not usually very happy. Or the bodice can be prolonged by basques so as to overflow the line of junction under a belt, thus creating two transverse lines—an obvious blemish ; or bodice and skirt rely on their own bands—with the risk of revelations when stooping.

As the two-piece type can so easily develop a masculine appearance, the bodice may be given some markedly feminine touches so as to neutralise that tendency. But when, for instance, the bodice becomes a shirt with collar and tie, with a masculine waistcoat above a plain short skirt having an inverted boxpleat down the front, the masculinity of the whole costume is very evident. That tendency began to appear towards the end of the 1860's and became conspicuous by the close of the century, following in fact, step by step, the progress of feminine emancipation.

The two-piece type has now won an accepted place in the modern woman's wardrobe and has lost its old implication of masculinity. No doubt it suits the mental attitude of the woman while at work, but of an evening, when her desire is to look more " feminine," she will instinctively revert to the older styles ; it used to be said of the blouse and skirt style that it was not " dressy " enough for the evening ; not " attractive " enough was meant.

B. The Open Dress Principle of construction :

A dress open down the whole front (over an under-dress) used to be called a " robe " from its resemblance to the robes worn by men and women in the middle ages and still surviving for ceremonial and other occasions.[1]

Originally an occasional garment (with sleeves) donned over the gown, it became after the Renaissance a permanent part of the costume, the gown becoming the under-dress (*Plate* 10). This new mode—" the robe " —typically Renaissance in spirit, offers the designer

[1] " Robings " or trimmings forming a " V " down the front of the upper part of the dress and being a stage towards the open bodice formation, may be seen in various brasses of the second half of the fifteenth century, e.g. that of Anne Boleyn at Blickling church, Norfolk (1479) ; that of the wife of W. Norwich at St. George of Colegate church, Norwich (1472) ; and that of the two wives of Sir Miles Stapleton, Ingham church, Norfolk (1466), recorded by Cotman.

more scope for the display of his art ; principally because the costume acquires " depth ; " in place of showing only one surface there are two layers, and by the deft use of colours and materials it is possible to modulate from one key into another on the under-dress. Moreover, by closing the robe at the waist, leaving it open above and below, the resulting angles point at the waist and thus draw attention to it ; the sharper the angles the smaller it appears.

The Robe principle supplies two Types : real and simulated.

(1) Robe with real openings : a type which flourished during the sixteenth, seventeenth and eighteenth centuries. The opening may be complete down the front, merely closed at the waist by a fastening, the complete open robe style ; or the opening may be limited to either the top (bodice) or to the skirt. One may find examples of all three styles in the centuries named. In the nineteenth century their use was occasional, but we have to recognise that the *teagown*, when it first appeared about 1877, was essentially an open robe. It seems to have been introduced as a kind of maternity gown. At least we are told that " young ladies are not expected to wear teagowns as this apparel is reserved for the married." A contemporary adds : " Moralists would strive to teach us that they are a sign of the degeneracy of the age." It would be more correct to regard them as a sign of the birth rate. By the end of the century they had lost their peculiar significance and were worn by the unmarried.

(2) Instead of real openings, these may be simulated by trimmings which were therefore known as " robings " (*Plate* 24*a*). And these might be limited to one or other portion of the robe to simulate a complete opening. It will be clear that these types are in reality simply closed dresses which are made to resemble " robes," but

unfortunately the name, at least in former times, was generally used for them. It would be more scientific, perhaps, to describe them as " hybrids."

It is necessary for the sake of completeness to mention two other sorts of hybrid. Just as the robe, originally an occasional garment, became incorporated into the costume, so, too, the Pelisse. This three-quarter loose outer garment of the late eighteenth century, became, just after the Regency, a style of dress, its outline being traced in robings, the result being known as a " pelisse robe." This very popular style during the early Victorian period presently changed its name to the " redingote," as its robings then simulated the outlines of a long riding coat.

The other hybrid arose from a modification of the " double-dress," by opening the front of the outer garment and shortening it (e.g. the short overskirt of 1866-70. See *Plate* 33). It is perhaps unnecessary to pursue these styles into their furthermost ramifications, where the overlapping of one with another defies disentanglement.

One might note here that the form of a woman's dress is necessarily affected by the amount of underclothing worn and it is very remarkable how variable this has been at different times. It cannot be explained simply by differences in the mode of living. The young woman of the Regency period, in her scanty garb, took very mild kinds of outdoor exercise as compared with the Girton and Newnham girl of the 'eighties wearing at least a stone's weight of clothes (*Plate* 37). Nor is it due to a variability in sensitiveness to cold ; the girl of to-day wears, even in winter, hardly any underclothing though complaining of the cold. A hundred years ago, even in hot weather, the young lady of that day would have shrunk from parting with a single petticoat.

The fact is that the amount of clothing is dictated far

more by the form of the costume ; we might almost say that the principal function of underclothing is to build up and support the shape of the dress. When it is not the form of the costume but rather the form of her body which the wearer wishes to demonstrate, then she naturally dispenses with underclothing.

Enough has been said to indicate the general principles on which Women's Costume has been constructed and the forms into which it may be resolved. Each has received the approval of Fashion for a considerable period of time because each has been appropriate to those times. Thus, the closed dress has always been with us ; in its " double-dress " form it lasted all through the middle ages, with a late Victorian and Edwardian revival.

It was essentially a mode for the static rather than the dynamic manner of life, except in its Edwardian form of flimsy materials.

The open robe, inspired by Renaissance artists, was an attempt to introduce some of the qualities of a picture into the Art of Costume ; it has supplied Woman with some of her most " picturesque " styles of dress.

The " bodice and skirt " style, though gradually appearing in the sixteenth century, did not become distinguished as a " two piece " construction till much later, entering into its long deferred heritage some eighty years ago, and it is still flourishing. In it we recognise the modern spirit.

From this description we see how Woman's dress is based on a constructional formula on which the edifice is built in various styles, each of which is distinguished by its manner of building. The style is very apparent, the basic formula is concealed ; both have to be appreciated if we wish not merely to *see* but to *understand* its Form.

CHAPTER IX

WOMAN'S SLEEVE AND GLOVE

In Woman's costume the importance of the sleeve is due to four principal circumstances. Its size and shape will largely determine the spirit of the whole, not only affecting the appearance of balance but also in many cases stamping a distinct character on the costume by softening or hardening the outlines of the bodice. Secondly, the size of the sleeve will affect by contrast the apparent size of the waist.

Thirdly, a woman's arm did not—until comparatively recent times—require as wide a range of flexibility at shoulder and elbow as did a man's. In fact its principal function was to be—ornamental.

Fourthly, it has to be remembered that her arm exerts far more erotic attraction than does his.

These four factors have been responsible for the many kinds of sleeve which have appeared in Woman's costume until—as we shall see—an entirely new one began to assert itself some eighty years ago.

Before that time the Art of Costume treated the arm as a thing usually in repose, and the design of the sleeve as an exercise in "still life." Its requirements were therefore comparatively easily served either singly or in combination—whether to harmonise with the costume, to supply a contrast to other parts, or to act as an independent attraction.

Sometimes the sleeve is, or was, a chorus to the costume, picking up and echoing from the wings the refrain announced by the principals ; sometimes it performs a duet, and occasionally it demands to play a star part.

The notion that a woman's sleeve should be designed

primarily to give the arm full freedom of movement would have astonished and perhaps shocked our more remote ancestors. For them the arm had other, more important, functions ; bearing these in mind we can classify the ways they have been expressed into two main groups, either by revealing the natural shape of the upper limb or by distorting it.

Let us examine each in turn.

1. The Natural Shape.

The extreme degree is, of course, where the whole arm is exposed bare of coverings. It is rare, however, for any region of the body which is recognised as exerting erotic attraction to be exposed completely and without any sort of modification. To do so too liberally diminishes or even destroys its potential in that respect. Consequently the occasions when the whole of the upper limb has been bared have been seldom, the first being in the evening dress of the early 1860's when, however, the bertha concealed the shoulders ; a few years later this was dispensed with and the shoulder strap substituted ; gloves then being short, all but the hand was bare (*Plate* 38).

In the 1880's a similar fashion for full evening dress was modified by exceedingly long gloves. But in the years following the first Great War, when costume moved so markedly towards nudity, the whole arm was often bare even in day costume—a unique exception to the general rule—and as a result the arm lost its erotic attraction (*Plates* 44 and 45).

The more customary practice has been to reveal not more than the forearm, a common fashion during the second half of the seventeenth and throughout the eighteenth centuries, both for day and evening (*Plates* 17 and 19).

The elbow day sleeve has to-day become so familiar that the forearm and hand have ceased to have any erotic attraction. This sort of sleeve presents an æsthetic problem, whether the elbow is to be exposed or not ; if the sleeve ends just above it the upper arm is awkwardly divided ; if below it, the forearm is similarly ill treated. A common practice has been (in the past) to conceal the joint by lace ruffles which give a less definite line of demarcation. One cannot but notice how careful our ancestors were to soften the edge of any garment where it borders the bare skin, an æsthetic refinement which is now dispensed with ; the modern practice, especially in summer frocks, is to end the sleeve plainly and bluntly, often half-way down the upper arm. It is evident that, in the case of those amputated sleeves ending in an abrupt stump, Art has given place to Utility.

Indeed ever since the arm and hand have in the last thirty years lost their attraction value, due to the necessity for constant exposure of them, the Art of Costume has been noticeably indifferent to their æsthetic claims ; and the sleeve, especially in its short form, has been uninspired.

The completely bare arm in evening dress generally has had some kind of shoulder expansion such as puffing (*Plate* 23) ; and such devices are also used when the sleeve is made of such semi-transparent stuff that the arm is visible through it.

When the puffing or similar structure is replaced by a mere strap, the inevitable suggestion is that the dress " hangs from the shoulders " instead of being fitted to the body ; with the implication that it might not belong to the wearer—an æsthetic objection which is apt to be drowned by moral disapproval. Thus a voice from 1869 : " They are really wicked, those ball dresses, wicked for cost and indecent for cut ; with only little gold straps across the shoulders that look as if a good shake would shake them off altogether."

Possibly that was the aim in view, but the æsthetic

objection became very conspicuous when the backless dress of the 1930's was hung from the neck by a couple of cords like washing on a clothes-line (*Plate* 45). Garments in suspense seldom look at ease, and it is a principle in the Art of Costume not to expose its mechanics.

We have now to consider the close-fitting sleeve which conforms to the natural shape of the arm. It is noticeable how through the early middle ages women shrank from a shape of sleeve so definite. It is difficult from such illustrations as are available to judge of their constructional details, but the specimens discovered in Greenland show that most sleeves were made in one piece with a gusset at the shoulder.

The top of the sleeve usually appears to be funnel-shaped, and that of the surcoat was either shorter than that of the kirtle beneath or it bagged at the wrist or had long streamers (" tippets ") attached to the elbows (*Plate* 1). At any rate a certain measure of disguise was given to the shape of the arm, and this has persisted until recent times : there would be some feature such as trimming at the shoulder or at least a cuff at the wrist, even in those epochs when the sleeve of the day dress most nearly approximated to the natural shape of the arm.

Sometimes, experimentally, the sleeve has been continued so as to cover part of the hand ; a fashion of 1891 attributed to Sarah Bernhardt, but in fact a mediæval revival.

From the prolonged habit of giving some degree of artificial outline to the arm in the day dress, but not nearly so often in the evening, we may conclude that its natural shape was not considered a thing to be lightly exhibited except when physical charms were to be emphasised. We may also conclude that our ancestors, perhaps wisely, realised the æsthetic difficulty of combining the natural shape of the arm with the general configuration of the costume. The close-fitting sleeve is prone to rebel ; when motionless it does not easily blend with the rest, while its outline in movement can be an awkward contrast to the shape of the body.

The practical objection to the close-fitting sleeve, that it interferes with flexibility, does not appear to have been considered important ; indeed flexibility was discouraged and a tight undersleeve, concealed, has been acceptable enough. The objection must therefore have been to its shape rather than to its inconvenience.

2. The Distorted Shape.

This can be effected either by making the sleeve pendulous or by expanding its outlines.

(a) The pendulous sleeve.

The extreme degree of the hanging sleeve of the twelfth century, when to prevent its trailing on the ground it was necessary to tie it up in knots, is one of the few modes which have never tempted a revival, although less formidable examples such as the " angel sleeve," clearing the ground, have been used for evening dress even in the present century, notably in Edwardian times.

The æsthetic function of the hanging sleeve is to supply flowing lines in harmony with the folds of loose draperies : with heavy materials it adds a note of dignity—at least to the stationary figure (*Plate* 7*a*) ; with flimsy materials which can float on movement, it is thought to add a bird-like grace. The arm, often bare, can emerge or retreat according to the exigencies of the moment.

The hanging sleeve formed the distinguishing feature of the fifteenth century houppelande (*Plate* 5), and a similar effect has been obtained by cloaks and mantles from time to time since, notably by the late Victorian dolman, where it was simulated by long side pieces hanging from the shoulders of that garment.

(b) The expanded sleeve.

This method of distorting the shape of the arm offers innumerable varieties both in degree and position, and these we may classify into expansion of the whole sleeve or of a part only.

Expansion of the whole sleeve :

The familiar " leg of mutton " sleeve was first introduced in the second half of the sixteenth century when it survived some eighty years.

It has had two great revivals, the first from 1827 to 1836 (*Plate* 26) ; the next from 1892 to 1895 (*Plate* 40).

It is obvious that this type of sleeve has the æsthetic drawback of making the whole costume look top-heavy, in extreme cases markedly so ; its use therefore indicates some powerful impulse demanding expression in spite of the conspicuous drawbacks. We find that whenever the sleeve, especially its upper part, has been grossly enlarged it has always coincided with a fashion for tight lacing. It appears, by sheer contrast, to diminish the size of the waist ; and to accomplish that end Fashion overrides aesthetics.[1]

The " leg of mutton " sleeve diminishes towards the wrist ; the " bishop sleeve," full to the wrist, appears to make the hand look small. We do not find this latter type fully developed until the period of the 1830's when the small hand was becoming the insignia of the Lady. We have, however, modifications such as a sleeve expanded into a series of transverse puffings, an Elizabethan shape which was revived from time to time during the Victorian era.

Expansion of one part of the sleeve :

Sometimes this has been at the top, sometimes at the wrist and occasionally at the elbow.

The shoulder enlargement seems to have been introduced about 1540 and was revived towards the end

---

[1] The size of some of the sleeves of 1827-1836 measured over three feet in circumference, the largest being known as " elephant sleeves ; " they rivalled the size of the hats.

of the Regency period. Its early form may well have been partly to conceal the junction of sleeve and bodice, but its æsthetic effect is always to diminish the apparent width of the upper arm ; the very opposite, in fact, of the " leg of mutton."

It is curious to note, however, that each time the " leg of mutton " sleeve has come into fashion it has been preceded for a few years by just such a shoulder expansion ; the Elizabethan was preceded by the 1540 shoulder (*Plate* 10) ; the huge sleeves of 1828 by the late Regency shoulder (*Plate* 24*b*) ; and the " leg of mutton " of the 1890's by the shoulder prominence of '89 and '90.

Not only has the expansion of the sleeve started on each of these three occasions at the shoulder, but it has gradually slipped down the arm, as it were, and terminated in an expansion, in due course, at the wrist.

Just as the first ballooned sleeve ending about 1640 (*Plate* 15) was followed by an elbow sleeve expanded by ruffles, so the second, passing through a brief phase of elbow expansion about 1839-40, developed into the bell-opening sleeve of the later '40's and '50's (*Plate* 29*a*) ; and the third, ending in 1896, passed through a phase of close sleeve frilled at the wrist expanding presently into a bell-opening by 1901-2.

In brief, it seems that inflation habitually starts at the top and passes right down the arm as far as possible before the impulse starting the expansion is worn out.

The point well illustrates one of the peculiarities affecting the Art of Costume—namely, that once a fashion has gained a certain measure of momentum in any particular direction, it seems compelled to go on to its utmost end as though driven by inexorable fate.

In less picturesque phrase, this is a characteristic of any strong psychological impulse ; it demands not merely satisfaction but over-satisfaction, the tidal wave of desire sweeping beyond logical limits.

We also see, in the case of the sleeve, how the focus

PORTRAIT OF LOUISE RENEE DE PENENCOUET DE
QUEROUAILLE, DUCHESS OF PORTSMOUTH (aged 35)

The brocaded over-dress reveals the contrasting colour of the sleeves
of the under-dress, with ruffled sleeves of the chemise at the wrist. Note
the degree of décolletage and the air of studied negligé in a costume
designed for colour rather than form.

From the painting by Mignard, 1682, in the National Portrait Gallery.

of attention gradually shifts from accentuating the smallness of the waist to that of the hand ; the target changes but the nature of the desire persists.

It is evident that the Art of Costume has paid much more attention to the sleeve in some epochs than in others. We find, for example, that in the nineteenth century there were over fifty distinct and recognisable varieties of form, far more than in all the other centuries put together ; and that most of them were constructed so as to check the free movements of the arm, especially during the period when the behaviour of the Lady was measured by the degree of her inability to move easily. The sleeve of 1840-50 was so constructed that the arm could not be raised above a right angle. In keeping with this restraint we find that the armhole was then singularly small, pointing to the absence of muscles. And previously, when the sleeve allowed flexibility at the shoulder or elbow, it seldom or never allowed it at both.

Immensely significant, therefore, was the introduction, about 1865, of an entirely new cut of sleeve in which free movement of the arm at both joints became easy (*Plate* 36). This was the " coat sleeve," based on the model of man's sleeve of that date. It coincided with the wave of emancipation and the beginnings of active outdoor exercise. The Art of Costume was thus compelled to acknowledge the presence of a new kind of impulse, a demand for greater physical freedom, and so we may regard the " coat sleeve " of eighty years ago as a herald of " the shape of things to come."

THE GLOVE

The glove has almost a literature of its own. Its æsthetic features, its psychological and sociological significance, have all been discussed and analysed by many writers. Here we are concerned with the glove as a part of Costume.

Until the innovation of the elbow sleeve about 1640 women's gloves had been large and loose, shaped, in fact, very much like a man's and worn chiefly for practical purposes such as riding and driving.

With the bare forearm of 1640, delicate close-fitting gloves to the elbow, or mittens, were worn indoors as an occasional part of the evening costume, a fashion lasting until the end of the eighteenth century, which, however, was mainly a gloveless period.

During the Regency period gloves reverted to the large loose shape, both wrist-length and elbow-length, but always plainly made and without ornamentation (*Plate* 23).[1]

It was not until the beginning of the ballooned sleeves of 1827 that the glove changed its essentially " practical " character and became ornamental ; it developed into a means for exploiting the smallness of the hand. Short gloves, excessively tight, for day and evening, with, as a variation, the evening mitten, controlled the size of the hand for the rest of the century except towards the end when the bare arm in evening dress was covered by gloves reaching nearly to the shoulder.

Among the upper classes gloves were also worn indoors and indeed often at night, so as to preserve the smallness and whiteness of the hand, characteristics with which the Victorian novelist would always endow his heroine. During that epoch a woman's hand acquired an extraordinary measure of erotic attraction coupled with social significance. It became the hall-mark of class, surviving as such until economic pressure compelled increasing numbers of young gentlewomen to engage in earning their own living.

[1]During the Regency period the fashionable day glove was the " York tan " of yellow-brown leather nearly to the elbow, and loose. The evening glove was commonly of white linen.

As a result the hand has now reverted to its natural size. We find that during the last eighty years or so the nominal sizes of gloves have had to be changed more than once to meet this expansion.

The Victorian attitude towards the woman's hand as a part not lightly to be exposed bare can be gathered from the long discussion in a ladies' magazine of 1876 whether it was irreligious for her to remove her gloves in church. So, too, the strict convention of handshaking in gloves, at least with members of the opposite sex, the wearing of gloves at family prayers and similar social curiosities, all illustrate how the Art of Costume can by mere concealment endow a part of the body with magical properties.

Æsthetically, no doubt, the tight glove gave the hand a new shape in which its breadth was reduced almost to that of the wrist itself; so that the arm appeared to taper off to a mere convexity instead of swelling out at the end into a bunch of fingers. The " filbert shaped " finger-nail of Victorian heroines was in miniature a replica of the shape of her hand. Her glove was in many respects analogous to the Chinese lady's crushed foot : a symbol of physical incapacity denoting rank.

That use of the glove has disappeared ; the bicycle and the motor car effectively destroyed it, and to-day with all hands employed in work it is not likely to be revived.

We see, then, the great importance which the Art of Costume has attached to the covering of the upper limb until modern times. Always treated as a more or less static portion of the whole composition, its sleeve—and glove—were designed to discourage free movement ; greater importance was given to making a design which could be absorbed into the rest of the picture, or which could illustrate in itself the spirit of the picture. Gradually instead of being in harmony with the rest of the costume the sleeve began, about seventy years ago, to strike out independently, often affording a contrast, especially in colour and material ; and as the upper limb shook itself free, the Art of Costume lost interest in the unruly member.

To-day the designer appears very often baffled by the problem how to devise a sleeve which shall be both practical for modern requirements and at the same time æsthetically satisfying.

CHAPTER X

WOMAN'S HEADGEAR AND HAIR

THOUGH it is true that during the last six centuries of feminine costumes the shape of the figure or of the waist, either one or both, has hardly ever been out of the picture, yet almost always it has been the head, with its covering and the arrangement of the hair, which has been the most consistently prominent feature in it.

Moreover, it has been here more than elsewhere that the sex has been most pronounced. The only exceptions to the rule appear to have been the tousled head of 1800 (perhaps) and, more certainly, the " Eton crop " fashion of the 1920's, both being war-products and imitative of the masculine.

Apart from these the distinctive facial features, including usually the hair, have been unmistakable. It is here we look to identify not only the sex but also the personality, particularly when the dress itself happens to be indistinguishable from dozens precisely similar. If it were not for the face most women (and men too) would be unrecognisable ; it would be strange indeed if the Art of Costume were to treat that region as of secondary importance.

It would be logical if the head covering and arrangement of the hair were adapted to match the face and that the rest of the costume were to follow suit ; circumstances, however, may compel a woman to " buy a hat to go with my dress," and that this is a common practice is evidenced by the unhappy mixtures so often seen. The modern custom of going hatless at least avoids one source of disaster, and the scarf, tied earache-wise over the head, suggests a painful evasion of a problem.

That a woman whose sole purpose is to express her

own personality should adapt her costume to her face seems reasonable ; but as she has also to express mass impulses and ideals of the social world in which she lives—and these seem to her to be very important—she must sacrifice some measure of individuality in doing so. This apparently she is generally willing, even eager, to do. If, for example, large hats are fashionable she must wear one, whether it suits her or not.

Obeying the dictates of fashion she will be prepared if necessary to alter her face to conform to the ordained model, and on that new foundation build up her costume. In fact, she will treat her face as though it were actually a part of her costume rather than a part of herself. As such, therefore, it deserves notice here.

The practice of face-painting, common to both sexes among certain savage races, has survived among women in spite of civilisation, and is seen in two essentially different forms. The Art of Costume is not concerned with that kind which merely attempts to simulate nature or to conceal defects, but only with the kind which transforms the natural face into a mask-like spectacle.

This " Sphinx motif "—which civilised man has never himself employed and therefore finds so striking when adopted by woman—has often been used to add the fascination of mystery not only in the dress but at times in the face, the mask being produced by paint, powder, patches and depilatories.

In our own country we find that eyebrow plucking with forehead shaving was fashionable—and of course condemned—in the fifteenth century (*Plate* 3), just as we find paint and patches in the eighteenth and plucked eyebrows and lipstick in our own day. The practice is perhaps a challenge based on the assumption that the Sphinx conceals a secret, but the fashion is not more curious than the moral disapproval it usually provokes.

After all, women change their faces with no more

eagerness than their names, and a morality which is shocked by nudity ought not to cavil when the face is clothed in pigment. If we are content to inquire why such enigmas exercise attraction it is perhaps because they appear to defy probability ; one expects to see above the dress—a face, and finds a phantasm with the charm that children find in a gollywog.

The æsthetic objection is more real ; the face is rendered as monotonous to look at as the drop scene of a theatre ; we long for the curtain to go up and the play to start. The normal function of headgear and hair is to support the performance of that matchless comedienne—woman's face ; the immense variety of each or of both which have been used at different times testify to its importance, and we may classify them in general terms according to the effect aimed at.

Thus, together or separately, the headgear and hairdressing may enhance the height or breadth of the head or modify its shape, and even the shape of the face itself. They may act as a picture frame or as a poster ; they may supply an æsthetic contrast, especially in colour, or may extend its effective range. They may tone down its less fortunate features, and the influence of the hair especially may spread downwards to modify the neck or more convincingly unite the head to the shoulders, making the composition a whole.

Or, on the other hand, they may emphasise that the head exercises an independent sovereignty, and this is notably the modern pose.

In brief, they add importance to the head and face.

These æsthetic effects are familiar enough to the artist, but there are also psychological effects possible. In a previous chapter reference has been made to the curious impression created by tilting the hat, with men ; so too with women, but here the nuances are much more varied and subtle. The backward tilt may give a youthful look without becoming childish ; a woman is not averse from looking " girlish," whereas a man does not care to look " boyish."

The sideways tilt at an angle either romantic or roguish, the demure tilt forward or the headgear modestly shielding the sides of the face, all have their obvious implications. And there have been times— though rarely—when the head has appeared to be almost inarticulate, so humble have been its trappings.

Headdress and hair are natural allies, though not always harmonious ones, and both usually adapt themselves to the spirit of the costume, but the headdress will, of the two, preserve more individuality. If the fashion of the dress expresses the prevailing mood of the community, the headgear selected to go with it, and the manner of wearing it, will still attempt a personal expression. For that reason we find, as we should expect, that in all epochs there has been a far wider choice of headgear than of dresses—enough, in fact, to satisfy the individual taste.

There have, of course, been times when the two, the inclination of the community and the taste of the individual, appear to have coincided, and then all wear the same sort of headgear ; the cloche hat of 1927-8 was an instance.

But when we have to rely only on records for our information we can be easily misled by a few notable illustrations ; we are apt to suppose that the bonnets and hats of the Regency period, for example, were just those made familiar by well-known portraits and fashion journals of the day ; in reality every conceivable type of headdress was worn.

It seems safe to say of any past epoch that its headgear varied more widely than its dress but that, broadly speaking, it tended to echo the dress, sometimes in louder tones, sometimes in less loud. This deviation from the set pattern can be discovered in certain brasses and monumental figures of the middle ages ; even then women had their individuality.[1]

Woman's outdoor headdress has a comparatively short history, at least as a distinctive article of attire. Writing of Englishwomen about 1575, Van Meteren records : " Married women only wear a hat both in the street and in the house ; those unmarried go without a hat, although ladies of distinction have lately learned to cover their faces with silken masks or vizards, and feathers. . . ." Until near the end of the seventeenth century her social life, among the upper class, was spent mainly indoors. Previous to that time when she rode or travelled about the country she usually wore a hat closely resembling that of the man of her time ; for short excursions she went bareheaded.[2] Chaucer's " Wife of Bath " on her pilgrimage to Canterbury is described as " Ywimpled well and on her hede an hat as brode as is a buckler or a targe." Otherwise the hooded cloak was the common mediæval head-covering (*Plate* 16).

In the second half of the sixteenth century[3] we find women beginning to wear either what we should call " toques " or hats frankly masculine (*Plates* 7b, 13), or going bare-headed perhaps with a scarf tied over the head. The high masculine hat was presently exchanged for the broad-brimmed plumed " Cavalier's," but until well after the Restoration the outdoor headgear remained curiously lacking in distinctive feminine characteristics— a remarkable contrast to the indoor headgear.

---

[1]For specimens of abnormal headgear shown in brasses, see those of Joan Peryent, Digswell church, Herts (1415) ; the wife of Sir W. Mauntell at Nether Heyford, Northants (1487), wearing a transitional form approaching the pediment headdress ; that of Jane Keriell at Ash-next-Sandwich, Kent (1455), with horseshoe ornament in front and no veil.

[2]In the 16th century the Mayor of Chester ordered that : " To distinguish headdresses of married women from unmarried, no unmarried women to wear white or other coloured caps and no women to wear any hat unless she rides or goes about the country, on pain of 3/4d."

[3]Women started wearing sugar-loaf hats about 1550.

The deduction to be drawn is that anything like prolonged excursions out of doors were only undertaken of necessity and that seldom, when " attractive " headgear would have been incongruous.

Towards the end of the seventeenth century, as we learn from contemporary plays, walking in the park became fashionable. Swift comments : " When I pass the Mall in the evening it is prodigious to see the number of ladies walking there ; and I always cry shame at the ladies of Ireland who never walk at all." He recommends Stella to buy a pair of good strong boots and use them.

As a result of the change of habits, outdoor headgear, in the shape of broad straw hats of the " milkmaid " style, acquired a new spirit ; they became coquettish. Ranelagh and Vauxhall Gardens worked wonders. Hats began to change their function ; from being protective they were becoming provocative or at least " affected." And when we say that a woman's hat is " affected " we only mean that she is too consciously striving to express an imperative idea ; the result would be more artistic if the effort were unconscious.

But in the eighteenth century the outdoor headgear provided a new technique of which she could hardly be unconscious ; during the last thirty years of that century the variety in shape and tilt was beyond reckoning (*Plates* 19, 21, 22), and in that phase of experimenting with a novelty, immense size became the principal note culminating in the " picture hat " which we associate with the portrait of the Duchess of Devonshire, followed by a more masculine shape with high square crown and wide brim.

(Once again we see how a new method of expression tends to be driven by Fashion to extremes, obeying the psychological law that in order to sustain an effect the stimulus must be continually increased.)

No part of woman's costume is more sensitive than

her headgear to abrupt social changes, and the twenty years of the Napoleonic war shattered the pre-existing inclinations and standards. As I have pointed out else-where (in my *Feminine Attitudes in the Nineteenth Century*) conventions were in the melting-pot ; there was no universal set pattern of behaviour ; woman's headgear became during that period much more individualistic in style with innumerable variations of shape and mean-ing. All moods were expressed except, perhaps, the demure ; military effects struck a patriotic note and our various allies supplied temporary novelties.

The romantic spirit which followed the war produced picturesque headgear (*Plate 24b*), increasing in size until it culminated in the immense hats of 1828-30 (*Plate 26*), sometimes trimmed with a hundred and twenty feet of ribbon, and decorated with such a riot of flowers and feathers that the very dogs in the street barked in protest.

This exuberantly romantic spirit was destined to desert the hat for ever ; for the rest of the century and after, the hat became almost a symbol of feminine emancipation, breaking out from time to time whenever that impulse became irresistible, as in the late 1860's and again towards the close of the century.

The conventional Victorian headgear (*Plates 35* and 36) was, of course, the bonnet, at first demure, close-fitting and shielding the sides of the face from observa-tion ; gradually expanding into a circular frame for the face, it became by the early '60's tilted back on the head so that at last the face was completely exposed.

The principle of the bonnet had been to obliterate the neck and limit the free movement of the head—the very opposite of the hat—but as the head became increasingly liberated from this restraint the bonnet declined during the last half of the century into being a mere head ornament : always a symbol of social class and propriety in opposition to the radical hat.

By the close of the century the bonnet, its function as a symbol having ceased, shrivelled up into nothing, leaving the hat sole mistress of woman's head. As such the hat now reverted once more to the picturesque role which it had abandoned for so many years ; large flower gardens adorned its wide surface, while feathered toques sustained for a few years longer something of the spirit of the bonnet.

A tendency towards increasing width in hats culminated in the enormous domed hoops worn on the head in 1908-12, perhaps the largest that women have ever carried as headgear (*Plates* 42 and 43). Unlike those of 1828-30, these were rigid and heavy ; the fine careless rapture of the earlier style was not repeated ; impressive without being romantic, their ponderous size seemed to cast a shadow of coming events. . . .

The first Great War of 1914-18, with its immense effect on the status of women in this country, left a mark, perhaps to persist indefinitely, on their headgear.

It has become in the main much more serious, in keeping with their outdoor costume. Attempts to recapture the gay " picturesque " note of former times have not had more than a moment's success. One has seen, of course, oddities of shape cropping up now and again, but the prevailing note of the last twenty-five years has been characteristic of this realistic age. The headgear is less individualistic and seems to be moving towards forming but a part of a civil uniform : less an expression of the feelings and more of the abilities, and the gaiety which the milliner attempts to introduce seems forced and out of harmony with this ungay world.

Indoor Headgear and Hair-dressing :

It is convenient to treat these two together as so often they have been blended to form, æsthetically, a single aspect of adornment ; and the periods when no head-dress was worn by day have been rare, chiefly during the reign of Charles I and Charles II, and since 1860.

During the last six centuries nothing has ever equalled in magnificence and artistry the headgear of the fifteenth; structures, at first immensely wide and later increasingly high, supported on wire frames, were draped with material and decorated with jewellery. The names usually given to them, such as " the horned headdress " and the " heart-shaped " are very familiar on brasses of the period, while from 1460 the " butterfly headdress " is conspicuous (*Plates* 2, 3, 4, 5, 6, 7*a*, 8*a*).

Mention has been made in an earlier chapter of the —apparent—absence of the " steeple headdress " in England ; we find, however, truncated cone-shapes and a few domed on the crown ; in fact, a careful search of the available records such as brasses and monumental effigies will reveal a great many variations of the types mentioned.

With all these the hair was stretched back from the forehead and almost concealed under the towering structure above. Indeed, it is a noticeable feature of the later middle ages that the hair is seldom visible *au naturel* ; it may be elaborately plaited and coiled in solid blocks on the sides of the head or surrounding the face so that it has the appearance of a wig ; or enclosed in an ornamental net or entirely hidden under the head-dress. But it is never allowed to flow loosely from the neck or to form ringlets. That is to say, it is deprived of its natural expression.

We have to remember that woman's hair, with its sexual characteristics, was always regarded as " provo-cative " and therefore not to be freely exposed to view ; such, at least, had been the teaching of the Church, which insisted that woman's head should be covered in church lest it should distract men's thoughts from higher things ; and there are still clergymen who seem susceptible in this respect.

The mediæval method was, then, to make the hair a part of the headdress and as unlike hair as possible.[1] The same principle persisted well into the sixteenth century, the head and neck being concealed under the " pediment headdress " which arched over the forehead with long side lappets hanging down.[2]

A highly significant change occurred about 1540 with the appearance of the " French hood " (*Plate* 10), in which the back hair was enclosed in a net while the small cap framed the head over the ears, allowing the front hair to be seen ; a modification, the " Marie Stuart " cap, had a veil hanging down behind. But at the same time the old style of hair-concealment also survived under a headdress flat on the crown with heavy veiling behind, obliterating the neck.

Thus there were two essentially different " schools of thought "—one daring enough to exhibit the natural hair, at least in part ; the other still reluctant to do so. Neither, however, venturing to expose the back of the neck (the spot always reserved, in the words of a French writer, for the passionate embrace of the lover).

During the Elizabethan period the escape of the hair became conspicuous, being dressed over arches of wire or trained over pads aided by false hair (*Plate* 8b), while some frankly wore a full crop of close curls ; at the same time the back of the neck began to be exposed.

In these rival modes, the " conservative " and the " radical," we see a curious analogy to the struggle between the Victorian bonnet and the hat, and in each

---

[1] The shape of the mediæval headdress (*Plate* 6) is best studied in sepulchral effigies where it is seen in three dimensions. They are admirably illustrated in Gardner's *Alabaster Tombs* and Crossley's *English Church Monuments*. For the sixteenth and seventeenth centuries Mrs. Esdaile's *English Church Monuments* may be consulted.

[2] In the brass of the family of W. de Gray, Merton church, Norfolk (1495), the younger daughters have hair flowing loose. See also the brass of Elizabeth Echyngham, Etchingham, Sussex (1480). A woman's brass at Felbrigg church, Norfolk (1480) and one at Brightlingsea, Essex, show hair reaching below the waist, a fashion indicating virginity.

case the restraining element was at last driven from the field.

These form two very important chapters in the evolution of feminine costume ; no doubt in each case the increased freedom of the head from its restrictions was irresistible ; at the same time the greater opportunity for displaying the hair as a means of sex attraction was an important cause of the new development (a point to be discussed further in the chapter on that subject).

By about 1620 the head covering was altogether abandoned, and a long period of side ringlets followed (*Plate* 15). In fact, the hair had established itself as a legitimate implement of attraction. That the platinum blonde is no new form of sex appeal may be gathered from *Pepys's Diary*, 1665 : " This day my wife began to wear light coloured locks, quite white almost, which, though it makes her look very pretty, yet not being natural, vexes me, that I will not have her wear them." For a brief period at the close of that century towering caps (" fontanges ") hid the hair from view, but it emerged once more to reach its supreme hour of triumph in the period of 1763-80. George Coleman (in his *Random Recollections*) describes the hair arrangement of a school-master's wife at that time :

" A twopenny toupee, pulled up all but by the roots and strained over a cushion on the top of her head, formed the centre of the building ; tiers of curls served for the wings, a banging chignon behind defended the occiput like a buttress, and the whole fabric was kept tight and waterproof by a quantity of long single and double black pins."

It is doubtful whether the credit for this stupendous erection should be given to hair or headdress.

In Hannah More's description, in 1777, of young women who had on their heads " an acre and a half of shrubbery besides slopes, garden plots, tulip beds, clumps of peonies, kitchen gardens and greenhouses "—

here surely are " headdresses " although the distinction is a fine one (*Plate* 21).

We may contrast the moral disapproval usually provoked when women cut their hair short—whom Prynne in 1628 described as " audacious, brazen-faced, shameless monsters whose prodigious and blushless impudency bids battle and defiance with Heaven itself "—with the effect of too conservative a treatment, as in 1756, when the lady in *The Old Maid* is asked how long had her hair been dressed. " Three weeks."—" Don't that lay you under the necessity of dressing your hair every evening ? "— " Oh, Lord, Sir, a head properly made up, with pins, paste and pomatum, will keep a month very well."

More fashionable ladies covered the summit with extraordinary ornaments such as glass models of ships and buildings, but in spite of such mechanical additions the structures had the appearance of being mainly hair, to judge from an account of 1768 :

" False locks to supply deficiency of native hair, pomatum in profusion, greasy wool to bolster up the adopted locks and grey powder to conceal dust. Thus my lady is dressed for three months at least during which time it is not in her power to comb her head." After nine weeks, at least in summer, it was time that such a head " should be opened and repaired as it began to be *un peu-hazardé*."

When such a structure added some two or three feet to the stature (the famous Duchess of Devonshire in 1774 wore on the top an ostrich feather four feet high) it is evident that hair and headdress have combined forces. Joseph Strutt in his *Manners and Customs of the English* remarked, in 1776 : " Do not the macaronies and fops of the present age fully equal, if not exceed, the preposterous patterns of their gallant forefathers ? Do not the ladies, now, who hang all sorts of fruit upon their heads, nay some who place thereon a sow and pigs, with other curious animals, almost, nay quite equal the broad wheel waggon, the coach and horses, and various other pretty inventions of the ingenious milliners, about fifty years ago ? "

Faced by this extraordinary example of the force of Fashion we may pause to take breath and ask what caused it. We have seen how Woman's hair had asserted its powers of attraction and was increasingly using them ; men had adopted the vast wig magnifying the importance of the head, and so the feminine counter-stroke of towering hair and headdress was a natural manœuvre, hoisting man with his own petard. The immense size is but an illustration of the tendency for a fashion, once started, to gather momentum beyond the control of reason or comfort, until either the impulse is exhausted or becomes checked by some abrupt change of social circumstance. It also illustrates—if illustration of so obvious a fact were necessary—how little relation Fashion bears to Beauty.

The nineteenth century introduced the novelty of making a marked distinction between the " day " and the " evening " headdress and hair arrangement, the distinction being always that the evening display should be much more conspicuous and " attractive " than the day. The day cap concealed the hair—sometimes entirely—while the evening cap became more and more a mere ornament to the head. Finally the day cap ceased to be used by younger women after 1860, at the time when the hat began to assert itself for outdoor use.

The hair-dressing during last century passed through four stages of evolution : at first short curls, the neck being free ; the evening coiffure becoming highly " romantic " towards 1830 with elaborate loops standing up on the crown. In the second phase the hair was looped over the sides of the face and covering the ears, by day ; glamorous ringlets in the evening, the neck movement being checked. The third phase had the hair massed at the back of the head with, in the evening, floral tributes. In the fourth phase the hair was massed on the top of the head by day, with fancy ornaments added for evening effects.

We have to note the Early Victorian device of covering the ears (a symbolic gesture of the " pure mind " which is deaf to temptation) ; and that during the second half of that epoch the hair was arranged more and more to liberate the head and to increase the apparent height, changes we may attribute to the emancipatory spirit of the period. The day cap had become so much associated with domestic service that the " young lady " naturally abandoned it, just as in modern times the domestic herself has declined to wear that badge of servitude. This is a striking instance of the power of a symbol : from having been originally an article of attire intended to hide a feature of sex-attraction, then becoming itself an object of " attraction," finally a symbol of servitude, the thing is now held in abhorrence and discarded—but only as such ; when it forms part of the uniform of a " superior " profession such as a trained nurse, it is still acceptable enough.

In the present century, indoor headgear having disappeared, the hair has entered a new phase of significance following the first Great War. Its modern characteristic is that it is arranged to display the natural shape of the head, the hair being cut short and kept thinned for that purpose.

Glancing back, then, over these six centuries we see a slow but in the main a steady evolutionary change. At first the hair, always viewed by the Church with suspicion as a dangerous implement of allurement, was to be kept hidden, together with the equally seductive neck, under a headdress. The headdress, assuming itself on that account the function denied to the hair, became highly ornamental and " attractive."

Gradually the hair, released from this restraint, employed all sorts of artificial aids to increase its powers of charm. Curbed from time to time by caps, it then emerged solus and became " woman's glory." Finally the head (and neck) escaped from the hair and relied on its own shape to complete the significance of the costume.

In short, the head has come to the surface exactly as did the hand and the leg. In all three cases the evolutionary process has been similar : a concealed region of the body with secondary sexual characteristics had been at first only occasionally revealed, and on that account condemned as " provocative." The magical charm of the concealed part became transferred to its covering (hair, glove, stocking) which was then regarded as " romantic " (a milder term).

Gradually the increasing exposure has worn out this attribute and the part has been accepted as " natural ; " that is, it is no longer specially " sex-attractive." Consequently the covering becomes less important and the Art of Costume pays less attention to it.

Of the three " liberated " regions we may say that the hand is now completely free of its magical properties, the head nearly so and the lower limb is free up to the knee. And as all three are now being used for work rather than for " charm " they have been allowed to appear in their natural shape. For the first time it has become possible to know what a woman's head is really like—at least, its outside.

It has seemed desirable, even at the risk of reiteration, to emphasise by these examples how false is the parrot cry that " fashion repeats itself." In reality we are witnessing not an oscillation of taste to and fro, but a gradual change forwards, or—if " forwards " seems too confident a term—at least a move always away from the past. And only those who have not examined the evidence can suppose that this long evolutionary movement can be attributed to—*dressmakers.*

CHAPTER XI

OTHER FACTORS AFFECTING FORM

O F these the principal is the accessory garment which is assumed for particular occasions such as out of doors, although a number are for indoor occasional use. According to their shape such accessory garments may radically alter the form of the costume beneath. Their function is either to act as a protection against the climate or in many cases as a means of extra display.

It is convenient to divide them into three main groups : a shaped sleeved garment covering most of the body, to which we may give the generic name " overcoat ; " a loose sleeveless garment covering the body— the " cloak ; " and one covering only the upper part, to which the old term " par-dessus " is appropriate.

The last named has always been essentially a feminine garment. Man's accessory garments have been few as compared to Woman's, and in general terms we may say that he used the cloak until early in the eighteenth century when it was gradually superseded by the overcoat. The length of his cloak was governed by the design of his costume : when this was broadened out at the hips, as in Elizabethan and Jacobean times, cloaks were short. As such they served to increase the shoulder breadth without hampering leg movement ; and also they did not interfere with the grasp of the sword hilt. It was this weapon of defence that forbade the use of long cumbersome cloaks which were therefore left to the elderly and " civilian " class. The overcoat, a peaceful garment, replaced the cloak when the sword ceased to be an essential. Long cloaks wrapped round the body as a protection against the weather when on horseback were less readily abandoned.

The long driving coat, often with double cape, appeared with the short-waisted fashion of costume towards the end of the eighteenth century, and gradually gave the form to the fashionable outdoor garment. Its long straight lines and wide shoulders gave an exaggerated " manly " appearance very much in keeping with the Regency style of dress.

During the nineteenth century the overcoat, hesitating between elegance and comfort, appeared in various shapes, at first fitting the figure and waisted as in the " Chesterfield," later with a loose sleeve and sack-back, the " Raglan " coat of the early '60's ; while the " Newmarket " preserved some of the features of the riding coat.[1]

We see that Man's overcoat does not in reality change the form of his costume ; it accentuates perhaps the solidity of the oblong frame, but it does not attempt to introduce fresh lines or novel features. In modern times it has steadily become plainer and plainer, having lost the velvet collar, the silk facings and linings which were fashionable at the beginning of this century, while astrachan collar and cuffs are now the undisputed property of the opulent alien. For ordinary folk it has become scarcely more exciting than a raincoat.

Women, on the other hand, have succeeded in preserving in their accessory garments a means of additional display, whether in the form of " overcoat," " cloak," or " par-dessus." Moreover, these have generally been designed either to change the form of the costume or to draw attention to it.

[1] Men's overcoats : The Chesterfield is single-breasted with fly front, shaped to the figure, formerly with quilted or velvet collar ; the mid-Victorian article often reached to the ankles.

The Raglan has sleeves set in to join up at the collar seam at the sides of the neck ; it is loose fitting and not defined at the waist.

The Newmarket is shaped, double-breasted with a seam across the waist, and always with velvet collar.

The Inverness cloak was a loose-fitting overcoat with cape attached at the neck.

In the former case, when the disguise is removed, a striking contrast may be revealed ; the long cloak, for example, may from the nature of the material alone afford a study in graceful folds ; its abrupt removal supplies a complete change of scene and entirely different " effects."

Large wrapping cloaks, completely concealing the costume, and designed to produce the maximum degree of contrast when removed, have been very frequently used especially over evening dress.

Allied to the cloak is the "mantle," notably a Victorian garment, sometimes three-quarter length, sometimes hardly covering the bodice, and infinite in its variations, sleeved or unsleeved, fitting or semi-fitting the figure. The fact that such mantles did not conceal more than a portion of the dress meant that they had to enter into the general composition, harmonising in colour and material with the dress. This entailed the well-dressed lady having a great many of them in her wardrobe.

The partial concealment of the figure by day, when mantles were used, was a characteristic Victorian trait for it was considered proper to reserve frank display of the shape for the evening. Some of the mantles, especially the dolmans of the '70's and '80's, were apparently made to emphasise a ladylike helplessness, being designed so that the arm could not be extended.

Their æsthetic defect lay in the fact that by concealing the waist the top half of the costume was converted into a triangle poised on the triangle of the skirt, thus radically changing the basic symbol " X " by turning its upper part upside down. The hardness of the outline would be softened by bordering it with trimmings—the besetting weakness of the Victorian designer when in difficulties—so that they dripped with beads, imitating in spirit the taste for excessive jewellery which was then fashionable.

We must allow for the fact that the coat, as an

accessory garment, was generally unsuitable as an adjunct to a large skirt, over which it fits with difficulty ; consequently it was not much favoured in the Victorian period until near the close, except for driving.

It hardly appeared until the narrow skirts of the Regency invited its use ; then its most notable form was the Pelisse, shaped to the figure with its skirt sloping away down the front to below knee level, and often of flimsy materials. The bodice portion resembled very closely the Spencer which was in effect a short jacket ; both garments served to draw attention to the shape of the bust, as can be judged from the lavish ornamentation which each displayed over that region.

The coat returned to favour as soon as the skirt diminished in size, and to-day it has survived all its ancient rivals. In modern hands it has acquired, so to speak, an individuality of its own and is now a highly expressive part of the costume. Its importance may be attributed to the increase of outdoor occupations necessitating walking ; the mantle belonged to the " carriage era."

The same change of conditions has obliterated the short " par-dessus " type of accessory which served the purpose of a shawl, protecting the shoulders and chest. Capes, mantlets, pelerines, caracos, visites, casawecks, polkas—their name is legion and their race is run. Were they to protect against Victorian draughts or too close a scrutiny of the figure—or, simply to draw attention to it ?

The shawl, denying independence to the arms, preserved a uniformity of outline and in its greatest meridian obliterated the waist, converting a crinoline costume into a perfect equilateral triangle. But its æsthetic value was as a means of introducing a kaleidoscope of colours on to a surface outside the costume.

In general terms the whole group of these cape-like accessories appear to the modern eye as savouring of prudery ; it would be a less harsh term to describe them as excessively " ladylike."

It will be seen, then, how important a part these accessories have played in Woman's Costume, especially in the last century when their choice was infinite. During the last half of the eighteenth and throughout the nineteenth centuries there was an elaborate etiquette for their correct arrangement, the exact kind for each social occasion and season ; they built up, as it were, a social barrier which those unversed in such niceties could not surmount, a barrier against the rising tide of democracy, which has now swept these curios of a forgotten Art into—museums.

We must not overlook a detail in the Art of Costume which can affect a considerable change in its Form ; I refer to the methods of fastening garments. Take, for example, an " equivocal " garment, one that can be equally worn open or buttoned up, thereby perhaps changing the whole spirit of the costume. When we spoke of the types of dress it must have struck the reader that the " open robe " could be converted into a closed dress simply by being buttoned down the front.

Fastenings, then, have their æsthetic importance. There are three kinds : the concealed, the visible and the conspicuous. Each may have its advantages ; invisible fastenings certainly help to sustain an air of inscrutability. Curiosity is aroused by an apparent miracle; how does she get into or out of such a garment? But further, such a method does not interfere with the play of light on the surface of materials, especially with highly refractile textiles such as satin, where the presence of buttons would be obtrusive.

The back-fastening dress, sometimes found in the fifteenth century, is a recognition of these objections and it was only abandoned in the present century for practical reasons (with which we are not now concerned). No lady's maid—no old-style " back fastenings." The visible but not conspicuous button-fastening dates from the thirteenth century.

We are, I think, entitled to question every button we see, and ask of it : " Do you mean me to see you or are you there, *faut de mieux*, hoping I shan't ? " After all, we ask such questions of kindred arts, and as there are alternatives available, we are entitled to require that a visible fastening device shall have an æsthetic as well as a merely practical function. It must be ornamental as well as useful.

The golden age of the conspicuous button, whether of shape, colour or substance, was certainly the third quarter of the last century, when buttons supplied not only colour but even pattern to the dress ; by their multitude they also distributed points of light over large surfaces of fabrics, assuming some of the qualities of jewels. In fact, buttons were often applied without buttonholes, simply as additional ornaments.

A still more conspicuous method of fastening, whether purposive or merely ornamental, is the visible lacing such as was often used across the front (and sometimes the back) of the bodice. Though occasionally used late in the middle ages this was essentially a Renaissance device revived in the eighteenth and late nineteenth centuries. The purpose is clear : to draw attention to the shape of the bosom and to suggest to the spectator an association with stays. This allusion will be discussed in the chapter on " sex-attraction " in Costume.

Finally we have the dress with no fastenings : one, that is to say, which is slipped on over the head ; it is enough to add that this is not only a modern but also the oldest method of all.

Invisible methods of fastening only concern us here in so far as they affect the æsthetic appearance of the costume. We have to note, therefore, the effect of tying a number of garments, one over another, round the waist—such as multiple petticoats. This practically necessitates a bulky skirt and some kind of bustle, so as to throw out the skirt to conceal the bunching of the undergarments. The Elizabethan method of fastening the " petticoat " (i.e. the separate skirt) is indicated in Kemp's *Nine Daies Wonder*, 1599, in which he describes how he happened to tread on the garment of " a homely maid that was but newly crept into the fashion of long wasted peticotes tyde with points . . . the point either breaking or stretching off fell her peticote from her waste, but as chance was, though her smock were coarse it was cleanly ; yet the poor wench was so ashamed . . . that looking before like one that had the greene sicknesse, now had her cheekes coloured with scarlet."

It is uncertain how many petticoats were usually worn in the eighteenth and earlier centuries, but as the legs were otherwise bare, drawers not having been invented for women, we may suppose that for warmth's sake they were multiple ; hence no doubt the prolonged fashion for the bustle or hoop, one or other being used during nearly the whole of the four centuries since the sixteenth. The only periods without either were from 1620 to 1680 (perhaps) and the first and last decades of the nineteenth century. (The bustle, it may be noted, was not necessarily confined to the back, but often, as in the late Regency and early Victorian periods, extended round the sides of the waist.) Horace Walpole alludes to bustles in 1783 thus : " . . . *on pretend* that certain invisible machines of which one heard much a year or two ago and which were said to be constructed of cork, and to be worn somewhere or other behind, are now to be transplanted somewhere or other in front, in imitation of the Duchess of Devonshire's pregnancy and all under-jaws to be advanced on the same principle."

The fastenings employed by men, in so far as they concern our subject, present some points of interest.

Although buttons were known as early as the thirteenth century they do not seem to have been much used by men until the sixteenth. Thus, while woman's cote-hardie, for example, might show a great many buttons both down the front and on the sleeves, the man's had them but sparingly ; perhaps the mediæval button was not a very reliable article ; he preferred the girdle or belt.

While the bulk of his clothing hung from the shoulders the short hose was (probably) secured by garters ; later when towards the end of the fourteenth century the hose had been prolonged to the fork, it was then tied to the doublet with laces or " points."

With the arrival of the true stocking in the sixteenth century, garters became visible and highly ornamental. At the same time buttons down the front of the doublet were conspicuous, and remained so long as that garment survived—longer, indeed, if we accept the waistcoat as its lineal descendant.

Since that time visible fastenings in the shape of buttons have been confined to man's waistcoat, coat and sleeve cuffs ; and it will be noted how many of these are in reality functionless. They have often served as substitutes for jewellery, being made as gay and costly as possible, and a faint trace of this survives in some of the fancy buttons which adorn the modern white dress waistcoat, and perhaps, too, in the cuff links which, it seems, are about to disappear from man's wardrobe.

Certain invisible methods of fastening concern us ; thus, the fly buttons introduced into the breeches in the time of Charles I, enabled the tailor to cut the garment with a better fit. The front flap, buttoned up on each side, was certainly present early in the eighteenth century and derived apparently from riding breeches.

The braces for holding up the breeches was a late eighteenth century device ; before that the breeches were cut full in the seat and hung (sometimes, it seems, precariously) on the hip bones, depending on the close fit round the waist. It is worth noting that this now aged and trusty servant of man seems likely after a century and a half to be discarded, the modern fashion being more and more to substitute for the braces elastic webbing let into the back of the trousers pleated round the top, or else to revert to the belt.

This enables the wearer to dispense with the waistcoat without exposing the trouser buttons, always a closely guarded secret. It is a psychological curiosity that the gaily worked braces which Victorian ladies were wont to embroider for gentlemen appeared at a time when the garment to which they were destined to be fastened could not even be named with propriety. That they seem to have disappeared when that prudish epoch faded is equally curious—or significant.[1]

Revival of Costume Forms.

The Art of Costume, like some other arts, shows at times an inclination to revive styles of Form which belonged to the past.

The familiar saying that " Fashions repeat themselves" is, however, very misleading ; in reality they never do. What does reappear is a similarity which is only superficial. What is far more remarkable and significant is the difference between the copy and the original.

This habit of borrowing from the wardrobe of ancestors is almost—if not entirely—confined to women's costume. We have, of course, to distinguish between

---

[1] When men started to use sock-suspenders some fifty years ago they were considered effeminate because they resembled the suspenders used by women since 1878. It was, in fact, one of the few items of theirs which men have borrowed ; another is the wrist watch which women were wearing as early as 1888 (as seen in a photograph of that date in my collection). When some ten or twelve years later men began to use wrist watches the same association of effeminacy was attached to the fashion, until the war of 1914-18, when all officers wore them without being " effeminate." Similarly " mannish " items worn by women cease to give that impression when the fashion becomes sufficiently widespread.

survivals and revivals ; for conspicuous examples of the former we go to men's clothes, for the latter to women's.

We may allow that the hooped skirt of the eighteenth century was a revival of the earlier farthingale, although the resemblance is superficial, but the first complete revival was the classical dress of the early Regency period. It was, in fact, a conscious attempt to return to the dress of the Ancients, a pose of short duration.

As soon as the Napoleonic war was over a revival of the Tudor style (of about 1540) became apparent. The puffed shoulder, the neck ruff on a smaller scale, the heavy bands traced round the lower part of the skirt, these together were traceable to Tudor sources—but entirely differing in spirit.

This is a characteristic of such revivals ; there is a resemblance, due perhaps to some striking feature mimicking, however indifferently, something in a former mode. Close examination will reveal a number of differences, apart from those due to material and work-manship. The principal change is in the whole spirit of the thing. The sprightly dress of 1820 had none of the severe formalism of 1540.

If the Form of Costume were entirely capricious, due solely to the whim of the designer, then no doubt we should frequently have exact repetitions of old forms, made as identical as possible, just as we have, for example, in furniture. But nothing even approaching such a reproduction has ever supplied a fashion ; and this, simply because the taste of the public demands an expression of its own ideals, set up by its own circumstances. No two historical periods can ever be sufficiently like one another in this respect to produce identical ideals. And so some resemblance in their fashions is all that is likely, or, indeed, possible.

We are, however, faced by the fact that all through the nineteenth century there was a series of these fashion revivals. How is this to be explained ? Although we may assume that the original and the copy had some influence in common which inspired them, we must guard ourselves from hasty conclusions as to its nature. Take, for instance, the " leg-of-mutton " sleeve which originated with the Elizabethans ; it was strikingly revived in the 1830's and again in the early '90's.

We know that each epoch emphasised the smallness of the waist. Also that the huge sleeve accentuates this. But why should that particular device have been selected at those particular epochs and not at others when small waists were equally in fashion ?

We discover that in the '90's, with the Diamond Jubilee approaching and loyalty in the air, curiosity was aroused towards the fashions prevailing in the time of Queen Victoria's youth. (The contemporary fashion magazines were full of this.) What more natural than to revive at least their most striking feature, the sleeve ?

But if we ask why did the women of 1830, in their turn, seek to revive an Elizabethan fashion, we know that the Romantic movement of the '30's was seeking for forms of expression, and it was natural that to them no historical period appeared more in keeping with that spirit than the great days of the Virgin Queen.

Push the inquiry to the point of asking what caused the Elizabethan leg-of-mutton sleeve, and we are driven to assume still more.

It is interesting to find that J. R. Planché, in the 1847 edition of his work on British Costume, regarded the fashions of the then recent 1830's as a revival of those of the reign of Henry VII, while the fashions of his own day (1847) he considered to be a revival of those of the Restoration of 1660. The profound differ-ence between these similitudes seems to have escaped him.

Of all Victorian revivals perhaps the nearest to approximate to the original was the Polonaise dress of the 1870's, so closely resembling the Polonaise of just a

hundred years earlier (*Plate* 21) ; and here the resemblance included the headgear and hair-dressing.
Both, it may be noted, followed a period of huge hooped
skirt with hard triangular outline ; a return to " curves "
in each case might almost have been anticipated. And
yet nothing of this sort followed the decline of the
farthingale in 1620.

Apart from these striking instances of revivals there
were innumerable borrowings of details, Tudor capes,
Marie Stuart caps, Valois collars and, in fact, items
from every epoch of which the costume was sufficiently
well known.

That this revival spirit was almost wholly confined
to the nineteenth century may, in part, be explained
by the interest aroused by Sir Walter Scott in "romantic"
historical episodes. By 1820 the Romantic Movement
was in being, and it is the " romantic " aspect of past
modes which were specially selected for revival, provided
they happened to suit the requirements of the day.

To-day in an unromantic and realistic world this
taste for such revivals has almost entirely disappeared.
It is unlikely that another William Morris will arise to
recommend a return to the costume of the middle ages
as the only style conforming to the requirements of
pure Art.

We are, however, at the present moment being faced
with what appears to be a definite " revival," as regards
Woman's day dress, of the modes of the middle '80's
(*Plate* 46). This has received the name of " The New
Look " and it represents the first attempt of feminine
fashions to get away from those associated with the war.

The Englishwoman is weary of the semi-masculine
garb in which she performed ultra-masculine jobs
during those years, and now there is a very natural
desire to appear more feminine. Under the present
economic restrictions she is prepared to accept—at least
until something better is allowed—almost any new

fashion which will help her to forget the old and to look more like—a woman.

The new style, recalling that of 1886, presents the sloping shoulder, the fitted bodice, the close sleeve reaching just below the elbow, the pinched-in waist and, especially, a fuller skirt with draped hip effects. The new skirt is accused of being extravagantly long, reaching to mid-calf level ; in '86 the skirt was said to be daringly short, reaching no further than—the instep. Though usually fuller than formerly, some of the new skirts are imitating the " hobble " of 1908-12, but most Englishwomen do not welcome this return to captivity.

It is too soon to judge to what extent this " New Look " is a straw indicating the direction of future fashions, or whether it is only a will-of-the-wisp ; but it is definitely symptomatic of a widespread yearning for greater femininity in woman's dress.

17. *Portrait of Mary Pettus, 1740.* Note the wrapping front, a style revived some 90 years later ; the loose elbow sleeves with large ruffles, and the square-cut décolletage edged with lace recall the style of a century earlier.

18. *Portrait of Charles Tottenham*, M.P., *c. 1745.* Note the riding boots of "Top-boots Tottenham," reaching above the bottom of the resplendent waistcoat, and the heavy turned-back cuffs.

Portrait of the Vanneck family, by Arthur Devis, 1752. Note the collarless coats, long waistcoats and small wigs of the men; the pointed stiff stomachers and huge pannier skirts of the women.

20. *Sir James Grant, Mr. Mytton, The Hon. F. Robinson and Mr. Wynne* in costur
the period, by Batoni, *c. 1760.*   For details see Chapter 6.

. *The Polonaise of 1777.* Note the hitched-up polonaise over the skirt which is itself hitched up over the petticoat. The style was closely copied a century later.

22. "*The Westminster Election*" *by Robert Dighton, 1788*. Note the tight buckskin bre
and coat cut away so as to reveal the thighs, with short square-cut waistco
male figure in the centre. Also the large feathered hat and high waist of the lady
to him. The costume of the man (left centre with hand in pocket) is " old-fashio

23. *Evening Dress in 1807.* Note the man's short waistcoat and cut-away dress coat, with legs exploited in tight knee breeches. The lady's high-waisted dress of crimson sarcenet is worn over a white satin petticoat. Note her loose York tan gloves.

(From *Le Beau Monde*, 1807).

24a. (left). *Brass of Lady Sacheverell, Morley, Derbyshire, 1558.*

24b. *Fashion Plate, 1822.* Note how the style of dress (a) is copied in that of 1822 (b). Note the similar design of sleeve, ruff and front-fastening dress.

"*Bond Street Loungers*" in *1820*. From left to right : Lord Sefton, the Duke of Devonshire, "Poodle" Byng, Lord Manners and the Duke of Beaufort. Note the varieties of hats and coats.

26. *Caricature of 1827.* "Nothing extenuate nor aught set down in malice."
The exaggeration speaks for itself. At all costs a woman insisted on
being noticed.

27. *Line drawing of Alfred D'Orsay, " The last of the Dandies," 1828.*
Note the " feminine " curves, the emphasis on the legs in their tight
pantaloons, and the lapelled waistcoat with its feminine point.

(From *Fraser's Magazine*).

28. *Portrait of Alderman Watkins, 1845.* The curves of the D'Orsay Dandies period have entirely disappeared giving place to a very purposive rectangularity. The waistcoat, very short, preserves the lapels and the distinctive colouring. Observe the short frock coat, the cravat, and square-toed boots of the period. The whole costume has a mercantile masculinity and the "H" formula is well marked.

9a, b. Two carte-de-visite photographs :

Man and Wife, 1860 (right). The man's waistcoat retains a slight lapel but is otherwise quite prosaic ; his necktie retains only a faint trace of the old " neckcloth." The lady's bell sleeves with puffed " engageantes," and the double skirt over an unfashionably small crinoline, were commoner than the fashion journals would suggest.

The first form of the " Walking Costume," 1862. The skirt is drawn up by interior cords revealing the ornamental petticoat. Note the touch of Victorian prudery blotting out all traces of feet and ankles so that she appears to be floating on air.

30a, b. Two carte-de-visite photographs :

The " heavy swell " of 1865 with Dundreary whiskers and light check trousers.

The Surtout of 1872. Note the narrow trousers. The tie and collar are approaching modern forms.

1a. *The Hyde Park Costume for 1885.* Note the proportions, the frock coat being exactly the middle half of the whole figure. The top hat is needed to preserve the proportions. Note too the emphasis on vertical lines.

31b. *Golfing Costume, 1894.* Note the Norfolk jacket and the woman's masculine cut of waistcoat and skirt now definitely " practical."

32a. *Gentlemen's country Walking Costume*
c. 1865.

32b. *Gentlemen's country Walking Costume*,
c. *1870*. Note form of knickerbockers and elastic-sided boots.

CHAPTER XII

THE PRINCIPLES OF COLOUR

THE importance of Colour in the Art of Costume is second only to that of Form ; sometimes indeed it appears to assume first place either in the costume as a whole or at least in a part of it, so that the spectator, vividly impressed by the colour, scarcely notices anything else.

Moreover, there will usually be a greater variety in the colours used in a particular fashion than in its form, so that, in common parlance, it will be the colour of a costume which is mentioned first in a description. " A man in a brown suit," " A woman in a red dress." Such expressions come more readily than an attempt to describe the form. In other words, colour makes the first impression on the spectator and usually the most lasting.

And as there is usually a wider choice of colours available, the personal taste in that respect is more conspicuous : people will accept the fashionable form but they will exercise choice in the selection of its colour. Apparently there is a vast difference of opinion as to what is and what is not " good taste " in colours, especially in combination. Moreover, if we judge one epoch by another we find that " good taste " changes to a remarkable degree so that when we condemn the colour taste of a period we are tacitly assuming that the taste of our own day is necessarily right, an assumption which posterity may perhaps dispute.

" Good taste," it seems, is a matter of opinion, but we can say that certain combinations of colours are, in fact, harmonious while others are discordant, without disputing the claim put forward by some that discords are very agreeable, in colour as in music. Indeed there have been times when discordant Art forms have been preferred to harmonious ones.

Each of the Primary colours, Red, Yellow and Blue, has its complementary colour composed of a mixture of the other two ; that of Red being Green (Yellow plus Blue) ; that of Yellow being Purple (Red plus Blue) ; that of Blue being Orange (Red plus Yellow).

In the Art of Costume the importance of the Complementary lies in the fact that a Primary tends to tint its surroundings with a faint halo of its Complementary, and vice versa ; so that the colour of one part of a costume will appear to affect that of another. Moreover, a costume which is to be exposed in the neighbourhood of other costumes, as at some social function, may be affected as regards its colour by their presence.

It is convenient to use the old-fashioned terms, " cold " and " warm " colours for those near the blue end and the red end of the spectrum respectively. Whether a mixture of the two is to be reckoned " cold " or " warm " will depend on the proportions used, though the cold colour always tends to outweigh the effect of the warm, in the mixture.

Thus, most tints or shades of pink are to be reckoned " cold." There is apparently a considerable variation in the sensitiveness of people's eyes to particular colours, especially to blue, and to many " pink " appears definitely a warm colour on account of the red in it, because they cannot perceive its blue element. They will therefore match it with other " warm " colours, and when one sees a woman wearing pink, orange and mauve in her costume, one must suppose she has a considerable degree of insensitiveness to blue.

It seems that the modern eye is less sensitive to this distinction than in former generations when, as in the last century, for example, there were customary " laws " on the subject ; thus, a " cold " colour must not be placed adjoining a " warm " without the interposition of a neutral to serve as a modulation from one chromatic key to another, a refinement now seldom observed.

(The term " hue " indicates the degree of variation from a standard colour ; " tint " implies the degree to which a hue is diluted with white ; and " shade " the degree to which it is diluted with black ; by " tone " is meant the degree of its luminosity.)

It is also noticeable that at certain epochs particular colours or combinations of colours were fashionable while others were eschewed, and that some colours have or have had special significance attached to them so that they have come to express recognisable ideas.

Moreover, especially in women's costume, certain colours were reserved for the married, the single or the aged ; that this was not based on purely æsthetic grounds is shown by the fact that such distinctions are now generally ignored. Mrs. Haweis, writing some seventy years ago, instructs us that two luminous colours in a dress are " vulgar " and that yellow was generally regarded as unladylike, while from other sources we learn that orange was not to be worn by the unmarried as it indicated " animal passions," but these are niceties now lost on us.

It is sufficiently evident that colours in the Art of Costume supply more than a mere æsthetic satisfaction ; they have—or had—a psychological significance.

We recognise this when we say that certain colours, as used in costume, have an " emotional tone." And this may be subjective or objective ; a sensitive woman can be cheered or depressed simply by the colour of her dress and the spectator of it likewise.

The most conspicuous example of an emotional tone in colour is—or at any rate *was*—black. In the second chapter I referred to the psychological significance attached to black, which has now lost much of its former emotional tone as a gloomy colour. Apparently black has been a symbol of mourning at least as far back as the thirteenth century, and in Chaucer's time its symbolism was well established. On the other hand it was a fashionable colour during the Elizabethan and Jacobean period, when its emotional tone seems to have been suspended.

When we see the lavish use of black mourning in the eighteenth and nineteenth centuries we can only regard it as a kind of emotional orgy sometimes bordering on hysteria. Thus the funeral expenses of a country gentleman in the year 1800 included twelve black bombazine dresses for the upper maidservants, twelve black bombazet for the lower, and a black velvet suit at £8 a yard for the chief mourner, together with black gowns for six clergymen.[1]

Since very early times white has been a symbol of purity—hence of virginity—and so the conventional colour for brides. In 1450, however, Sir W. Plumpton was married " in a garment of green checkery," his bride being in red with a grey hood. It is curious, also, to find, about 1600, that yellow was fashionable for the occasion.

Blue, being the natural colour of the sky, has likewise symbolised purity. (In early Italian pictures of the Virgin Mary her robes are commonly of that colour.) On the other hand, we find that during the first half of the seventeenth century it was regarded as a menial's colour : thus Ben Jonson in his *Masque of Christmas* speaks of one " in a blew coat like a serving man." Consequently it was not a colour then worn by gentlemen.

But in the middle ages blue was one of the more lasting dyes and less likely to fade than others such as

[1] At the funeral of Mr. Pepys, forty-one suits of mourning were provided for those attending the ceremony. This custom of supplying mourning garments continued in the form of gloves, which the undertaker served out to each guest on arrival, down to the end of last century. Thirty years earlier hat bands were also provided ; these hung down to the waist and were worn by men.

green ; hence blue came to signify constancy and green inconstancy. Thus Lidgate :

> " Instede of blew, which stedfaste is and clene,
> She wered colours of many a dyverse grene."

The popular colours for men's clothes towards the end of the fifteenth century are indicated in Caxton's *Dialogues in French and English*. There a purchaser is advised to go to the market : " there shall ye find clothes medleyed, red cloth or green, blue-azured, yellow, red, " sad blew " (dark blue), murrey, raye (striped), checquered, scarlet in grayne." From the ensuing dialogue between customer and seller we gather that scarlet is the most expensive. And when, after bargaining, the former asks for as much cloth as he will need for " a surcote, for a cote, for a hewke (cloak), for a pair of hosen," he is told he will want fifteen ells (yards) of cloth two and a half ells wide.

The emotional tone of red has generally been fully appreciated from its association with the colour of blood ; it has therefore always been employed to inspire feelings of fear or awe, as in ceremonial robes, and it still has that significance in its use as a signal of danger.

Enough has been said to indicate that colours have emotional tone, and that circumstances change their implication. We may attribute this to association of ideas derived from familiar objects, even sometimes from passing events.

On this account their use in the Art of Costume affects us, perhaps unconsciously, causing a particular hue or combination of hues to strike the observer as pleasant or unpleasant, as the case may be, and so much is this the case that the colour of a costume may blind us to its form which we find ourselves unable to judge with impartiality.

It follows that in criticising the colours favoured in some former period we can hardly do so fairly unless we know whether these colours signified to the original wearers precisely what they mean to us. We have also to know under what conditions they were seen, and this applies of course chiefly to costumes worn indoors.

We must allow for the comparative darkness of domestic interiors, at least until the end of the sixteenth century ; that window glass did not become at all large until the eighteenth ; and that in the present century there has been an increasing amount of daylight admitted into our houses.

Artificial light has similarly progressed ; mediæval torches and candles, candles until the eighteenth century, then candles and oil lamps until the introduction of gas about 1830, and electric light about 1890, and in recent years an increasing use of electric light of a kind giving off an appreciable amount of ultra-violet rays.

Such has been the progress, and it will be noticed that artificial illumination has not only increased in intensity but that it has steadily passed from the red end of the spectrum until now it approaches the other extreme.

The effect of this change of quality of light on the colours of costumes is important ; broadly speaking, we may say that red rays tend to kill the blue colours, and that blue rays kill the red colours. The old-fashioned candle-light favoured red, but the modern lighting will reduce the red in a mixture such as purple, turning it dark blue or at least lowering its shade.

These practical points necessarily affect the choice of colours for evening wear, and we can therefore understand why yellow was a popular colour in the candle-light of the eighteenth and early nineteenth centuries, and again in the very yellow electric light of the 1890's.

The intensity of modern illumination tends to drive

the more brilliant hues out of fashion simply because they are no longer necessary ; in the times, now gone, when drawing-rooms had shadows, luminous hues were appropriate, and the further back we go the brighter were the colours used, and necessarily so in the dim illumination of the middle ages.

Consequently when we witness a stage reproduction of a mediæval "interior" seen under the fierce blaze of modern footlights, the colours of the costumes, though perhaps strictly authentic, appear in fact extremely distorted.

The reader is to be reminded that until the introduction of aniline dyes for textiles about 1860, all colours had necessarily been obtained from vegetable sources. In 1472 the Dyer's Company was established in London, and the opening up of the Cape route to the Far East brought many new dyestuffs in the sixteenth century, cochineal coming from Mexico. The introduction of Eastern carpets and rugs in Elizabeth's reign doubtless suggested new colour combinations.

The range of vegetable dyes and their practical application steadily increased until the advent of the aniline dyes. Of these, Solferino and Magenta were the first to be used in textiles. Both are mixtures, Solferino being composed of Red 83%, Blue 17%, Magenta of Red 67%, Blue 33%. Those who are not very sensitive to blue may find these two colours almost indistinguishable. (Mauve is Red 37%, Blue 50%, White 13%.) From aniline bases an infinite range of hues is obtainable, and although at first such chemical dyes were prone to fade they are now, in fact, faster than vegetable dyes.

When we examine the colours used in Costume we should bear in mind that wool takes a dye better than silk, and silk better than cotton ; and that, formerly at least, it was impossible to dye cotton fabrics with certain dyes, so that those colours could not be used with that material.

We have next to consider the various methods of using colour in the Art of Costume.

These may be classified as follows :

1. The monochrome costume, in which a single colour is used, with perhaps some minor accessories of a different colour either in harmony or contrast. This type has been much more used in modern times than formerly by women, especially in the tailor-made costume. It has seldom been used by men as a pure single colour, though a mixture of hues closely blended will produce the effect of a single colour. " Heather mixture," for example, is almost a colour in itself.

2. The two-colour costume. In this the two colours may be (a) distributed fairly equally in distinct masses vertically or horizontally in stripes or bands, or the upper half of the costume being of one colour, the lower half of the other ; they may also be combined to form patterns, or blended to form a mixture as in shot materials. (b) The two colours may be unequal masses, one supplying a background to the other—that is to say, having the effect of colour on colour. And here the two may vary in chromatic intensity (" luminosity "), sometimes an intense colour on one less intense, or vice versa ; the two either harmonising or contrasting with each other.

The art of using " colour on colour " in costume can best be studied in women's fashions of the period 1870-80.[1]

3. The polychrome costume, in which three or more colours are used. These likewise may be in distinct masses or combined into patterns, and variations of luminosity employed. It is obvious that coloured

[1] Audsley's *Taste versus Fashionable Colours* (1863) advises ladies on suitable colour selection in dress, and from it we learn that at that period the following were considered harmonious blends : Crimson and purple ; yellow and crimson ; yellow, purple, scarlet and blue ; green, scarlet, and blue ; orange, red and green ; orange, blue, scarlet and claret ; lilac and cerise ; lilac, yellow, scarlet and white ; lilac and scarlet. Not all such mixtures would appeal to modern tastes.

linings to garments such as cloaks which may be seen open, introduce an additional colour, and important accessories of this sort afford different layers of colour to a costume. Thus flat surfaces can be given a " three dimension " appearance very effectively. Further, the addition of semi-transparent materials, such as lace, will modify the tone of the colour beneath.

We have to bear in mind how much the tone of a colour depends on the nature of the textile, some surfaces being completely dull while others are highly luminous ; a velvet and satin of precisely the same tint or shade will nevertheless have a very different tone on account of the nature of their surfaces.

The several colours may be used without any definite relation to the parts of the costume—and this especially in women's dress—or each may be confined to a particular region, thus breaking up the costume into parts—a common masculine device. The former method accentuates the *toute ensemble*, the latter emphasises individual features.

We may note in passing the curious reluctance of human beings, especially men, to use different colours for the two sides of the costume ; piebald effects have only appeared in men's costume in the latter part of the fourteenth and early fifteenth centuries. It was, of course, the conventional attire of the court fool and the clown, the distracted colours symbolising distracted wits.

The purposes for which colours are used in costumes may likewise be classified, thus :

1. To increase or diminish the apparent weight and size of a region, dark colours tending to increase the former and reduce the latter, and light colours the reverse, thus affecting the appearance of balance.

2. To make a region more noticeable by light hues and luminous surfaces, or less noticeable by dark hues and dull surfaces.

If a costume has a noticeable " high spot " of colour

we may assume that the spectator is specially invited to look at it.

By this means a costume is given a sort of " foreground " and " background."

3. To affect the emotional tone of the whole costume by the use of colours which have acquired symbolic significance. And this emotional tone can affect the wearer as well as the spectator. Writers from Ovid onwards have discussed colours that invite and colours that repel, colours that suit particular emotional states which psychologists have explained by—wave lengths.

4. To lead the eye in a particular direction by means of coloured " pointers," e.g. angular trimmings pointing towards the waist. Such pointers have therefore a special significance, implying a desire expressed in dumb show.

5. To produce an optical illusion, vertical stripes seeming to increase height, and horizontal stripes breadth.

The outlines of Form can be accentuated by being imitated in colour on the surface of the costume, or, if necessary, Form can be camouflaged, e.g. by large irregular patterns.

Coloured patterns are of two types : the Free and the Restricted.

By a free pattern I mean one which is distributed over a surface without being confined by any obvious demarcation ; a restricted pattern has well-defined borders to each repeat. These borders have the effect of lines and so lead the eye to follow their course vertically or transversely as the case may be, while a squared pattern distracts by drawing the eye in different directions.

The effect of a free pattern depends on the size of its elements ; if these are small, such as dots or minute floral designs, they appear to blend with the ground colour and so affect its tone ; if the pattern elements are large they distract attention from the rest of the costume and especially from its form.

It is evident that pronounced patterns markedly affect other features of the costume, sometimes advantageously, sometimes the reverse, and it is a device which this Art will therefore use only for a specific purpose.

Floral designs are perhaps the commonest type of pattern, and it is noticeable that men have very seldom used this type, except in brocades. (We observe how women have always associated themselves with flowers, often borrowing their names for themselves, a thing men have never done.)

Patterns can be formed in various ways : in the weave of the textile, by colour printing on the textile, or by added trimmings. Woven patterns are of great antiquity —at least in the Far East. Brocade, in which the coloured pattern is raised, is mentioned in the wardrobe accounts of Edward IV—" a blue clothe of silver broched uppon satyn ground." Printing materials in colour dates in this country from about 1690. In them the effect is to flatten the colour so that it is non-luminous or nearly so ; hence printed colours require daylight, and cannot rival woven patterns under artificial light.

Finally we have also to note that a pattern can be produced in a textile simply by changing the nature of the weave so as to alter the tone of the part patterned.

Thus in damask there is no alteration of hue, but the pattern stands out by its difference in luminosity ; similarly a diaper pattern can be produced in velvets by double pile. All such are examples of patterns in tone rather than in hue.

From these considerations we may, I think, conclude that, broadly speaking, a costume in monochrome is, æsthetically, somewhat severe and less venturesome than in polychrome. There is less possibility of disaster, but as the eye soon ceases to notice a single colour, a natural desire not only to attract notice but to retain it will tempt the use of the latter.

In the monochrome, Form becomes all-important ; in the polychrome less so. And always colours are used first to catch the eye and then to retain it, so as to impress an idea on the spectator. We learn from the art of advertising that while it is easy to make the public glance at a poster, it is much more difficult to make them read its message.

So, too, in the Art of Costume.

In the foregoing pages reference has been made to the psychological " tone " of colours. We have to distinguish this from the æsthetic " tone," which depends on its degree of luminosity.

In coloured fabrics this is governed by a combination of factors which need to be considered.

In the first place, every colour has its own natural " chromatic intensity " which is, in effect, a measure of its visibility. Thus, red, green, yellow and blue have a descending scale in that order ; and it may be added that not only is red more " visible " than the other three, but the field of vision of the human eye is widest for that colour and progressively narrows as that scale descends to blue. (Red and green are therefore the two colours habitually used for signals, being not merely more easily seen but seen through wider angles than other colours.)

In the second place, the luminosity depends on the nature of the surface of a fabric, whether polished or dull, the animal products of silk and wool having a higher degree of natural polish than flax and cotton.

And thirdly, the luminosity depends on the nature of the texture, a close weave allowing less light to pass through the meshes and therefore reflecting more from its surface than a coarse weave.

The æsthetic tone of a fabric therefore depends on a

combination of these factors ; moreover, it will also vary, perhaps momentarily, as folds and creases are formed by movements producing shadows.

In the next chapter the effect of texture on tone will be further considered, but here, in so far as colour-tone is concerned, we may note that two different colours may have the same tone and that two materials of the same colour may yet have different tones.

To some eyes the former will therefore appear a harmonious match, irrespective of their colours, while the latter combination will appear discordant although the colours may be identical.

This no doubt explains, to some extent, the wide difference of taste in colour mixtures which Costume habitually exhibits. Some people seem more concerned to match colours, others to match tones.

A lack of sensitiveness to differences of tone seems to be an English characteristic, and is perhaps due to the effects of our climate, which lowers the natural tones of our surroundings.

Yet in former times our ancestors appear usually to have been discriminating, instinctively employing the higher tones for the important regions in their Costumes, and the lower tones for the less important. They seemed to realise that as a composition is viewed, the eye will tend to travel towards the higher, sometimes not stopping until the face is reached with its natural high tone (unless lowered by paint or powder) ; sometimes purposely arrested at some region to which special attention is meant to be drawn, where a brilliant item of ribbon or jewellery will signal " stop ! " The modern woman's preoccupation in lowering the tone of her face by constantly powdering her nose, may be attributed to increased visibility and a lack of confidence in her appearance under that condition.

But the modern indifference to tone in Costume appears to have accompanied the general use of low-toned textiles in Costume ; and if this Art is destined to move progressively nearer the blue end of the spectrum with diminishing chromatic intensity and less luminous surfaces in its fabrics, the slight differences of tone between a smudge and a blur will cease to inconvenience even the Argus-eyed.

CHAPTER XIII

THE USE OF COLOUR IN COSTUME

WE may now pass on to examine what colours were used in former times, and the methods of using them. In order to study this matter we have enough of the actual garments themselves for the last couple of centuries or so, although we have often to allow for varying degrees of fading which has taken place in them. Pictures, too, supply useful, indeed essential, information, at least as regards some social classes and types of costume, though they are usually portrayed under daylight conditions only.

But when we attempt to explore still further back beyond the time of the portrait painter—that is to say, beyond about 1500—we enter the obscurity of the middle ages, and we cannot accept the colours used in illuminated MSS. and wall-paintings as reliable evidence.

The reason is that the artist's palette was limited, and he naturally used the colours which gave him the most brilliant effects, in particular red, blue and gold, without attempting exact reproductions of the original costumes.

Nevertheless we do find colours described by contemporary writers ; Margaret Paston, for instance, evidently favoured scarlet—judging from her frequent reference to it in her letters—and other sources of information indicate that scarlet was, in fact, a colour commonly used, together with blue and green.

The clergy before the Reformation appeared to have worn garments much like laymen, and in the will of a Yorkshire rector, dated 1431, we find him leaving two green gowns, one murrey, one sanguine colour and two black. Chaucer's *Canterbury Tales* give us some notion of the colours worn by different classes ; thus the Knight's son, a youth of twenty, wore a garment embroidered with red and white flowers ; the Yeoman was in green and the Reve in blue ; the Merchant in motley ; the Doctor of Physic in purple and light blue ; the Parish Clerk wore red hose, sky-blue kirtle and white " surplice."

The singular fashion for piebald colouring, white and red, white and blue, black and red, white and black, especially in men's hose, was introduced in the reign of Edward II, and had probably originated from heraldry. There is, in fact, sufficient evidence for concluding that in the fourteenth and fifteenth centuries the general taste was for bright colours, especially red, blue and green ; yellow is seldom mentioned (*Frontispiece*).

Two factors no doubt affected the popular choice of colours, one being the fashion for mummers, who traditionally dressed in parti-coloured garb ; the other being the custom of nobles to put their retainers into easily recognisable liveries. Thus, in the reign of Henry VI, the Earl of Warwick came to London with a train of six hundred men all clothed in red jackets embroidered with his emblem, the ragged staff.

In fact, colour, as visible as possible, was used as a means of distinguishing occupation and rank, a natural expedient in the conditions then prevailing of bad illumination.

Indoors the finer shades and tints would have been very ineffective, for instance, in those gloomy apartments which served as bedrooms shared by a number of people ; one gets a faint notion of their conditions from the advice given, late in the fourteenth century, to young women, that the last to get undressed should extinguish the solitary candle " by her mouth or her fingers and not by throwing her chemise at it."

We may summarise the mediæval use of colours as being mainly based on utility ; primary colours, except yellow, were common, and garments of one colour were usually contrasted with the colour of another or of the lining. Patterns were unusual except on embroidered robes of ceremony ; but the most noticeable feature, perhaps, is that the colours had but little emotional tone. For that reason mediæval colouring in the Art of Costume seems to us somewhat naïve, much as children use a paintbox to " brighten up " a piece of paper.

Colour is used in simple masses, with effective though perhaps rather crude contrasts. Technical difficulties no doubt limited the scope, and the possibilities of complex combinations of hues were as yet incompletely realised, at least in Costume. The finer work was reserved for the embroidery of ecclesiastical vestments (for which this country had been famous long before the fourteenth century).

The Art of Costume, however, was still under the influence of heraldry, and we find that mantles were lavishly decorated with heraldic devices. The mediæval mind in England had yet to come under the magic spell of the painter on canvas using oil paints, by which the traditional use of precious metals and jewels as colourful adornments to Costume was destined to be transmuted into more subtle pigments. To be effective the mediæval coloured ornament had to borrow the luminosity of polished metals and cut gems ; before more delicate combinations could be appreciated, what was lacking was, simply, better illumination.

The effect of the Renaissance was to introduce something of the warmth of Italian sunlight into our colder homes, and with it a new conception of the use of colour in Costume. Losing its crude and " posterish " effect, it became in the sixteenth century highly complex.

The great novelty was patterns. Thanks to improved domestic illumination, delicate patterns enriched with polychromatic hues could now be appreciated. This is the feature which stands out more than any other in the Tudor period, and it implies a higher degree of sensitiveness to combinations of colours and indicates a growing power of synthesis.

For we do not, when we look at a close pattern, disintegrate its colours in the mind's eye ; we blend them together and judge them as a combined effect. That the Tudor patterns tended to " stare " out from the grounds may be regarded as the first stage in the understanding of this novelty.

Patterns may be subsidiary to the ground colour of a textile or may stand out in vivid contrast, and the latter is the type we associate with the costumes from about 1530 for another hundred years.

The introduction of Oriental rugs and carpets in the Elizabethan period doubtless stimulated an interest in this method of using colours, and resulted in Anglicised forms of patterns always boldly designed, sometimes floral in type freely distributed over the material, sometimes stylised arabesques, and occasionally geometrical.

We have, of course, to recollect that portraits of the period do not usually show everyday costumes ; more probably many, in both sexes, were " gala " dress, the masque being the fashionable entertainment of the time. As regards Elizabethan and Jacobean embroidery, I cannot do better than quote J. L. Nevinson :

" Embroidery, being worked on linen, in the home and with designs taken from samplers or pattern books was cheaper than silks or velvets and seems to have been used mainly for indoors, undress or masquerade wear . . . bright colours are the most common, while monochrome pieces (usually green or red) are comparatively rare. In a polychrome piece one may expect to find royal blue, pale blue, grass green, pale green, cream, bright yellow, pink, carmine or crimson. Rarer colours are purple, dark green, olive, yellow-brown, sepia, salmon-pink, pale vermilion, and shades of reddish mauve."

As regards coloured stuffs a noticeable fashion for black and white or black alone prevailed during the last quarter of the sixteenth and first quarter of the seventeenth centuries. The Italian warmth, noticeable during the earlier Tudor period, had cooled under our skies ; the late Elizabethan and Jacobean costumes, though striking in their patterns, were essentially " cold " in hue, with almost a granite hardness in keeping with that adamantine age.

The distribution of colour mass was vertical rather than horizontal ; sleeves were often of a lighter hue than the body of the costume, but apparently in women's dress there was no distinction in colour between bodice and skirt.

By the time of Charles I patterns had ceased to hold an important place, giving way to luminous colours in fabrics, especially silks and satins. Striped materials began to appear, and in Dutch pictures of the period we observe a feature in women's dress which seems to have been quite uncommon in our country—namely, a definite two-colour scheme, with bodice or jacket sharply contrasting with the skirt.

In men's costume the slashing which persisted during the first quarter of the century provided a two-colour effect, while the cloak and its lining of contrasting hue supplied vivid masses of colour. The lavish use of lace accentuated the ground colour and enriched it by contrast, while ribbons began to break up colour masses or rather to overlay them with movable contrasts.

The popular notion that the Puritans wore nothing but drab and sombre garments is an exaggeration derived from Loyalist lampoons and satires. Perhaps, too, the contemporary term " sad-coloured " for a cloth commonly worn has misled readers : actually it meant merely a dark brown. When, for example, we read of

" a suit of sad-coloured cloth lined with flowered silk, the ground buff with peach and green coloured flowers," it does not sound exactly " dismal."

So, too, in the wardrobe expenses of a Kentish gentleman during the Commonwealth, though there are frequent purchases of " sad-coloured " cloth, he also bought " three yards of gold lace for a waistcoat," together with scarlet cloaks, green stockings, etc.

No doubt the Restoration produced a natural outburst of colour in the costumes of the last part of the seventeenth century. We read of a gentleman's " rich suit of phillamot[1] brocade laced with silver and gold lace trimmed with scarlet taffeta ribbons ; white silk stockings upon long scarlet ones ; black shoes with scarlet strings and garters. Gloves trimmed with scarlet ribbons." Colour was used lavishly all through the century and with striking contrasts. Taste, after the Restoration, does not appear to have been restrained, and colours were laid on in variegated fashion. Mr. Pepys's " new gowne of purple shagg trimmed with gold," and his " black cloth suit trimmed with scarlet ribbon " were exactly in the taste of the day.

We notice that colour was being used to give " depth " to the picture ; the surface is not an even layer, and added ribbons of diverse hues over the ground colour have an effect no longer " posterish " but " theatrical." That is to say, the æsthetic effect is apparently best viewed at a certain distance. We might even deduce that much of that sort of finery was intended for outdoor inspection, such as the fashionable saunter along the Mall.

The eighteenth century is, of course, famous for its brocades ; the Spitalfields weaving industry founded by refugees after the revocation of the Edict of Nantes in 1685, introduced a refinement in the art of silk weaving which captivated the tastes of the fashionable world.

[1] Phillamot—dead leaf colour.

At the same time chintzes became extraordinarily popular. Defoe, in his *Weekly Review* (1708), tells us : " The general fancy of the people runs upon East India goods to that degree that the chintz and painted calicoes which before were made only use of for carpets, quilts, etc., are now the dress of our ladies . . . even the Queen herself was pleased to appear in China silks and calico." And the less fashionables were clothed " in calico or printed linen, moved to it as well for the cheapness as for the lightness of the cloth and the gaiety of the colours."

Silks watered and shot with colours such as claret, rose-pink, old gold, dead leaf, and brown, were used in large surfaces bearing delicate patterns of floral brocading and figuring. Stuffs with narrow stripes in the weave came into use, and the printed textiles, especially cotton (an invention introduced into this country in 1676) not only extended the range of colours but supplied patterns which were softer and more delicate in design so that they no longer " stared."

Up to about 1780 the colours were almost invariably harmonious, harsh hues being avoided. In short, we may say that if the colours of the former century were of the theatre, those of the eighteenth were essentially of the salon. The " focal length "—so to speak—had shortened, and to-day, as we examine specimens preserved in museums, we instinctively approach close to them in order to relish the delicacy of their colour combinations and patterns.

The practice of employing pairs of principal colours in a costume—a man's coat with its contrasting lining, his breeches contrasting with his stockings, a woman's open robe contrasting with the colour of the exposed petticoat, in fact a series of happy matches, is very distinctive of the portraits of the period, in which it is hard to find a colour solitary and standing out as an oddity.

It was seldom that colour was used obtrusively as a " pointer ; " we might say that the spirit of the period was to present a composition as a whole without undue emphasis on a part ; at least, any emphasis was to be supplied by Form rather than by Colour. Patterns appear to be absorbed into their grounds, and their colours have that peculiar quality of appositeness which characterises so much of the porcelain of the period, such as early Derby, Dr. Wall's Worcester, and Champion's Bristol.

In the last twenty years of that century, however, a change in colour taste became very evident, accompanying the aggressive note of the " high waist " fashions in both sexes. A brilliant splash of colour, standing out in isolation, as though to signalise a particular region ; a loudly coloured sash on a white dress marking a waist which clamours for notice ; a scarlet coat above buff breeches exposing the shape of the male leg ; a huge bow of coloured ribbon on a huge hat—in a word, colour used in staring patches and strongly contrasting with the ground and a colour unmatched by another, these were the methods employed.

The effect was to break up the balance of the whole colour scheme by introducing the novelty of a " high spot." For this purpose a primary colour on white or near-white was frequently used, and where two colours were employed they tended to be selected from near the opposite ends of the spectrum—scarlet and blue, for example, whereas earlier in the century the pair would have been closer—the greens and yellows, the pinks and blues, the browns and orange. Polychromatic designs tended to change into two coloured designs. No longer was there a general blending of hues, but rather a strongly accentuated contrast.

The effect was restless, emphatic, dynamic.

All through the period of the Napoleonic wars colouring in the costumes of both sexes was in the spirit just described : bold and at times even coarse. The widespread use of white for women's dresses with a striking dash of colour supplied by some accessory such as scarf or the like was very characteristic, and the military uniforms of the men, brilliantly hued but not designed on æsthetic principles, meant that in any social gathering the sexes were in violent contrast. The civilian's evening suit with coat of chocolate, brown or olive green, decorated waistcoat, drab breeches and white or pink silk stockings would have added to the kaleidoscope of the evening.

It was, of course, an epoch of extravagant behaviour, and therefore of extravagant costume, in both sexes ; it was scarcely likely that colours would be out of keeping with that exciting age. War, with its continued emotional strain, compels a heightening of any other emotional appeals if they are to be perceived, so that colours tend to become coarser, more blatant, if they are to be effective in their aim.

But with the restoration of peace the tension lapsed, and in the 1820's and '30's a more picturesque and romantic spirit prevailed. Strong pure colours became " tints "—that is to say, diluted with a modicum of white softening their hue.

At this point the costumes of the two sexes, so far as their use of colour was concerned, parted company. In men's clothes there was a chromatic decline ; yet it was they and not women who showed greater originality in at least one respect : men struck out boldly into the use of three colours in their costume ; thus, an olive green frock coat, a waistcoat of floral pattern on a cream ground, and trousers of a bright jade. Or, if you please, an ultramarine surtout, light fancy waistcoat and violet trousers.

The youthful Disraeli's evening attire of green velvet trousers, canary waistcoat, lace ruffles and silver buckled shoes, was in the spirit of the Dandies. A curious feature may be noted : whereas in the eighteenth century the knee-breeches were as dark as, or generally darker than the coat, the pantaloons and subsequently the trousers of the nineteenth were always lighter in colour—a principle which has persisted unless the whole suit is of one material. Thus men's costumes were developing the rule of " dark above light " just when women's were reversing that order. The lighter trouser is doubtless to draw attention to the shape of the male leg. The darker skirt is to give extra weight and therefore balance.

The trousers had also inherited the light hue from the nankin pantaloons, and presently acquired stripes and chequered patterns. The use of strongly defined check patterns is always significant ; these while catching the eye tend to camouflage the shape. It is to be noted that about the middle of last century—the height of the " trouser taboo "—a check pattern would draw attention to those unmentionable objects while leaving their outline decently obscure. Thus a fashion journal of 1850 remarks : " Check materials are not worn by the ladies, being entirely given up to the nether integuments of the sterner sex."

By the middle of the century the coat had become definitely sombre, while the waistcoat alone tried to preserve traces of the ancient splendour of the male costume.

In the privacy of domestic life, however, the Early Victorian gentleman cherished his " morning gown," a survival from the former century, and as late as 1850 we find this chamber attire consisting of an Oriental robe with tasselled cap and brilliant scarlet slippers, in which the wearer would lounge his mornings away in the manner of Ouida's guardsmen.

It is surely significant that something of this tradition still survives, and the modern man's peacock instincts, suppressed in his suits, burst forth in his pyjamas and dressing-gown, recalling the plumage of the mating season. Obviously the male desire to use colours as a means of sex attraction is not wholly dead.

That in his working clothes bright colouring would be inappropriate is equally evident, and the gradual decline of colour—other than in the bedroom—is merely an indication of his prosaic occupations. Work—and railways—together have driven the colour out of men's clothing. The monochrome suit of a single material and colour throughout became noticeable about 1860, but until quite recently that type has been considered as rather " slack ; " the old two-colour convention, black coat and striped trousers, or for special moments the three-colour convention in which the waistcoat presents a colour of its own, these are not yet quite extinct.

We have also to allow for the fact that the man of fashion is no longer the idle butterfly of old, and fashion itself is set by a class now " engaged in gainful occupations "—in other words, on a much broader but also lower social basis. Colour is no longer a distinguishing feature of class, and something of the sort is overtaking women's costume for similar reasons.

We must now retrace our steps to examine the manner in which women's costume has employed colour during the last hundred years or so. Thanks to the invention of the Jacquard loom an immensely increased range of coloured textiles was available, and the 1830's was notable for the use of printed materials, cottons and woollens, having all-over patterns in polychrome, usually floral in nature.

These, together with half-tints of secondary hues, pale blues and cyclamen, rose and delicately striped stuffs, adorned that age of romance. Gradually the primary colours were considered somewhat " vulgar ; " the Early Victorian feature was the accessory garment, the shawl, mantlet or the like which added colour on colour, and a progressive use of trimmings.

These, coloured, began to be used as " pointers " to emphasise the lines of the figure ; narrow striped silks (" Pekins ") suggested a ladylike slimness, while a wealth of shot silks, always harmonious in hue, illuminated the picture. It was the swan-song of the vegetable dye.

The aniline dyes in the '60's encouraged an orgy of intense colours, especially those containing an element of blue, such as magenta, solferino, purple, green-blue, pink—colours, that is, that have an astringent quality. In addition, scarlet petticoats and scarlet striped stockings, vivid gloves and—perhaps still more original—broad horizontal stripes of colour contrasts across the skirt. But the impression created by a widespread use of aniline dyes was not always favourable. In *Punch* of 1877 we have a masculine complaint : " Ah—she affects aniline dyes, don't you know. I weally couldn't go down to suppah with a young lady who wears mauve twimmings in her skirt and magenta wibbons in her hair." Mrs. Haweis in *The Art of Beauty* complained that the new colours of her day (1883) were too pure though she speaks of magenta and mauve as " exquisite colours."

This craving for contrasts was further exemplified by the growing taste for two widely divergent colours, the lighter for the bodice, the darker for the skirt. It was in vain that the warning was uttered : " glaring colours would be contrary to good taste " in the face of such mixtures as " a bronze green dress with a drab paletot, ruby red trimming and a white bonnet."

And presently three and then four colours appeared in a dress. " An open dress of blue and green over a bronze green skirt;" " olive green dress with plastron of two shades of maize, ribbons of two shades of carnation;" " turquoise faille, deep green plush, apple blossom and silver embroidery." In the words of a contemporary, " there is no limit to the number of colours and materials in evening dresses " (1882).

The second half of last century was marked by a

chromatic struggle between colour mixtures that were harmonious and those that were conspicuously discordant ; it was as though a school of thought was striving to express dissatisfaction with existing conditions, and was hoisting a banner of discontent.

At the same time colour was being used extensively to exploit particular features, and to draw the eye towards them. In this medley of opposing impulses where colour became more than a symbol of a mental attitude—even a weapon—the brief Æsthetic Movement of cretonne costumes, peacock green, brick red and the " greenery-yallery " ridiculed in *Patience*, hardly checked the general tendency, until in the '90's the taste for violent discords became generally accepted, and the fashion for huge sleeves of one colour against a dress of another produced some arresting combinations.

A skirt of copper-and-black check, bodice olive green with sleeves of glacé purple shot with green ; mixtures of peach and orange, green and pink, lilac and pale blue, mauve and light green, pink and cerise were all acceptable, while a day dress, the skirt of purple zibeline, bodice of dahlia satin, turquoise ribbon round the neck, two shades of purple with pink flowers in the hat, and sealskin coat lined with pink, was described as " a brilliant success." The notable colour for evening in the '90's was yellow in all its tints and shades.

We cannot dismiss so marked a divergence from the normal taste in the Art of Costume as a mere accident. The '90's, so far as women were concerned, was a revolutionary era analogous in many respects to the '60's, and both were marked by violent colour contrasts in costume.

During the present century there has been a gradual decline both in the intensity of colours used and their combinations ; this change has been accompanied by a greater interest in Form, as the modern woman, who in reality came into being as the result of the upheaval

of the '90's has developed more and more into a
" working woman." We see a greater use, by day, of
darker shades and monochrome effects which might
often be called " monotonous effects," a long run of
beige followed by a longer of black ; and the evening
dresses, either keyed down to suit the intense illumination
of our rooms, or making nervous efforts to be arresting
by odd colouring from which the old inspiration is
clearly absent.

In this survey of colour in the history of English
Costume we observe conspicuous variations in the
effective range ; sometimes colours seem to have been
designed to be appreciated at a certain distance—
" poster effects," in fact—sometimes they were evidently
intended for closer inspection. In evening costumes we
can almost estimate from their colours the size of the
appropriate rooms.

We note, too, their psychological significance, their
reflections of social unrest, periods of serene calm, sombre
moods with shadows of fear, emotional disturbances
affecting a community and exhibited in its change of
colour taste.

Under these varying conditions are we entitled, then,
to pick out an epoch and say " this was the age of
perfect taste " ?

It would be easier to say " taste perfectly adapted for
the conditions of that age "—but this perhaps applies to
all. For human taste is no more than the natural and
inevitable reaction to circumstances, and perfect taste
can only be exhibited by a community which is living
in perfect conditions. Such an epoch must be left to
future historians to describe.

Although it would be rash to attempt a definition of
" good taste " in colours, we may go so far as to note
that, of all periods in our history, it is the middle of the
eighteenth century which receives the widest approval
in respect to taste in colours. I think this may be

attributed partly to the fact that its colour combinations were simple harmonies which can be easily understood ; partly that they satisfy the natural liking for a " good match," and partly because the colours used are familiar in the English garden. They please, æsthetically, as a tune of Handel's pleases, by being simple, complete and satisfying.

But we recognise, too, that no art can remain stationary ; it must move on. And as we compare one epoch with another we see evidence of this movement in colour use as well as in Form.

We can watch the sense inherent in our ancestors struggling to overcome imperfect conditions, such as poor illumination and materials, finally bursting forth riotously until restrained by the elegance and discrimination of the eighteenth century. There, in a very small select world, it became possible for the fortunate few to exercise their artistic taste in a manner which posterity admires and envies.

But such conditions were, in fact, unstable, and with a wider world the nineteenth century had to cater for a vastly larger section of the nation for which science then supplied the materials. As one sex receded into eclipse the other became more glowing ; colour piled on colour marked the Victorian sunset and the Edwardian afterglow.

We can hardly fail to notice the close association of colour in Costume with class-distinction and sex-attraction. Colour was once used to impress spectators with the importance of the wearer—that is, as a symbol of social rank, for which purpose we still employ it in ceremonial costumes to an extent which would provoke ridicule if used for ordinary wear. Gradually it shifted its aim towards the opposite sex, which then became the principal target.

With the development of democratic ideas, and the notion that display of social rank is vulgar—a change which has become increasingly apparent during the present century—one of the two chief incentives for using colour in costume has subsided.

But in so doing it has also lost much of its appeal to the opposite sex, and men have almost entirely discarded colour as a weapon of attraction. With women the tradition still lingers, but its use to draw attention to particular physical features has become—or seems to be becoming—superseded by a franker display of those regions themselves. Colour is no longer needed to point out the obvious.

It appears, therefore, that women, too, are losing their interest in the main uses of colour in costume. In this case, if the principal incentives to its use are diminishing with both sexes, it is probable that the æsthetic interest is also likely to fade.

Stripped of this interest, the Art of Costume is being driven more and more to depend on Form in order to express its hidden meaning, and to satisfy the impulses surging in a community.

From being a picture, Costume is becoming a building, and the painter is turning into an architect.

CHAPTER XIV

TEXTURE AND MATERIALS

GARMENTS are made of woven materials—Textiles—and their texture is the disposition of the fibres composing them. The weave may be coarse with large mesh, or fine with small ; and the fibres themselves may have been subjected to various processes before being woven. The woven textile may receive further treatment which may affect the appearance of the finished article. Thus it may receive a polished or glazed surface, or by the addition of " dressing " the mesh may be practically closed.

We are not concerned with the methods by which these results are obtained but only with the results, which may be that the textile is given a surface which is rough, even shaggy, velvety (i.e. with a pile), crinkly like crape, smooth, dull, polished or shining.

All these qualities will affect the luminosity of the finished article quite apart from the natural luminosity inherent in the nature of the material itself. Thus, silk is more luminous than wool and wool more than cotton, but in the finished textile the nature of the weave may alter this order.

Sometimes the word " tone " is loosely applied to mean this luminosity of the finished textile, but to preserve clarity I reserve the word " tone " to denote the degree of luminosity inherent in the colour ; the luminosity of the textile, apart from its colour, I call its " radiance."

Thus, satin has a high degree of radiance whatever its colour ; but white satin has a higher tone than black satin. It is evident that the æsthetic quality which we observe in a textile is in fact a combination due to texture, radiance and tone ; and when viewed from a certain distance their effects blend so that it becomes impossible to distinguish them apart, unless one of them is very pronounced.

When " dressing " is added to a cotton fabric, glazing its surface, its radiance can be raised nearly to that of silk while the natural radiance of silk almost disappears when it is woven with a pile as in velvet.

As we look at a costume (on the living model) composed of various coloured fabrics with varying degrees of texture, radiance and tone, we more or less unconsciously compare these with the corresponding qualities of the bare skin especially if they are in proximity to it. In fact we instinctively accept the skin as a kind of standard, recognising that a woman's is in all three respects more refined than a man's.

The Art of Costume has therefore usually kept the coarser textiles for men's clothes (or for women's when they are engaged in masculine jobs) ; [1] normally it uses the finer for women's clothes, the finest of all for their evening wear. It has commonly interposed between the edge of the textile and the bare skin (e.g. of the neck and hands) some material of a wholly different nature, in texture, radiance and tone, especially an edging of white such as collar, cuffs, ruffles.

By this device the abrupt change of texture is modified or concealed. It is noticeable, however, that to-day both sexes are gradually abandoning this æsthetic refinement ; the man's collar has sunk almost out of sight together with his cuffs, while women wear neither.

The fact that not only the colour-tone of a fabric but also its radiance will affect the natural tone of the skin when put near it was formerly more appreciated in the

---

[1] It is curious, however, that the use of feathers as ornamental additions to the costume, introduced near the end of the thirteenth century, remained until the eighteenth exclusively a masculine habit. Since then it has, of course, become a material exclusively used by women.

FLORENCE NIGHTINGALE (seated) AND HER SISTER

Note that the sleeves are in the mode of not later than 1836. The flat white collars are plainer than was then "fashionable." The coiffures approximate to the style of the date, 1839.

From the coloured drawing by William White, 1839, in the National Portrait Gallery.

Art of Costume than it is to-day. For the radiance of the fabric will overflow on to its surroundings, and when the natural tone of the face is lowered by paint and powder it becomes necessary to place some material near to restore it.

As such materials are worn by women more usually in the evening than in the day dress, we can understand why a lavish make-up, which may pass muster in the evening, will often resemble in daylight a painted corpse, suggesting that the exponent is unable to distinguish between colour and tone.

It is noticeable that when men to-day wish to look as " masculine " as possible they wear fabrics of the coarsest texture ; and although women will wear such fabrics in their tailored suits for day use, they will resort to much finer ones when they wish to look as " feminine " as possible. Even the most modern don't wear evening frocks of Harris tweed.

It also seems to be—or to have been—the custom that in a costume comprising materials of widely different textures, the coarser should be used for the less attractive and the finer for the more attractive regions. Thus, in the " bodice and skirt " type of dress it is the bodice which is given the finer textured material (and also the higher toned). With men's morning coat and trousers, on the other hand, it is the legs which are thus favoured. By studying this differential use of materials in a costume we are often informed which is the region to which the wearer desires to draw particular attention.

Similar principles apply to the accessory garments ; those more " remote " such as the overcoat will have a coarser texture than the man's suit, and a woman's jacket will be of coarser material than the bodice beneath. In short, the natural inclination is to use the finer textures to exploit the shape of the body from their approximate resemblance to the texture of the skin.

And if we examine the textures, radiances and tones

of a combination of materials forming a costume they appear to rise progressively in quality towards the head, so that the eye of the spectator is drawn upwards in following their lead.

The Art of Costume will use its materials—texture as an ally to colour—so as to present a composition of a range of values over which the eye is persuaded to travel from the less important to the more important ; and in an ingenious composition a change of material always has a significance.

The history of Costume reveals that up to the nineteenth century there was not much real distinction between the materials used by each sex. Although no doubt men wore for ordinary purposes a good deal of cloth, yet women would wear that too, especially for outdoor occupations such as riding and driving. It was the custom, at least till the end of the seventeenth century, for women's dresses to be made by men tailors using stocks of materials common for both sexes ; while for gala wear both used silks, satins, velvets and even ribbons.

But the nineteenth century marked a distinct cleavage. We have already described this separation as applying to colours, but in fact a separate range of textiles became the property of each sex until, towards the close of that century, the New Woman began to purloin those of men. Women's tailor-mades of the last quarter of that century were often of materials hitherto used only by men. The same epoch marked man's final surrender of silks, satins, laces, and ribbons as he settled down to a monotonous woolly existence.

Nevertheless although his textile perquisites are being steadily encroached on by women, there lingers at least a tradition that he has a prior claim to some though " respect to the cloth " has now vanished.

We have also to note that formerly, for women's costume, certain kinds of texture were considered appropriate for different ages, the finer woven—such as glacé silk and the delicate fabrics such as muslin—for the youthful, the velvets and ribbed silks for the matron. In other words, radiant textiles for the youthful face, less radiant ones for the " not so young."

Variations in texture and radiance can be introduced into a costume by using different materials, for a number of æsthetic purposes ; to give the effect of " light and shade " in order to accentuate one region and distract attention from another ; to emphasise form, to affect balance, and—in short—to serve the same functions as are performed by variations of colour.

For although, theoretically, we distinguish between the tone of a colour and the radiance inherent in a material, in practice the two may be indistinguishable. In a dull black woollen material, for example, we are chiefly conscious of its tone, *dead* black ; in a black satin we are chiefly conscious of the radiance of the material.

As we might expect, with the gradual improvement in artificial lighting and the wider admission of daylight into our houses, so there has been a corresponding decline in the radiance of materials used in costumes. This is well exemplified by the fate of satin ; worn by men in the sixteenth and seventeenth centuries *by day*, its use by men became restricted to their evening wear in the eighteenth century and ceased to be used by them in the nineteenth except for details such as the waistcoat and finally only the necktie.

Its use by women has likewise declined though more slowly ; it has now vanished from the day frock and is becoming rare for the evening, and the material itself has become less brilliant. Indeed in the fierce blaze of modern illumination satin is an eye-watering spectacle. If lighting improves still further we shall presently be driven to clothe ourselves in sackcloth and ashes.

The same cause has encouraged the use of woollens

and duller surfaces ; these began to appear, tentatively, for " home evening dress " in the '80's, but women have always been reluctant to wear in the evening any material except silk (real or artificial) and muslin. An attempt, just before the recent war, to introduce printed cottons for that purpose was not favoured.

The range of visibility of the materials in a costume is adapted to the circumstances under which it is to be worn, and a discriminating taste will avoid the stronger radiances in daylight except when, as in certain epochs, social functions designed for display are held in the day-time.

The use of animal fur in the Art of Costume introduces a texture unlike that of any other material. When employed merely as an accessory outdoor garment its effect is to provide the greatest possible contrast between it and the costume presently to be revealed. The old saying that " every woman looks well in furs " is no doubt based on the fact that the texture of the face appears to stand out surprisingly smooth and clear in contrast.

But fur employed as a trimming has other functions. The furs of all native animals (including wild cats) were much used in the middle ages to trim robes and mantles. Fur indeed is still used for that purpose ; it defines a border and adds a quality of richness—or seems to if we happen to know that the fur is an expensive one. But as a dress trimming it has never been wholly acceptable ; the suggestion of " hair in the wrong place " is inescapable.

The materials used in textiles are Wool, Silk—real and artificial—Cotton and Flax, wool and silk being animal products, cotton and flax vegetable. Any two or more of these may be woven together to form composite textiles, but the Art of Costume has generally hesitated to employ two very different media in the same costume, unless for quite separate regions of the body.

In men's costume the Elizabethan needle-embroidered trunks were of linen though worn with silk doublet, and early last century the cloth frock coat might be worn above nankeen trousers.

In women's costume the mid-Victorian use of a cotton blouse above a silk skirt and, in the Seventies of last century, the use of silk textiles and woollen blended in the same costume was a startling breach with tradition.

A brief sketch of the development of each of the principal materials used in this art will indicate its progress. Wool was the chief material used all through the middle ages supplying most of the garments for both sexes. Edward the Third, by importing Flemish weavers, immensely improved the technique of cloth-making and developed the industry until it became the recognised staple of this country.

The effect of the Black Death in 1346-9, by reducing the supply of labourers, was to encourage the conversion of vast areas of agricultural land to sheep-farming, for which less labour was required. Consequently the wool industry became more and more important ; weaving was mainly carried out as a domestic industry and appears to have been widely spread over southern England from East Anglia to the borders of Wales.

Norwich was one of the principal centres for the weaving of fustian which in this country was then made entirely of wool. (Thus an Act of 1504 refers to " worsteds, stammins, fustians and all other woollen cloth.")

It was also famous for its worsteds, a cloth of long-stapled wool combed straight and smooth, as distinguished from woollens which are woven from short-stapled wool crossed and roughed in the spinning. The fabrics made from worsteds are known as " stuffs," and are stiffer and rougher than woollens.

Fustian was a coarse twilled cloth with a pile like corduroy. (" Of fustian he wered a gipon "—Chaucer.)

Frieze or Falding was a coarse napped cloth of the period. ("All in a gown of falding to the knee" —Chaucer.) Linsey-woolsey was a mixed cloth of linen and wool ; Camlet an imported woollen of Angora goat's hair much used in the fifteenth century ; and Russells, a worsted with a satiny surface made in Norwich, appearing in the sixteenth century.

We get some notion of the materials and their colours commonly worn in the fifteenth century from the mention in contemporary wills of various garments bequeathed to relatives ; from which we also gather that even second-hand garments were of value. Thus in 1418 a man leaves : " a gown of blew worsted furred with protes and polles of Martrons ; a gown of gray russet furred with Ionetis and wylde Catis ; a gown of grene frese furred with blak Lambe ; a Doublelet of defence covered with red lether ; a cloke of blak russet ; a Doublelet covered with blak gote Lether." (" Russet " was a coarse woollen homespun of a reddish brown). In 1431 a woman leaves : " a blew gowne, a grene kyrtell, a blak cote furred, a russet gowne lynyt with whyte blanket." And another in 1479 leaves : " my furd gowne, a rede girdill harnest with silver and gilted, a musterdevlis gown with a velvt colar, my cremesyn kirtill, my blew girdill and my red girdill."

(Musterdevilis was a kind of cloth : vis *Paston Letters* : " My mother sent to my father to London for a gown cloth of Mustyedevyllers "). From sources such as the above, which are quoted by Clinch in his *English Costume* from wills in the Court of Probate, London, we get the impression that mediæval cloth was strong, rough and enduring, very much like Welsh flannel in fact ; and, as such, fit and cut would have been of minor importance.

Silk fabrics were imported as a luxury into this country from the earliest times. The mediæval Samite was a costly silk believed to have been similar to satin.

From the Household Accounts of the Lestrange family of Hunstanton, 1522, we learn the cost and materials of making a gown : " 11 yards of tawny satin for a gown for my mistress, £4 11s. 8d. 2½ yards of tawny velvet for the same gown, £1 13s. 4d. Rolle of buckram for same, 2s. 8d. Stuffing clothe for the pleates, 11d. For making the gown, 5s."

The use of silks did not become common here until the sixteenth century, but the weaving of them was not established until the reign of Charles the First. Later it was said : " The English formerly wore or used little silk in City or Country, only persons of quality pretended to it ; but as our national Gaudery hath increased, it grew more and more into mode and is now the common wear . . . and our women, who generally govern in this case, must have foreign silks. . . . Of the same humour are their gallants." (*Brittannia Languens or a Discourse on Trade*, 1681.)

The Revocation of the Edict of Nantes in 1685 established large numbers of Protestant refugees in Spitalfields, Coventry and Norwich, and by 1713 the silk manufacture in this country was " come to be above twenty times as great as it was in the year 1664."

Velvet, which had been imported as early as 1400, was one of the products of these Spitalfields weavers. It has had some important variations, uncut velvet or " Terry " being much used in the last century together with " Genoa velvet " (a velvet with a double pile, the upper being stamped into patterns).

Artificial silk is of course the great textile invention of the present century.

Cotton was being imported here by 1430 and Fuller in 1662 tells us : " As for Manchester the cottons thereof carry away the credit of our nation and so they did a hundred and fifty years agoe." Our supplies of raw cotton came entirely from Asia Minor and the East Indies until the end of the eighteenth century when it began to be imported from the Southern States of America.[1]

Printed calicoes were first made in this country in 1676, the early calicoes having the weft only of cotton, the warps being of linen. The cotton chintzes of the eighteenth century have been referred to in a previous chapter ; a more important cotton textile was of course muslin. This began to appear here, imported from India, about 1670 and a century later its manufacture started at Bolton, Glasgow and Paisley. An immense output resulted and the fabric in various forms supplied one of the important materials for women's costume, especially ball dresses, throughout the nineteenth century.

Linen woven from native flax has been made in this country from the earliest times. The first guild of Flemish weavers was established here in 1386, but it was not till the reign of Charles the First that the industry became important.

It is noticeable that except for accessories and under-garments men have seldom used cotton or linen as compared to their adoption by women, which—as soon as supplies became adequate—has been marked. Men have relied on wool for all ordinary wear, with silk and velvet for gala costume.

The use of gold and silver thread, burnished, has been to increase the luminosity of a fabric and was therefore appropriate enough when and where illumination was poor. In the form of " lamé " metals have been used in fabrics for women's evening dresses, especially in the Regency and Edwardian periods, while " gold thread " has of course decorated men's ceremonial robes and military uniforms from very early times.

As we cast an eye back over the centuries we cannot

[1] The art of mercerising cotton fabrics, thereby giving them an artificial lustre, was invented by John Mercer in 1844 who treated the material with caustic soda. In 1895 Messrs. Thomas and Prevost put on the market a cotton textile thus treated and having the lustre of silk.

but notice how certain materials seem to have been prominent in certain epochs ; we associate coarse woollens with the middle ages, velvet with the sixteenth century, ribbons with the seventeenth, silks with the eighteenth, cottons with the nineteenth and artificial silk with the twentieth. We may perhaps anticipate artificial wool as the probable feature of the next half century.

Each epoch retained of course the " novelties " derived from the preceding, until the present century has begun to discard some of its inheritance. We to-day lack the wealth of the nineteenth when every possible variety of textile, except artificial silk, was available to a large section of the community.

Some seventy years ago the first signs of a decline in quality began to appear, silks being heavily " dressed " to improve their appearance—in the shops—but shortening their lives ; and it is very noticeable how the Edwardian silks, especially the taffetas, only forty years old now crumble to pieces like burnt paper.

It seems that the Art of Costume is becoming more evanescent in its aim ; it no longer aspires to construct heirlooms and this is not entirely disadvantageous—at least, to the maker of clothes. Yet it means that there can be little permanent satisfaction in such work. Leaving no lasting memorial of its accomplishments it cannot claim a high place among the Arts.

The nineteeth century added to women's costume muslins in a bewildering variety and also materials valuable for their lustre such as glacé silk and alpaca, together with combinations of materials of which lustre was a feature. We have to associate this with the fact that it was an epoch in which domestic illumination was rapidly improving and therefore the nature of certain textiles had to be frequently modified in keeping with it.

The shot silks and the corded silks were equally remarkable, together with patterns woven in or printed on fabrics of all kinds, both for the dress itself and for its accessories. With so much at its disposal the Art of Costume could hardly restrain its hand reaching, in the '70's, to combinations of three or four different materials in a single dress. Such exuberances a modern generation, austere by compulsion, condemns as " bad art."

Men's costume seems to have been more easily satisfied. The Scotch tweeds and " shepherds' plaids " were added in 1832, but fine cloth, kerseymere (a woollen with a double twill) and cashmere (a fine worsted) supplied most of their wants. We find however that a taste for mixed materials, coat, waistcoat and trousers each of a different fabric, survived until the last quarter of that century together with such curiosities as sealskin waistcoats.

Some fifty years ago a material much used for professional men's suits was " Oxford mixture," a dark grey in two shades, the darker being called " Oxford " and the lighter " Cambridge." For the conventional " morning coat " a black vicuna (a very soft woollen), a black fine serge or a herringbone cheviot was popular.

" Saxony," suitable for coats and waistcoats, was a somewhat soft material, technically a species of flannel, which had originated in the eighteenth century and is still in use. The ordinary flannels, however, did not begin to be used for suits until the early years of the present century and are to-day immensely popular for trousers. Worsteds and cheviots still hold their own.

For evening dress suits the old smooth shiny broadcloth was beginning to disappear some fifty years ago, being replaced by a very fine twill with a shiny surface and later by the fine black " pin head " which is now in general use.

A noticeable feature of the last half century has been the looser cut and the preference for coarser woven textiles ; in a word, comfort has become the first consideration.

Until quite modern times certain materials had a class-distinction of their own, but since the beginning of the Industrial Era the finer fabrics have had their inferior imitations—velvet and velveteen, satin and sateen, silk and artificial silk mark progressive stages in this process during the last hundred years. To-day this democratic extension is even in reverse and a textile, corduroy, formerly the sole property of the labourer, will now on occasion decorate chromatically the lower half of the Middle Class male and female.

CHAPTER XV

MOBILITY IN COSTUME

IF we try to visualise the costumes worn by previous generations we are unconsciously apt to regard them as pictures or stationary arrangements of garments immobilised by the brush of the painter.

Even the costumes themselves, if they exist, are visible only in museum cases, stuffed and petrified. It needs an effort to appreciate that the original wearers actually moved about in them, even, on occasion, ran.

Henry the Eighth in his youth was a great athlete, Charles the Second a fast walker, facts not revealed by the Court painter or appearing in the modes of their day.

Contemporary writers have often complained that the fashions of their epoch were inconvenient ; abundance of ridicule has been poured on them, moralists have lamented their wickedness and artists their lack of beauty, but seldom has any one criticised the modes of his day for their lack of mobility.

Yet this has been, on the whole, the most conspicuous and persistent feature in the long series of fashions which the Art of Costume has provided for those with any social pretensions ; in them the need for mobility has always been treated as a minor consideration ; its absence, indeed, almost as a desirable quality. It implied that such functions were provided for by menials.

Consequently there is hardly a style of costume which could be revived exactly and used for everyday purposes under modern conditions. It is an art form from the past for which we have no practical use. We should find them all intolerably restricting to the amount of mobility which we have come to require in our clothes.

Why is it then that our ancestors were willing to accept such restrictions ? Their complaints on that score seem to have been singularly few. Nevertheless, even if the wearers of those uncomfortable modes made no murmur, there was all the time a background of criticism on this very point which, I think, deserves to be noticed.

Turn from the fashions of the elegant world to the clothes worn by their contemporaries in the lower social strata and we see there this criticism silently expressed. For though the costume of the working classes often bore traces of fashion (sufficient for us to be able to date them approximately) yet it was always adapted for practical use. And the degree of such modification is a measure of the impracticability of the original.

As soon as some passing fashion happened to produce a shape of garment that could be made serviceable to the workers it was likely to be adopted by them, with modifications, and then might and often did persist for generations.

We can trace the countryman's smock frock back to the mediæval tunic ; so too the hooded cloak. Various trades and occupations acquired and preserved distinctive garments derived in the first place from the fashionable world of generations back, a custom which has now practically vanished. The sleeved waistcoat which railway porters wore until this century was in fact the " gentleman's " waistcoat of the eighteenth century and had been inherited from the ostler of the coaching days, much as the gentleman's dress suit has become the waiter's uniform.

But the artisan can now wear very much the sort of costume worn by his social " betters," largely because this has now become not merely cheaper but more mobile in design ; as a result any fashion to-day is spread over a much larger section of the community than formerly. It represents now the taste of the actual majority ; formerly it represented only that of a minority which diminished in numbers, though not perhaps in importance, the further back the history of fashion is traced.

And the further back we go the wider appears the gap between the costume of the worker and that of the " fashionables." It is however surprising to find that no matter how far we go—no matter how wide the gap —still, the artisan was not entirely free from the restricting influence of current fashion which had filtered down to his level. In the illuminated MSS. of the thirteenth and fourteenth centuries we see pictures of labourers digging, ploughing, etc., in garments cumbersome indeed as compared with the modern. Even in those times utility was not the first consideration in the costume of the labourer and only by slow degrees has that come to the fore.

As for the rest of us, with all our improvements in domestic appliances we still cling to traditional forms of clothing, modifying them for work or play only with reluctance, and returning as quickly as possible to the old encumbrances of skirt or trousers.

It is in fact evident that the Art of Costume has not considered freedom of movement as important, and formerly, indeed, strenuously opposed it. This was especially the case with women's dress ; certainly until the eighteenth century, and probably much later, the average woman in easy circumstances spent most of her time indoors and perhaps never since childhood ran a yard.

Some of us are old enough to remember ladies who seldom went beyond the garden gate except to church on Sundays, while for the younger folk a country walk was an adventure.

Physical restriction by clothing, corsets, long skirts and abundant petticoats may have been tolerated by a sex compelled by convention to lead an indoor life, but it is strange that men should have accepted styles of clothes which, with their greater activities, must have been even more galling.

However they do not seem to have protested against the rules of their own making. Jeremy Bentham as an undergraduate mentioned in 1765 that he had walked from Oxford to Farringdon " in green silk breeches bitterly tight," but he accepted them as a necessity.

Men indeed have frequently worn garments as inconvenient as any worn by women ; picture, for example, a gentleman of A.D. 1400 trying to walk fast in the fashionable long piked shoes, or an Elizabethan in a wide ruff attempting to drink soup. Who is not moved by the experience of that stout Regency buck whose skin-tight breeches, as he was attempting to bow, suddenly broke loose from their moorings and collapsed round his ankles ?

Indeed we have only to recall the attire of " a man about Town " at the beginning of this century ; on a hot summer's day he preserved his rank in starched shirt, high collar, frock coat and top hat, for to be less uncomfortably clad was to confess oneself " no gentleman." And when at that time attempts were made to introduce the cummerbund as a substitute for the waistcoat they were rejected as " not quite English."

For four centuries the English gentleman has suffered tortures from starched garments but without making audible complaint ; in brief, it is evident that though Fashion has perpetually changed the nature of its chains they have never been struck off. When I was an undergraduate in Cambridge it was imperative that the bottom of the trouser legs should be turned up, whereas at that time in London it was equally essential that they should be turned down, if one was to pass as a gentleman. Consequently the traveller to town had to transform them at about Hatfield.

Such was the grip of Fashion fifty years back ; but

is it wholly relaxed to-day? It would need a degree of moral courage few men possess to go to the City in pullover and shorts. Few women have the nerve to walk down Regent Street in slacks; for shopping in the Outer Suburbs perhaps, but for the West End, definitely no. At what precise spot on the map slacks must be exchanged for a skirt is, however, uncertain.

Until comparatively modern times this kind of voluntary bondage was not merely tolerated but eagerly sought by both sexes; no doubt the knowledge that the wearer perfectly represented the ideal of the hour was an adequate reward for the trivial discomfort entailed. The Art of Costume is, after all, but a visible expression of the overwhelming power of the herd instinct which overrides the claim of the individual. Even now it only grudgingly makes concessions to utility; its concentration is on the expression of mass impulses, and in so doing it supplies to the "slaves of Fashion" a mental comfort which far outweighs convenience and mobility.

We must assume that this applied also to earlier times whose costumes we know only from pictures; their degree of mobility we can only guess (the vast skirt of the fifteenth century gown tells its own story). When we turn to the eighteenth century of which actual specimens are available for examination we are struck by at least two features. One is the stiffness of some of the garments, due either to the nature of the material or to the addition of stiffening devices such as corsets and hoops in the case of women's garments and wiring and buckram to splay out the skirts of men's coats (*Plate* 19).

The other is a structural obstacle to free movements; a small armhole indicates the absence of muscle in the wearer and in itself tells of immobility. This is especially noticeable in women's dresses of the eighteenth and early nineteenth centuries. The set of the sleeve may show that the arm could not be raised to a right angle. The man's sleeve was often cut in the Magyar style, with the shoulder piece coming some way down the arm and fitting tightly ; and in the sixteenth and seventeenth centuries the added welt or " wing " over the shoulder joint must have impeded movements very considerably (*Plates* 11 and 12).

Reference has been made to the cut of the eighteenth century breeches before braces had been invented ; one can hardly imagine the wearer of such a garment running far without incurring disaster. So too the ruffles at the wrist of the huge turned-back cuff were elegant obstacles and also the various ornamental accessories which at different times have limited the movements of important joints in man's body (*Plate* 18).

We can understand why the gentleman of the time would be tempted, in the privacy of his home, to assume a loose gown in place of his stiff coat and, discarding his wig, feel at last " at ease." The analogy to the Victorian lady removing her stays and tight dress and " slipping into something loose " in her boudoir is exact. All of which goes to prove how very important it was (and in a measure still is) for the chosen few to be very uncomfortable. It is evident, however, that modern requirements are forcing the Art of Costume, against its will perhaps, to give more consideration to mobility and this will necessitate some profound change in technique.

In fact this is already happening. If we apply a critical eye to modern designs in the costumes of both sexes we can hardly fail to recognise that the greatest inspiration and originality is to be found in the most mobile forms such as those for sport and similar activities. Whereas the less mobile types, such as those for indoor use and especially the evening, are so often unconvincing as works of art or mere weak replicas.

The art is passing through a transitional stage ; we

have not yet shed all our shackles but at least we do recognise their futility as insignia of social superiority. High heels no longer indicate the carriage class of woman and there is scarcely a discomfort left in the whole of her wardrobe which she does not now share with the rest of her sex.

The hold which Fashion exercises on both sexes is still very great—in some respects greater than ever— but, happily, it ordains that the day costume shall be much looser in fit. In other words, Fashion has grudgingly allowed greater play between the body and its coverings, and this for both sexes.

This fact introduces new æsthetic problems of construction which are not yet completely mastered. The Art of Costume has never really accepted the fact that the human body has moveable joints. We have only to glance at illustrations taken from various epochs in the past to see how the Art has tried to conceal the very existence of the larger joints, passing over them, as it were, or obliterating them with various disguises such as padding, puffing, excrescences and the like.

In both sexes this has always applied to the hip joint, always to woman's knee and—since the invention of trousers—to man's likewise ; always to man's elbow and generally to woman's. Restriction has always been applied to man's neck and in both sexes always to the joints of the spine, while gloves and footwear have effectively immobilised the joints of the extremities.

Man's knee breeches and woman's elbow sleeves are the only costume designs in which important joints have been accepted as facts and the costume made subservient to them ; it is a little strange that in this age of freedom both have been again suppressed by coverings which check movement. However, we may suppose that an increasing measure of mobility will be granted us, sufficient at least to affect some of the basic principles of costume design. A demand, on practical grounds, for more mobility will open a wholly new chapter in the Art, introducing novel æsthetic problems.

When the body moves, garments have to readjust themselves and they tend to fall into creases and folds, disturbing the original form which had been designed for the body at rest. The effect of movement will depend in part on the stiffness of the fabric, in part on the closeness of the fit, and also on the amount of underclothing between it and the skin. The most obvious example is a woman's skirt ; when this was made of heavy material supported by layers of petticoats movement hardly disturbed its original shape, but a skirt of light material with little underclothing, battling against a breeze, recalls an umbrella inside out.

A close-fitting garment necessarily moves slightly more slowly than the body itself and this " time-lag " produces awkward stresses and strains very noticeable when a dress, for example, is worn over little or no underclothes. The appearance of " drag " suggests effort, of which the wearer may be less conscious than the observer, and this is very conspicuous in the modern evening frock, tight round the hips where it is dragged over knobs, while it sags into creases elsewhere (*Plates* 45 and 48).

It is evident that with thin fabrics mobility requires that they shall be sufficiently loose if this æsthetic blemish is to be avoided. It is curious that the modern woman should insist on having skirts so tight that they presently acquire a visible "seat ; " men's trousers have a similar defect.

The development of mobility in Costume has been extraordinarily slow and this fact alone is sufficient to teach us that in the Art of Costume mere utility has always been a minor consideration. Perhaps the strangest example of the reluctance to adapt the means to the end is supplied by the history of military uniforms. A hundred and fifty years ago a soldier with his hair smothered in powder and pomatum, a huge cocked hat on his head and a rigid leather collar round his neck preventing him from seeing the ground, in a uniform incredibly tight, fought battles and even won them ; fifty years ago " smartness " still meant tightness, and it was not till the recent war that the soldier's clothing— in which he had to risk his life—was designed to help instead of to hinder him.

But we can best trace the development of the idea of greater mobility in the history of that class of civilian costume which requires it most—namely, the " sports costume." For centuries that sort of clothing was hardly considered worthy of notice as a form of this art, and indeed it scarcely existed as a specialised kind.

We see in mediæval illuminated MSS. ladies depicted wearing apparently indoor clothing while engaged in such sports as hawking by the river-side, and women clad in voluminous gowns and mantles sitting astride on horseback before the side-saddle, a sort of boxed-in seat, was introduced (it is said) in the reign of Richard II.[1] Nevertheless until the nineteenth century many women continued to ride astride wearing costumes indistinguishable from men's riding-suits.

Thus in *The Spectator* Addison comments on " the ladies who dress themselves in a Hat and Feather, a Riding-coat and a Perriwig . . . in imitation of the smart part of the opposite sex. . . . The highways about this great City are still very much infested with these Female Cavaliers."

The real side-saddle of the nineteenth century encouraged the use of the voluminous riding-habit with its inappropriate concessions to propriety.

Man's hunting costume produced the hard " top hat "

[1] With some hesitation I have repeated the oft-quoted statement about the introduction of the side-saddle by Anne of Bohemia. She may have improved the model but it is certainly the case that illuminated MSS. show women, in this country, riding in the side position at a much earlier date, e.g. in Saxon times. (See MS. Cotton, Claudius B IV.) Both positions are illustrated in the Ellesmere " Chaucer " of the Fifteenth Century (*Plate* 16).

and the " cutaway " coat and breeches which became
the basis of the gentleman's ordinary attire, except of
course his boots. The curious stigma attached to men's
boots, derived originally from the filthy state of the
roads, has persisted to modern times ; the illustration
of " Top-boots Tottenham " recalls the nickname given
in the eighteenth century to a member of the Irish
Parliament who had ventured to enter the House for a
critical division, wearing his riding-boots and who was
heavily fined for so doing (*Plate* 18).

Riding and shooting remained the only active sports
that were fashionable until the Crimean War experiences
encouraged a new conception of outdoor activities. By
the 1860's it was correct not merely to look on at cricket
but to play it, and a noticeably looser cut in country
suits accompanied the change (*Plate* 35).

By 1870 the " Norfolk jacket " and knickerbockers
were making a hesitating appearance and lawn tennis
and the " penny farthing " bicycle presently compelled
further relaxations, but the " Norfolk," based on the
shooting-jacket, did not become comfortable until golf
in the '90's enforced a looser cut of sleeve (*Plate* 31*b*).

But not only were these " sports costumes " adapted
but slowly to the needs of those sports, but it is to be
remarked how still more slowly did their influence
infiltrate into the costume for ordinary wear (*Plate* 41).

In fact during the thirty years or so before the first
Great War threw its decisive weight into the scale, a
sort of contest persisted between the idea of " smartness "
and the idea of " mobility." On the one hand there was
the rigidity of social etiquette, always trying to enforce
an artificial standard of dress marked by its smart
discomfort, and on the other a movement derived from
the various forms of sport towards a style of dress which
its opponents condemned as " slovenly."

Daring women were experimenting with " rational
dress," and some were secretly discarding stays, while

in the masculine field petty engagements were fought over stand-up or lie-down collars, starched or soft shirts, the Chesterfield or the Raglan overcoat, and the "topper" or the "bowler." Parliament nearly collapsed when Mr. Keir Hardie, the first Labour M.P., invaded the House wearing a workman's *cloth cap*.

From this distance we can see that the Victorian resistance to greater mobility in the costumes of both sexes, as exemplified especially in "sports costumes," was a more or less conscious resistance to the removal of a class barrier. The riding and hunting costumes had been acceptable enough, for they were sports of the County set, but the more democratic varieties entailed wearing costumes from which the symbols of class had vanished. The Edwardian years provided the last stand of smartness against the new spirit.

Elegance and long skirts put up a brave if hopeless resistance ; these, it is true, entailed much brushing off of mud in spite of their being held up in the manner dictated by Fashion—in the fingertips, not the whole hand—and women's hats grew larger and larger when at length the skirt tightened into the "hobble." It seemed almost a defiant gesture at the threat of greater freedom promised by the Suffragettes (*Plates* 42 and 43). Men from the beginning of this century were studying how to relax their bonds while retaining the appearance of smartness. The dinner jacket, dating from—if not the product of—the Boer War, was a case in point. Could it be worn in the Dress Circle ? (Not, of course, in the Stalls.)

Could the Norfolk jacket be worn within the Four Mile Radius, that mystical circle wherein Fashion reigned ? Should the starched dress shirt have one or two studs and under what circumstances might a turned-down collar be worn ? Such were some of the problems besetting the Edwardian male.

On Sunday the rigour of Costume was redoubled, for

then at least the influence of sports was taboo and men garbed themselves in the armour of respectability, the top hat and frock or tail coat and lavender gloves, in which they looked as though they had been to church.

The history of women's " sports costumes " is specially important, partly because it had ultimately a far more profound effect on the rest of their wardrobe than had men's " sports costumes " on theirs ; and partly because its stages admirably illustrate the growth of mental as well as physical emancipation.

Moreover, the growing taste for outdoor sports has affected woman's costume in its function of sex-attraction which is gradually shifting from the costume to the body itself. A healthy physique has become a principal form of attraction and the growth of outdoor sports for women is probably the chief cause of this change. The Art of Costume has had to adapt itself to this and provide for women not only physical freedom in their " sports costume " but also to endow it with a measure of sex-attraction.

Women's " sports costume " dates from some eighty years back. It began with the " walking dress " of 1862 which was, for the first time in the history of Fashion, a style specifically designed to enable women to take active outdoor exercise (*Plate* 29*b*).

" At last," a contemporary was moved to exclaim, " it seems that Fashion has taken a step in the direction of common sense ; it is said that the new fashion is not likely to become popular for the reason that many women have not got pretty feet ; short skirts for outdoor wear are really a necessity."

The Victorian woman shrank from indulging in outdoor sport because it might entail exposing the shape of the body under conditions when it would not be attractive. Thus the bathing costume, which had in 1865 displaced the old " bathing gown," consisted of tunic and knickerbockers of materials which "secure perfect liberty of action and do not expose the figure" (*Plate* 39).

This, at the very time when the ball dress was exposing as much of it as possible, provoking a gentleman's comment : " Did you ever see such a sight ? " " Not since I was weaned."

The croquet dress set free the ankles, and at the end of the '70's lawn tennis necessitated a cautious measure of ladylike running restrained by a costume comprising, for instance, " a cream merino bodice with long sleeves edged with embroidery ; skirt with deep kilting reaching to the ground ; over it an old-gold silk blouse-tunic with wide sleeves and square neck. The tunic looped up at one side with a ball pocket sewn to it. Large coal-scuttle straw hat." And, of course, gloves (*Plate* 37).

When, in the Nineties, the bicycle brought with it the need for still greater mobility, the skirt would be weighted with lead " so that no possible peep at the knickerbockers can be obtained."

This feminine dread of betraying anatomical secrets persisted until the first World War, and although a modern generation can afford to smile at that attitude of mind it was, after all, a perfectly logical one, if the premise on which it was based is accepted—namely, that any and every part of the body would and indeed should, if seen by a man, provoke unruly emotions in his breast.

Woman's struggle for physical freedom and greater mobility in her costume entailed the sacrifice of easy means for exciting attraction (often mistaken for admiration) ; we can hardly be surprised at her hesitating to exchange an effective ankle for an athletic leg. Still, there were women willing to make the sacrifice but the Art of Costume persistently frowned on their efforts and the feminine " sports costumes " were invariably unæsthetic until some fifteen years ago the modern tennis costume was arrived at. In this, practical utility is combined with artistic design and a pleasant measure of sex-appeal. So too are Art and Utility seen blended in the modern skating costume where the short bell skirt preserves its independent shape in movement, concealing the width of hips and supplying an air of balance, while the material over the body may be sufficiently elastic to move without " time-lag." The costumes worn at games in girls' schools during the last half century or so show a curious sequence of concessions reluctantly granted, but the games played are far in advance of the costumes, which are often inappropriate and always inartistic.

Stockingette fabrics move without " time-lag." They appeared first in the " Jersey costume " introduced by Redferns in 1879 and popularised by Mrs. Langtry in the form of a coloured jersey (" recommended only for those whose figures are perfect ") and worn above a serge skirt. Although woven stockings had been used since the sixteenth century for the lower leg, it took three hundred years before women ventured to use that type of fabric to reveal the shape of their figures. And the Victorian lady, nicely brought up, shrank from revealing any part of her physique except for the purpose of sex-attraction.

For centuries the Art of Costume evaded the problem of mobility by supplying Woman with a form artificially constructed and comparatively rigid. In this her body could move discreetly without disturbing the essential outline of its camouflage.

This principle more or less applied to the costume of both sexes ; the designer could plan a structure without having to allow for its being disarranged by movement. Weight, for instance, hardly mattered ; sleeves could be heavy and even hanging to the ground. Women's skirts could trail behind in graceful folds on the ground ;

men's breeches could be tight and their coats stiff with ornament.

They could have lace collars and ruffles as a reward for keeping stationary. Either sex could stand—or sit—surrounded by gorgeous raiment. It was in fact almost as static an art as architecture.

Any movement would be leisurely without straining delicate fabrics. In the case of men doubtless they doffed a good deal of their finery in the practical affairs of daily life ; in women's attire there was that ample foundation of undergarments, from corset to petticoat, on which to build a solid immoveable structure. We must assume that our ancestors, both men and women, even those of the highest rank, did move about to some extent, but it is significant that they preferred to have their portraits painted in costumes which seem to deny that possibility.

Immobility, with all that it implied, was something to be proud of. When we compare all that with the requirements which this art has to meet to-day we see how fundamental is the change. The prior need is now —mobility.

In place of " living pictures " we demand " moving pictures " and the designer has to start from that novel basis. It follows that modern costume can only be judged fairly when it is viewed in movement, for that is now one of its principal functions and that spirit is affecting the whole conception of dress. This perhaps explains why men's lounge suits and country garb and women's tailored and " sports " costumes are generally more successful and " alive " than those for less active occasions (*Plate* 47).

The designer is being driven to think in terms of movement rather than in terms of attitude ; the old costumes of " posture "—in both sexes—are becoming things of the past, expressive of ideals no longer existing and the inspiration for designing them is, very naturally, fading.

An Art destined more and more to exemplify movement, but as yet in an experimental stage, will inevitably
show reluctance to abandon the traditional forms
entirely, so that in the last thirty years or so, during
which this change has been becoming noticeable, there
have been some curious hybrid effects ; attempts to
unstiffen man's dress shirt and waistcoat while clinging
to the old style of coat, or a wavering as to the ideal
length of the evening frock and its hip-grip—to say
nothing of the curiosities worn on women's feet, pedestal
heels, built-up insteps, sandals and latticework on
which they stride to greater freedom.

This wavering between the old conception and the
new is surely excusable, for Costume is the most conservative of the arts. It hates change ; it prefers
variations on familiar themes. It is fundamentally
traditional in spirit and only the pressure of events
compels it to progress. It is now being driven by such
circumstances towards, perhaps, an entirely new form
of this ancient but living art—one in which mobility will
dictate design.

CHAPTER XVI

PRINCIPLES OF SEX-ATTRACTION

SEX-ATTRACTION was described in the first chapter as being one of the three principal functions of the Art of Costume, a fact which is generally accepted by those who have studied the subject, especially if we allow for indirect forms of attraction.

Some of these may of course fulfil more than one function ; if, for example, a person's costume indicates wealth, unquestionably that feature increases the person's attractiveness, just as does the possession of a large income.

But in a given case is it displayed for that purpose or merely to impress spectators with the wearer's social rank, or perhaps to give him (or her) a confidence which would otherwise be lacking ?

With an individual especially we cannot always be sure. A mink coat admits of so many explanations.

Similarly, when we suppose that a particular style was at some past period intended to be sex-attractive we are assuming that a feature which attracts us now must therefore have attracted them then. On the other hand there have been fashions in the past which may have been attractive to their generation but which instead of attracting us now tend rather to repel.

We may even call such modes " indecent." By that term we really mean an attempt to appeal to our sexual instinct by means which are inappropriate either to the occasion, circumstances or personality, thereby rendering it repulsive.

We have also to recognise that the margin between " attractive " and " repulsive " is exceedingly narrow and oscillating according to circumstances.

There are no doubt general principles which persist from generation to generation and costumes clearly inspired by them do not leave us in any doubt as to their original purpose, but if we wish to approach this aspect of the Art of Costume intelligently we have first to disabuse our minds of preconceptions based on modern taste. We must avoid the error committed by Victorian writers, such as Thackeray, of judging the tastes of one age by the prejudices of another.

So far as we can we have to accept the contemporary premise, that a particular kind of dress or the display of a particular region of the body was intended to be attractive and was presumably accepted as such.

After all no approved fashion was ever *intended* to be indecent ; the most outrageous was meant to be attractive, not repulsive. We may, if we are sufficiently satisfied with our own superiority, deplore the bad taste of our ancestors, comforted by the knowledge that they cannot deplore ours.

It is well to recollect that some of our social habits of dress, speech and behaviour—on which we pride ourselves as being so frank and wholesome—would have been regarded as being extremely indelicate by most of our ancestors and, for aught we know, may be so regarded by our descendants.

The standard of good taste in this respect has not progressively improved but has merely fluctuated to and fro ; the recent decade of 1920-30, for example, compares unfavourably with the period of the Restoration of 1660 which has always been held up for moral disapproval.

The principles of sex-attraction in Costume may be grouped as *direct* and *indirect*. The latter can be dismissed briefly. Any display of some social advantage such as wealth or rank expressed in the costume would be, indirectly, a form of sex-attraction. And in modern times we should have to include the costume that suggests proficiency.

Direct forms of attraction are concerned with the physical features of the body and these are largely those which are known as " secondary sexual characteristics." In men, height, breadth of shoulders and shape of leg have been the three which the Art of Costume has repeatedly attempted to exploit. In women, it has been the shape of the figure, waist and hips ; in a word, the distinctive curves of the female body (*Plates* 42 and 48).

But in addition woman has employed the device of intermittent concealment of regions which are not intrinsically " sex-attractive " but become so from the fact that their occasional exposure is professed to be a privilege. What attracts the man is not, in such cases, the part revealed but the privilege of being allowed to see.

It is well recognised that concealment of any region endows it with mystery which excites a desire to penetrate it. Thus the woman's gloved hand and the semi-concealed ankle acquired a high degree of attraction, only lost because nowadays all concealment of those parts has lapsed.

The backless dress of the 1930 (*Plate* 45) period was no doubt an attempt to discover a territory which had hitherto been unexplored (at least within living memory), and for that reason it excited a passing curiosity, but this method of arousing interest is limited by the fact that the area of the human body is not inexhaustible ; consequently it becomes necessary, from time to time, to conceal regions previously exposed so that they may, as it were, lie fallow.

A phase of nudity is therefore often followed by a phase of concealment ; if we choose to describe this as a return to greater " decency " we are assuming a motive for which we have no proof. It is safer to regard such manœuvres as the unconscious tactics of an instinct.

It is noticeable that man has seldom, if indeed ever, troubled to employ this ingenious device of intermittent concealment in order to add to his attractions. Probably in a woman the act of " undressing "—even if it is only the removal of a glove—is itself attractive from the associated idea of physical surrender. For the same reason women have frequently practised the display— or simulated display—of undergarments, from revealing a portion of petticoat to exposing the top of the shift at the bosom (or what resembles that garment), wearing bodices that look like stays, as in the front-lacing effect seen in so many fashions from Tudor to Victorian times, or dresses which themselves look like chemises or nightdresses (*Plate* 38).

Thus, in 1800 an old lady described seeing her grand-daughters partly clothed, as she supposed, in but one petticoat and powdering gown apiece, and was astonished to learn that in reality they were fully dressed for the opera.

The illusion of appearing half-clad with its obvious implications admits of infinite variations. On the other hand concealment has sometimes been extended to regions normally exposed *au naturel* : we may instance those forms of bonnet such as almost concealed the face in the 1840's ; or the arrangement of the hair to hide the ears, and in the same category we may include feminine face-painting, patches, veils and the wearing of masks, the object of which is to arouse speculation.

When woman poses as a riddle, man will always seek for the answer, and so in the Art of Costume the essence of charm is—to provoke curiosity. This Art is well aware of the danger of monotony. " Quel est le plus grand ennemi de l'amour ? C'est l'habitude." This maxim alone suffices to explain the perpetual variations played on that theme.

Familiarity with the costumes of generations stretching back some six centuries will convince the observer that though both sexes have always introduced this well-worn motif into their respective compositions it has generally been far more stressed by women than by men ; that it has sometimes inspired works of art which are æsthetically beautiful and also, not infrequently, designs which are æsthetically bad.

We have to admit that human beings regard sex-attractiveness, in costume, as much more important than beauty, and the relation between the two seems almost a matter of chance ; and when a particular mode does not happen to attract us it is difficult to admit its claim to beauty, so hard is it for a human being to be completely unbiased by sex-feeling. The kind of costume which most of us regard as beautiful is the one whose sex-appeal is uttered in discreet tones ; we do not like its message bawled at us.

As English people we cannot ignore the powerful influence of prudery in the Art of Costume. Prudery is the persistent fear of sex, and the prude will therefore detect the trail of the serpent in places where the less circumspect are blind to it, and the less particular even welcome it.

This search for the dreadful fascination becomes by practice an absorbing hobby, and the prude obtains from its pursuit a satisfaction akin to that which the common mind obtains from satisfying the instinct. Indeed prudery may be regarded as a rarified and subtle form of sex-satisfaction whereby a warm glow of moral disapproval can be extracted from quite commonplace spectacles and will even rival the heat of passion itself ; we must always remember that no form of sensuous pleasure surpasses that derived from moral disapproval.

To the prude quite dull bits of the body become, as it were, enchanting if they happen to belong to the opposite sex ; and by association of ideas this exciting halo becomes transferred even to inanimate things and words. When the Victorian lady could not mention " trousers " or refer to a " chest of drawers " without embarrassment, we may assume she was an accomplished

33. *Fashion plate of Afternoon Dress, 1874.* These bustle curves, with those formed by the looped-up overskirts may be contrasted with the elliptical curves seen in plate 38.

34. *Fashion plate of Summer Costumes, 1878.* The lady wears an early example of a
" tailor-made," a Norfolk jacket over tightly swathed skirt with tunic. Note
the emphasis on the vertical lines to accentuate slimness of figure. The
gentleman wears a S.B. " University " coat, the fore-runner of the " morning
coat." The necktie has become insignificant but the trousers still clamour for
attention.

(H.R.H. Princess Louise Marguerite and H.R.H. The Duke of Connaught).

35. *Photograph of Archery group with other sports, 1862.* Note the old-fashioned beaver hat on the old gentleman while the young man wears a " chimney pot " in the mode of the day. The girl in a crinoline dress wears a " pork pie " hat. The others show varieties of male sporting costumes.

36. *Group photograph, 1866.* Note the almost modern lounge suit, of one material ; the crinoline worn by the girl on the right is smaller—and more fashionable—than that worn by the seated lady who has a paletot over her dress.

37. *Photograph of Tennis Costumes, 1884.* Two figures on left show basque bodice, pleated overskirt with " waterfall " back, over pleated underskirt ; boater straw hats. Third from the left shows draped overskirt, and the lady on the extreme right has a flounced skirt with " bag " bodice. Feathered hat.

38. *Fashion plate of Evening Dresses, 1878.* Note the subtle use of elliptical curves and pointed angles. Contrast with plate 42 as a method of sex-appeal. The figure on the left wears a simulated cuirasse bodice, suggestive of corset-lacing. The back is *en princesse* with attached train, and the whole is as tight as possible, so that it was dangerous to attempt to sit down.

39. *Bathing Costume, 1886*, of turquoise blue flannel
edged with torchon lace, with cap of same.
(From the Cunnington collection).

40. *Fashion plate of Garden Party Dress (Peter Robinson), 1895.*
Note ballooned sleeves and yoke of bodice above gored skirt
of different material and colour.

41. *Fashion plate of Lounge Suit, 1906.* Note length
of jacket and narrow cut of trousers accentuating
the vertical lines.
(From *The Tailor & Cutter*, portraying Mr. Winston Churchill).

42. *Dress of black face cloth piped with puce velvet; Beaver Hat with twelve ostrich feathers, 1908.* A study in curves, of which the composition is entirely built.

(From the Cunnington collection. Photograph by Peter Clark Ltd.).

43. *Fashion plate of tailor-made " Hobble skirt " Costumes, 1912.* Note
the long, close-fitting tunics with high waists and " Empire "
effects ; and the unbalanced effect of the huge hats.

44. *Ascot Dress of printed linen, 1923.* Note absence of curves. Waistband gives
bad proportion: pattern of material has no relation to the dress or to the
wearer, unless there is some Freudian significance.

(From the Cunnington collection.   Photograph by Peter Clark Ltd.).

45. *Backless Evening Frock, 1930.* Note the clumsy method of suspension and the meaningless nature of the pattern.

46a. *The " New Look."* Grey and white spot silk surah afternoon dress showing Victor Stiebel's " Washerwoman Skirt." It is evidently inspired by the modes of the middle 'eighties, both as regards the pannier drapery, the sleeves and even the hat. See 46b below.

(Costume by Victor Stiebel at Jacqmar. Photograph by Peter Clark Ltd.).

46b. *Dress of spotted red sateen, 1886.*
(From the Cunnington collection. Photograph by Photopress).

47. *Tailored Afternoon Dress in black rayon silk, 1947.* Note the marked " X " symbol of its line.

(Costume by Hardy Amies. Photograph by Peter Clark Ltd.).

48. *Evening Gown, 1947.* The modern emphasis is on the body rather than on the dress, as a means of sex-appeal—the dress being allowed to fade, as it were, into the background.

(Dress by Debenham's. Photograph by Ernest)

prude ; and if the gentleman of her day was thrilled by the word " chemise " in print it is obvious that a generation so gifted had sources of mild excitement which a modern world may well envy (*Plate* 39).

It used to be claimed that prudery was not only an English accomplishment but that it was in our blood. The United States of America however have frequently demonstrated that they too are possessed of it to a high degree, from draping the legs of furniture to obliterating the word " bastard " from drama.

Moreover, research into our own social history fails to reveal the presence of prudery to any extent earlier than about the middle of the 1830's—that is, if we may take contemporary literature as a guide. In English costume prudery began to become manifest about 1840 (*Plate* 29).

We should expect of course the mental attitude to precede the expression of it in clothing and we cannot understand the fashions which subsequently ruled the English social life unless we realise the grip exercised by prudery.

A convenient and reliable test of its presence is the use of circumlocutions and euphemisms in speech and writing, and especially the avoidance of plain words denoting parts of the body. As early as 1818 an observer (Lady Susan O'Brien) was commenting that the language of society was growing " more refined. No one can say ' breeding ' or ' with child ' or ' lying-in ' without being thought indelicate. ' Cholic ' and ' bowels ' are exploded words. ' Stomach ' signifies everything."

And presently when " legs," " breasts " and "stomach" disappeared from novels and speech, as had happened by 1840, and were replaced by " limbs," " bosom " and " the liver," we may deduce a high tide of prudery. The Victorian lady, it should be understood, consisted— below the diaphragm—of nothing but the liver until the ankles were reached, and the Victorian gentleman was constructed on nearly the same principle. Their prudery may have started as a psychological reaction to the exhibitionism which had distinguished the twenty years of the Napoleonic wars, or—more probably—as an expression of the sedate bourgeois mentality. That extraordinary phenomenon, the Victorian " trouser " taboo, followed a long period of exploiting the male leg ; the earliest example I have come across of this avoidance of the horrid word is in *Oliver Twist* (1837-9):

" I tossed off the clothes ; got softly out of bed ; drew on a pair of——"

" Ladies present, Mr. Giles," murmured the tinker.

"——of shoes, sir," said Mr. Giles, laying great emphasis on the word.

This mild joke would have been quite pointless a decade or so earlier, but Dickens's finger, always on the pulse of the people, was seldom misled.

The Victorian prudery, once well established, served as a kind of regulator by which a constant but safe emotional pressure could be maintained ; its practical value in the general improvement of behaviour has not received the credit it deserves now that we no longer, we think, require this ingenious refinement of sex-appeal.

Its effect on the Art of Costume was naturally very marked. The lure of the gentleman's legs subsided ; the shape of trousers accurately fitted their new name " inexpressibles," becoming less and less anatomical in cut while their colours gradually faded out of the picture (Cf. *Plates* 36 and 41).

In women's costume the growing disguise of expanding skirt culminating in the crinoline but lasting in various forms throughout the century, together with the lavish drapery of the shawl concealing the figure, the abundance of cloaks, mantles, burnouses and similar wrapping garments, all spoke of a desire to hide the physical outline except on those particular occasions when, as in evening dress, sex-appeal was legitimately practised.

But always there was the ladylike assumption that any results therefrom were unsought for and were ordained by a Higher Hand. The condemnatory words " bold," " fast " and " immodest " signified that the offender had used her gifts designedly.

The present generation may find it difficult to appreciate the atmosphere of hypersensitiveness to sex allusions, real or fancied, which prevailed throughout the Victorian era and even after, among nicely brought up families. One recalls that young lady, engaged in repairing an undergarment, who hastily thrust it under a cushion because her father happened to enter the room ; the daughter reproved for having accidentally used the word " nightdress " in a gentleman's presence ; and the shocking case of the little girl who, being told it was not nice to go down in her *déshabillé* to say good night to her grandpapa promptly removed the indelicate garment and went clad in her—innocence, explaining " I mustn't see gentlemen in my nightygown."

Yet does not the tradition still linger ? How the plain word " drawers " is shunned : how the more masculine " knickers," and now the still more masculine " pants," is preferred ; and does not the official mind describe a pregnant woman as " an expectant mother," while the coarse Victorian " W.C." has become a lavatory. Surely this shunning of plain words is evidence of the prudish mind. . . .

The psychological antithesis of prudery is exhibition-ism, and this in costume is the desire to expose physical features of the body with the intention of arousing the emotions of the other sex. It is obvious that the degree of exposure is relative to whatever is considered the norm ; in times of excessive prudery a woman's naked hand was considered an indelicate thing to expose unduly ; in times of exhibitionism to conceal the shape of the breasts was held to be prudish.

We may perhaps regard as the happy mean costume which does not deny the secondary sexual features but does not aggressively flaunt them. We have always to distinguish between exhibitionism of an individual—which is probably consciously assumed, and that of a group—in other words a " fashion "—which by most of its members is probably subconsciously assumed.

In the periods when a considerable measure of nudism was fashionable we cannot assume that all who followed such a fashion were doing so " with intent " ; all we can safely deduce is that there was such a spirit in the air.

Exhibitionism has been indulged in by both sexes, sometimes concurrently—as in the last decade of the eighteenth century—but not always. The following extracts from *The Times* indicate masculine comments on feminine fashions, the feathers worn on the head, and the scantiness of the rest of the costume, at the close of the eighteenth century :

Jan. 6, 1796. " We saw a feather in Drury Lane theatre that cost ten guineas. We should have thought the whole goose not worth the money."

Jan. 27, 1796. " The only new fashions that remain for our modern belles are certainly puzzling and difficult. There can be nothing new but going either dressed—or naked."

Dec. 11, 1799. " If the present fashion of nudity continues its career the Milliners must give way to the Carvers, and the most elegant *fig-leaves* will be all the mode. The fashion of *false-bosoms* has at least this utility, that it compels our fashionable fair to wear *something*."

We recognise that the modes of the fifteenth and sixteenth centuries were mainly a phase of male exhibitionism. The Jacobean fashion for exposing the whole of the breasts (*Plate* 13) was a phase of female exhibitionism, while during the last thirty years of the Victorian era women's evening dresses were constantly charged with being indelicate. Thus, in 1888 : " The excessive nakedness of modern full dress is sometimes a pain and more often an embarrassment to those who only observe. The lowness of the bodice and the total absence of sleeves leaves an impression of general nakedness." The bearded man of that time was a complete contrast.

The period following the Great War of 1914-18 was perhaps the most marked epoch of exhibitionism in both sexes that this country has ever experienced, though it scarcely affected men's ordinary costume but was very marked in women's.

We tend to assume that a phase of marked exhibitionism in woman's costume denotes a relaxation of conventional morals because no other explanation seems apparent ; thus, the post-war period of 1920-30 appears to offer many analogies to that of the Regency years, and it is tempting to attribute both to the effect of great wars which loosen restraint. For both these periods there is abundance of information to corroborate this. But if we are going to read standards of morals from fashions of dress we ought not to ignore that singular epoch : the last thirty years or so of the fifteenth century.

Then it was that feminine costume appears, in our eyes, to have been practising most of those devices of " exhibitionism " which we readily recognise as such in the other two periods mentioned. We have of course to rely on second-hand information derived from illuminated MSS., effigies and brasses, together with contemporary comment, but there stands out conspicuously the extreme decolletage, the eyebrow plucking, the extraordinary posterish headgear and the tight-fitting dress revealing the shape of the breasts—in a word, the same kind of display that we see in the Regency and the 1920-30 periods. Here, then, is evidence, tantalisingly incomplete, suggestive of a similar phase occurring with the upheavals of the Wars of the Roses, and their aftermath. If the Art of Costume is a faithful record of contemporary mass psychology its study will be as necessary for the social historian as any other contemporary data.

These waves of exploiting the physical aspects of sex are necessarily at the expense of the Art of Costume, as an art, for then its æsthetic claims are sacrificed in order to obtain the desired display of the body (*Plate* 48). On the other hand, occasional outbursts of exhibitionism do serve a useful purpose ; they correct the overloading of the body with clothing, a process which if unchecked tends to choke the artistic expression by its own exuberance.

The desire to pile Pelion upon Ossa has frequently been the bane of this art. When for example a fashionably dressed lady, some sixty years ago, staggered under a stone and a half of winter clothing in order to keep abreast with the modes of the day, some kind of lopping to get rid of the redundancy was clearly called for, to the advantage of the art of the costumier.

A phase of exhibitionism supplies the pruning knife ; subsequently the Art of Costume, refreshed by the process, blossoms again with renewed vigour.

The weight of women's clothing has fluctuated far more than men's. At the beginning of last century a woman could dress on sixteen ounces of clothes, a record she equalled and sometimes surpassed in the decade 1920-30. The fashion for " slimming " which persisted after as much clothing had been scrapped as possible may be regarded as an extension of the process to the body itself.

These periodical fluctuations, however, can be accepted as perhaps useful and not on the whole detrimental to the Art of Costume. But it becomes evident, I think, that in aiming at sex-attraction the costume and the body, though sometimes in alliance, are frequently in secret opposition. When large areas of the body are triumphantly nude it is seldom that the costume, shrinking in the background, retains much intrinsic beauty.

Sometimes one and sometimes the other claims pride of place, and the Art of Costume is most successful when the body is least conspicuous ; surely therefore prudery must supply the most favourable medium in which this art can express itself, unhampered by its rival ?

Not only has it then the field to itself on which it can build whatever design it pleases, but moreover it has at its service all those mystical symbols which allude in veiled terms to the forbidden subject, and which prove more attractive than reality itself.

Thus it can combine the charm of a work of art with the charm of subtle allusion without offending the most delicate susceptibilities.

But during an exhibitionist phase the Art of Costume is gravely hampered ; it is constantly causing offence so that any artistic merit it may have is misjudged ; any success it may obtain is apt to be attributed to the body and not to the costume covering it. Indeed the artist is mortified to discover that his function has become a subsidiary one and so in despair he falls back on the costumier's last resource—transparent materials.

The dress is not more than a window-frame.

Under such conditions the artist must wait for public taste to change, knowing that sooner or later it will demand something more expressive than mere flesh.

In ordinary times, too, this art has its peculiar difficulties. Its methods of sex-attraction have frequently exposed it to a good deal of hostile criticism, either because it fails to attract or because it succeeds. There have always been some who, on moral grounds, would disapprove of its making any attempt to be " attractive " though permitting it to be " charming." How to be one without being the other is a problem indeed.

There is a tendency to-day to consider the Edwardian modes for women as decorously stately ; yet at the time they were condemned by the Vatican as " immodest and unholy." The difficulty with which this art has always to contend is that while some would have it austere the majority wish it to express human aspirations ; as such it can hardly avoid the most powerful influence to which humanity is subject.

But while one may be chary of criticising the morals of this art it is often permissible to criticise it adversely on æsthetic grounds. We are justified in charging it with sometimes committing a blunder : that in trying to express sex-attraction its designs may be intrinsically ugly and therefore repulsive. This surely is the worst offence it can commit.

If mere nudity were itself the most powerful means of attracting the other sex then it is unlikely that the Art of Costume would ever have been invented ; but in fact it is the universal experience that Costume can add an extra attraction to that inherent in the body, and the extreme exhibitionist who recklessly disregards the aids of costume is likely to be disappointed.

It is significant that phases of semi-nudity do not last as long as phases of lavish concealment. The latter may therefore claim to represent the normal, the former supplying mere interludes, and we may conclude that in the long run the latter is more to the taste of the community.

Probably there always has been and always will be a wide difference of opinion as to how far this art may legitimately attempt to express this fundamental instinct; but it is certainly very remarkable that all through the Saxon and Anglo-Norman periods in this country, extending over a period of some eight centuries, the costume of both sexes appears, by our standards, to have been almost entirely without those expressions of sex-attraction to which we have become accustomed during the last six centuries.

And as during those dark ages the normal instinct was presumably not suspended we must conclude that it found other, perhaps cruder, means of expression. At any rate the fact remains that ever since the fourteenth century the Art of Costume has never been without evidence of such influences and that frequently they have been very pronounced.

It is tempting to assume that either we have in these six centuries become more depraved, or else that the Art of Costume has supplied a harmless and convenient way of sublimating an impulse which might otherwise disrupt society.

This latter view is supported by the fact that the conscious knowledge that a costume is " attractive " supplies in itself a measure of satisfaction to the wearer and so appeases a very human desire. In other words, an attractive costume may allay as well as provoke the sexual instinct.

In that case the Art of Costume during these six centuries may claim to have been on the whole an elevating influence on social morals, and if we were to return, as William Morris wished, to the garb of the eleventh or twelfth centuries, morality would also take a retrograde step. As it is, this art has enabled a civilised community to advance its standard of behaviour, and especially in its attitude towards the manifestations of the primitive instincts of sex.

CHAPTER XVII

SEX-ATTRACTION IN MAN'S COSTUME

IN the preceding chapter a distinction was drawn between direct and indirect forms of attraction, and the history of men's costume during the last six centuries shows a gradual transference from the former to the latter type.

In spite of natural fluctuations and occasional reversions to the more primitive method, the tendency has been to shift the appeal from the particular to the general and eventually from the general aspect of the costume to that of the character of the wearer himself, a progressive change which, as we shall see, the feminine technique has been very slow to adopt. Man's costume presents, in pictorial fashion, that process which the psychologist describes as sublimation, together with a gradual discarding of the artificial aid formerly supplied by his clothes.

We may ascribe this change to a variety of causes such as an increasing refinement of manners, an increasing pre-occupation with matters and interests other than sex-attraction, and especially we have to recognise the effect on man's costume of the change in woman's taste.

After all, the methods of attraction which one sex finds successful reflect the taste of the other ; if man claims that his costume no longer employs the cruder forms of appeal, the credit is not entirely his. When the girl of to-day says she does not like her boy friend to be dressed in a conspicuous manner it is she who really dictates the style he has to wear.

This aspect of the Art of men's Costume covers some six centuries from the time when it was discovered—or

SEX-ATTRACTION IN MAN'S COSTUME

to be more correct, rediscovered—that it could be used
as an implement of sex-attraction.

We should naturally expect that its first essay in that
direction would be crude ; and the crudest way in
which one sex can compel the notice of the other is by
displaying the distinctive physical features of sex.

In an earlier chapter we have seen how the male
costume in the days of Chaucer provoked disapproval
and the subsequent fashion of the cod-piece, a protruding
bag-like structure of material covering the male organ,
became a conspicuous feature of man's costume from the
fifteenth to the middle of the sixteenth century.

This fashion seems to have been accepted by the
majority as a natural display of a sexual feature and its
general adoption is evidence, I think, that it did not
offend the conventions of the time when the display of
the male leg in tights, often parti-coloured, up to the hip
had become the mode.

It is true that in the Sumptuary Laws of Edward IV
it was enacted that " no knight under the rank of a lord,
esquire or gentleman, nor any other person shall wear
any gown, jacket or cloak that is not long enough, when
he stands upright, to cover his privities and his buttocks
under the penalty of twenty shillings."

From which we must conclude that a privilege enjoyed
by the higher aristocracy could hardly have been
regarded as indecent or repulsive to women. If it were,
the cod-piece would not have survived, as it did, for over
a hundred years.

It is also to be noted that although the extreme degree
of leg exposure was fairly soon obliterated by lengthening
the cloak, the cod-piece persisted without provoking as
much disapproval, on the score of decency, as, for
example, woman's bathing costume has done in modern
times.

We must assume that women in the fifteenth century
accepted the one as men in the twentieth have accepted

the other, and it would be dangerous to attempt to draw moral inferences from either. The change in conventional " decency " which took place in men's costume between the Renaissance and, let us say, the Restoration of Charles the Second, had a curious replica in the development of man's bathing costume. This in the strict age of the Victorian era was, by modern standards, extremely indecent ; that conspicuous scarlet triangle gradually developed into a sombre costume even acquiring a skirt reminiscent of the Restoration petticoat-breeches.

It would be fallacious to deduce from his bathing costume that the modern man is more bashful and the modern woman more shockable than their Victorian grandparents. In his diary (1873-4) the Rev. Francis Kilvert, a young curate, describes the " very short red and white striped " bathing drawers of the period which, however, were a novelty to him. " At Shanklin one has to adopt the detestable custom of bathing in drawers. If ladies don't like to see men naked why don't they keep away from the sight ? " At Seaton " unaccustomed to such things I had in my ignorance bathed naked. . . . Some little boys who were looking on at the rude naked man appeared to be much interested and the young ladies who were strolling near seemed to have no objection." To-day even the most advanced curate would hesitate to copy Mr. Kilvert's example, but whether that would be evidence of greater refinement or greater prudery the reader must decide.

Nor is there, I think, sufficient evidence to decide how far such variations in the so-called " decency " of man's costume affect its degree of sex-attraction. " Whatever is—is right " seems to sum up woman's taste in such matters.

In an earlier chapter we have traced the exploitation of the male leg exposed in tights, at first to the hip and eventually from the knee to the ankle only, ultimately to vanish entirely. We may regard this as a transference from a primary to a secondary sexual characteristic, the male leg having a distinctive shape of its own.

It is noticeable that the traditional significance lingered during the Elizabethan and Jacobean periods when the pointed doublet seemed to direct attention towards the sexual region after the cod-piece itself had disappeared (*Plate* 12). Eventually this was followed by a complete covering of that region under the petticoat-breeches and subsequently by the long waistcoat of the first half of the eighteenth century (*Plate* 18).

It would be unwise to assume that such an apparent increase of male modesty implied a more austere code of morals. The lesson we can deduce, however, is that human beings rapidly accustom themselves to anatomical facts displayed by the other sex which therefore cease to appeal ; and that on the whole concealment is more effective than revelation, a lesson which man appears to be learning quicker than woman.

In tracing the history of sex-attraction exercised by man in his costume we see that, while the leg display persisted in varying degrees until well into the nineteenth century, minor features of secondary sexual characteristics had their phases of emphasis.

Man's gloves have a history of their own. His hand can hardly ever have been without interest to women ; it represented his power of taking and holding. All through the sixteenth century his gloves were highly ornamental and served no other purpose, being carried in the hand.

The fashion for scented gloves worn by both sexes in the seventeenth and eighteenth centuries, and the nature of the scents used such as musk and ambergris with their well-recognised aphrodisiac properties, indicates their function as a crude form of erotic appeal. In this respect it is to be observed that men continued to use scent until near the close of last century, and that now they have abandoned it together with so many other artificial kinds of charm.

The hand with its ruffles, its rings and select cane in the eighteenth century, exhibited a high degree of elegance, and its novel feature was a delicate skin which in the case of the exquisite had to be protected by a muff in the day and by chicken-skin gloves at night ; we must assume that in the by-play of sex-attraction it too had its moments.

Gradually, and all through the Victorian age, the glove became significant of social class ; in that sense it possessed an implied attraction while the absence of gloves stamped a man as hopelessly " not quite." Unlike the hand of a lady, that of a gentleman could, if he chose, be exposed bare, provided of course that gloves were carried (*Plate* 31*a*). To-day the signet ring is disappearing and the glove has become wholly utilitarian ; man's hand has abandoned any attempt to be attractive. All that woman demands of it is that it shall be strong and clean.

This progressive decline in the exploitation of particular regions in order to appeal to feminine feelings has extended all over the body from man's head to his heels. The choice shoe of the eighteenth century with sparkling buckle, and red-heeled for full dress, gave way to forms growing less and less conspicuous, once the eccentricities of the Regency period had subsided.

From tasselled Hessians to elastic-sided boots was a decline indeed.

And for evening dress we have seen in the last fifty years patent-leather buttoned boots and pumps with bows becoming less and less until to-day men's feet are hidebound in the commonplace.

But this apparent indifference on the part of man to the sex-appeal of his costume is perhaps even more noticeable in its loss of colour. Brilliant colours naturally catch the eye and all through the animal kingdom such colours are employed to enhance sex-attraction. It is common knowledge that whereas at one time, on the occasions when man sought to win the admiration of the other sex, his costume was as gorgeously coloured as women's, during the last hundred years or so it has steadily lost that quality.

Contrast his evening clothes to-day with those of two centuries back, when an elegant was described as wearing " a black velvet coat, a green and silver waistcoat, yellow velvet breeches and blue stockings."

The facile explanation that his present sombre attire affords such an admirable foil to the colours of his partner's dress is irrelevant ; men don't dress to supply backgrounds to anybody.

But two centuries ago they dressed to display their wealth and rank ; to-day these are secrets a gentleman would blush to reveal. When we reckon the immense cost incurred in former times by any man with social pretensions, it is clear that those peacock effects must have been thought essential ; we may be thankful they are so no longer.

We find Pepys buying suits representing £100 in modern money ; Steele giving £40 for a periwig, Goldsmith paying twenty guineas for a blue velvet suit and £8 for a pair of blue silk breeches, sums corresponding to four or five times those amounts in our currency.

The Hon. John Spencer on the occasion of his marriage in 1756 is said to have worn shoe buckles worth thirty thousand pounds. If this was an instance of masculine sex-attraction it was doubtless as effective in its way as the heart of woman could desire.

Enough has been said to illustrate the general tendency in man's costume to abandon, one after another, the more obvious forms of display which, we like to assume, had been adopted by former generations largely if not principally for their sex-appeal.

We have seen how they featured particular regions of

the body ; then gradually changing this to a more general effect how they reinforced any physical attraction by the exhibition of evidence of wealth and social rank, especially in gala dress.

At this point we may not improperly inquire how far those efforts to win feminine admiration were successful. What results were due to those splendours in which the beau and the buck, the maccaroni and the dandy, exercised their charms ? Was it his coat or his waistcoat or breeches which won the gentleman of *ton* his victories ? [1]

As we gaze at those magnificent garments in the passionless atmosphere of a museum their story seems incomplete. We require to know what agitating emotions were stirred thereby in the elegant females who had been the target of those shafts.

For evidence on this important point we naturally turn to contemporary reports and especially novels where we may expect to find the heroines' opinions illuminating.

Here however disappointment awaits us. The novels written by men are from the nature of the case unreliable, and even so, where a masculine bias in favour of those weapons might be expected, the authors never venture to assert that their heroine succumbed to the hero's costume. His handsome bearing, fine features, skill in horsemanship, combined with the attractions of wealth and a title, these seem sufficient to bring the story to a satisfactory close.

Naturally we look for more revealing information from women writers, such as Fanny Burney, but her *Evelina* is singularly obtuse. She is content to speak of

---

[1] In the reign of Queen Anne the curious fashion for wearing the upper part of the waistcoat open to show the frilled shirtfront was said to have a killing effect on the other sex. " A sincere heart has not made half so many conquests as an open waistcoat " (*Tatler*, No. 95).

This affectation of youth finds a faint echo in modern days when it is considered essential that the bottom button of the waistcoat should be left undone.

Lord Orville's " elegance of person," but when subsequently she is asked " what coat had he on ? " she can only reply, " Indeed I never looked at it."

Turn to Jane Austen and she is equally uninformative. True, we learn from Marianne that " of all manly dresses a shooting-jacket is the most becoming," but that does not carry us far ; and observe, a shooting-jacket is definitely not intended to be appealing. It is meant, primarily, for other game.

In fact Jane Austen's young women are so unobservant that they appear to be oblivious of the privilege of living in the very epoch when, as we like to think, man's garb with those seductively tight breeches, was almost indelicately attractive. Yet it wins no comment—no, not even from Lydia Bennet.

We pass on to Charlotte Brontë ; Jane Eyre tells us of Mr. Rochester's noble brow, fine eyes and breadth of figure but his clothes entirely escape her notice, which is strange in one so observant of her rival's alluring attire.

If we consult novels of subsequent periods the same reticence is observed ; while the hero is entranced by the heroine's dress which he attempts, inadequately, to describe, she on the other hand is oblivious of his—unless he happens to be wearing a very old suit charged with cigar smoke, when she is immediately captivated.

From such sources the evidence seems to indicate that the Strong Silent Englishman of those days was at his best when clothed in his worst, a true symbol of our rough island story.

Such novels had however one man dressed in the height of fashion—the villain.

It appears that it is the masculine costume for sport, and especially the sport of war, that arouses feminine admiration to its highest pitch—that is, it is just the clothes a man wears when his thoughts are wholly directed to other aims than sex.

In the recent war man's battledress, designed on the most repulsive lines, proved to have an appeal which was at times even embarrassing ; while when he does dress up to attract, his clothes are unobserved ; all that stands out is his " elegance of person," or, in modern phrase, " he looks all right to me."

The conclusion is forced on us. All those costly garments in which our ancestors swaggered before the ladies, those velvet suits and silk breeches, those colourful waistcoats, the ruffles and ribbons and sparkling jewels, were they, perhaps, after all, not designed to be sex-attractive so much as " sex-supporting ? " Were they not just to give the wearer self-confidence in the presence of his own sex, his rivals, while he engaged in the most dangerous of all sports ? The extravagant sums spent on clothing by gentlemen about the court of James the First can hardly have been for any other purpose than to advertise their recently acquired wealth. One of Buckingham's court suits of white velvet was covered with eighty thousand pounds' worth of diamonds. Sir Walter Raleigh's court shoes were decorated with six thousand pounds' worth of jewels. We read of a knight spending five hundred pounds on his cloak to attend the coronation. These figures must of course be multiplied several times to obtain their modern equivalents. Such displays were doubtless confined to a small group of courtiers all anxious to give an impression of their importance. We may suspect that much of the gorgeous masculine dressing in the eighteenth century was due to the returned Indian nabobs setting the pace in exhibiting their wealth, not as lady-killers but simply as *nouveaux riches*.

In contrast to the extravagance of the court circle, however, the following extract from the Household Book of Thomas Cony, Esquire, of Bassingthorpe, Lincs., *c.* 1606, is of interest :

" Item, that I, Thomas Cony of Bassingthorpe did

spend in and upon myself and my wife in apparel and jewels, as also upon servants'-liveries and other necessaries in nursing and bringing up of nineteen children for the space of fifty-three years, reckoned compotus compotand, in my conscience is most true, at least £856."

Evidently we shall have to rectify the accepted views of man's peacock adornments. It seems their real function was to express his importance and to give him the necessary assurance—in the eyes of his fellows—for they were assumed to impress his own sex as much as the other.

Is it not the case that he dresses—and always has done so—in his most splendid attire not when his aim is to charm women but to impress men? At ceremonies of state or civic pomp, then it is that a man appears at his most resplendent. For mere sex-attraction tennis flannels will do.

It follows that in the austerity of modern times it is no extraordinary hardship for a young man to be deprived of the opportunity for obtaining exquisite clothes ; happily it is not now necessary for him to display his income on his back and as for sex-appeal, he has, one hopes, discovered the fallacy of his forebears —if indeed they *were* under the delusion that those fine feathers did attract ; he now uses his costume to attract only by inference. He seeks to dress so as to emphasise two features of his personality and both are highly attractive.

In the first place his costume is markedly youthful in design as compared to the usual modes of former times. The modern style allows a man of fifty to pass himself off as in the prime of life.

When we contrast such a man, clean-shaven and physically fit, in a trimly built lounge suit, with—let us say—his grandfather at that age, a portly whiskered gentleman in a heavy frock coat and bulging waistcoat, whose charm of person had long vanished, then surely we realise that his general set-up has helped to knock off at least a decade from the modern man's years.

And if there is no longer anything in his costume to cause immediate surrender to its charm, at least he has another ten years in which to prolong the siege.

It is no great disadvantage that the style of clothes does not extol any particular region ; the head is not glorified by a romantic hat or flowing locks, the virile beard has been swept away, the leg no longer displays its shape in skin-tight breeches. His costume adds nothing to his inches and timid attempts to introduce poetic colouring are not encouraged. In a word, the man of to-day is content to wear pedestrian prose ; and our descendants viewing specimens of the modern suit hanging impersonally in glass cases may well marvel at their absence of charm.

They may conclude that the male of this epoch was wholly devoid of sex-attraction—a judgment we are tempted to pass on the costume of our Saxon and Anglo-Norman ancestors.

But in fact the modern man's clothing has acquired a subtlety which does not survive in a museum. It is designed to express the wearer's masculine competence ; this is effected by a harmonious combination of details, their correct choice, the perfect cut, the quality of materials, which together tell that the man is proficient. You may not, to-day, be able to tell a duke by his clothes ; you can however tell a dud.

In the modern world an air of proficiency in whatever happens to be a man's job is itself a powerful weapon of sex-attraction.

The girl who says she does not notice what a man wears so long as he looks her-idea-of-a-man is, of course, paying his costume the highest possible compliment. She means it has become a part of his personality.

If we turn our eyes back to the modes of the past, however much we may admire their elegance, their grandeur or their artistic beauty, they do not suggest to our minds any extraordinary competence possessed by the original wearers. They may sometimes suggest a virile race ; they don't suggest an able.

It is evident that man's costume has undergone or is undergoing a revolutionary change of function. It will be recalled that the Art of Costume was described as having three aims : to express social rank, occupation and sex-attraction.

The first two have almost disappeared from the dress of the Englishman, and the third, if it has not entirely vanished, has certainly become much subdued. This change has taken place during the last hundred years and particularly during the last thirty or so, while a new function has begun to take their place.

This expression of what I have labelled " proficiency," physical and mental, has yet to develop. What further changes in man's costume will result from it we cannot guess, but when we hear the complaint that his clothes have become " so dull " the criticism seems singularly inept. For it may well prove that at last they are becoming really interesting.

CHAPTER XVIII

SEX-ATTRACTION IN WOMAN'S COSTUME

IN the preceding chapters reference has been frequently made to methods of sex-attraction in Woman's costume ; and as I have treated this subject at some length elsewhere (in *Why Women Wear Clothes*) it will suffice here to summarise this important branch of the Art of Costume.

We have to bear in mind that not only is any physical feature, if it is distinctive of one sex, always attractive to the other, but by association of ideas the same charm becomes attached to kinds of garments and styles of clothing.

In the case of Woman, the exposure, real or simulated, either of parts of the body or, equally, of parts of the clothing not usually displayed becomes, as it were, an intimacy which is in itself attractive.

If we analyse the various methods of attraction employed in Woman's costume we see that they are designed either to draw attention to the wearer herself, or designed to draw attention to some particular region of her body. And in order thus to catch the eye of the spectator there is necessarily some measure of æsthetic exaggeration used. The composition may bear signs of artistry and arrangement which not seldom verge on caricature.

It is apparent that Woman's costume can be very " attractive " without being very beautiful ; in fact beauty is only accidental. We discover, as we survey these six centuries of her endeavours to captivate Man by her attire, that most methods of exploiting localised sex-attraction—that is, of drawing special attention to particular regions—tend to be detrimental to the beauty of the whole picture because they disturb the balance of the composition.

It appears that the practice of localised sex-appeal is being gradually replaced by something more general, and the modern tendency is to employ an entirely different technique in the day dress and in the evening. In both, the whole body and not a particular part is featured, but in the evening frock the body is allowed to be far more important than its covering, which indeed is becoming so irrelevant that the spectator is scarcely aware of its presence. The modern young woman in her flimsy dance frock worn without any sort of under-clothing is tacitly insisting that her charms are wholly anatomical (*Plate* 48). In her day costume, on the other hand, the appeal is exerted by the effect of the whole with its practical air ; for she is beginning to rely, as Man has learnt to rely, on the persuasiveness of the *toute ensemble* with the secondary implication of physical and mental fitness.

It is evident that of the two kinds of appeal the physical is the less subtle form of art, but nevertheless it exercises a more immediate influence and therefore it is not likely to be discarded, at least by those individuals whose chief weapon it happens to be.

As we survey this aspect of the Art of Costume during the last six centuries, we cannot but notice the immense pains taken by women to draw attention to their physical allurements and chiefly by the method of localised appeal. To heighten the effect of one region others may be skilfully obscured, or their attractions veiled ; ingenious exaggeration lends its artful aid and the laws of art are broken with impunity. For happily feminine fashions change so rapidly that Man has no time to detect their artistic flaws.

It is natural that for the purpose of sex-appeal Woman's costume should so habitually draw attention to her distinctive characteristic—the curve—as exemplified by the shape of the breasts, the waist and the hips. At least one of these has (with the exception of the 1920's) always been emphasised in her costume during the last five or six centuries, while at various times other curved regions such as the head and neck, the arm and the ankle have also been given prominence, their natural curves serving to reinforce the impression created elsewhere.

The curve, being such a well-recognised feminine symbol, its use both in the design of the costume framed to display the natural curves or to supply artificial ones, is to be expected. The greater the emphasis of this sort the nearer does the resulting costume approach to what is condemned as " sensual ; " by which is meant, simply, that the sex-appeal has become too blatant. Or, to be more exact, it has reached a point where it has become deliberately assumed by the wearer. At that point Man has usually objected.

It is perhaps necessary to state that all such devices of sex-attraction are the more appealing to the normal man the less consciously they are assumed. Their essential charm lies in the fact that Woman uses them instinctively, without calculation ; for the intention to attract tends in fact to repel. Women will frequently employ, for example, sexual symbols in costume without being in the least aware of their primitive significance ; all they are conscious of is that such symbols please the masculine mind ; and men, too, may be equally unable to say why they are agreeable.

In criticising devices of sex-appeal in costume we have to bear in mind that the two sexes view these things from very different standpoints ; to men, in their dispassionate moments, such things seem inherently ridiculous ; to women it is always a serious subject ; their children's lives are at stake.

It seems that the accepted technique of sex-appeal in Woman's costume may be regarded as threefold : that of concealment to provoke curiosity ; that of allusion to provoke associated ideas ; and that of exposure to provoke surprise, which, however, soon passes into indifference. As we should expect therefore, the two former have been habitually employed while the third is used intermittently and seldom for long at a time. (*See Appendix A.*)

As an example of all three the following letter written by a girl in 1786, presents, somewhat crudely perhaps, the orthodox pattern : " I have no patience with the men. I have been talked to, admired and complimented for my beauty these five years ; but though I am arrived at the age of nineteen I have almost lost all hopes and am monstrously afraid I shall increase the catalogue of old maids. What a horrid idea ! To make the matter a thousand times worse I have had the galling mortification to see above half a dozen of my most intimate friends—the ugliest girls you can conceive—settled perfectly to their satisfaction.

" I begin indeed to think there is nothing at all in beauty. What a deal of pains I have taken to improve my face and shape ! But if you cannot put me in the way to make something of myself after all, I will actually unfrizzle my hair, throw my rouge into the fire, stuff a cushion with my bustle, press down my handkerchief to my bosom and—in short—appear exactly as Nature made me. I am absolutely weary of taking so much trouble for nothing." A similar letter, dated 1789, is equally revealing : " I am reckoned handsome yet have no peace because my female friends are always finding fault with my dress ; they exclaim against my manner of putting on my little round beaver ; they tell me my handkerchief is frightfully open before. Yet I declare that I do not know how to believe all this as all the male sex to a man say quite the contrary."

On æsthetic grounds it may be questioned whether

there is any part of the body which does not acquire increased attraction by some measure of veiling, or whether it is possible to design a dress artistically satisfying in which extensive areas of bare skin are exposed. No one has yet designed an artistic bathing costume. Skin and dress material are such different media that the two challenge each other, often discordantly, so that if costume were designed solely on artistic principles the amount of bare skin exposed would be reduced to a minimum. Nevertheless exposure of those areas most obviously characteristic of sex has been frequently employed because the appeal is crudely effective.

Thus, in the fifteenth century, decolletage began to be practised often to the extent of uncovering the upper half of the breasts, and in the late sixteenth and early seventeenth centuries the whole of the breasts were often exposed in the unmarried (*Plate* 13), a fashion which a contemporary condemned as " an exorbitant and shameful enormity." We have to remember, however, that at that time girls were married at fifteen or so, the exhibition being in fact to indicate their virginity ; nor did they often appear at social functions in the presence of strangers. This fashion is frequently depicted in sepulchral monuments, as in the Tansfield tomb, Burford church. The complete exposure of the breasts disappeared as the marriage age advanced, but partial exposure of the bosom in varying degrees has continued in evening dress though never in day. Thomas Nashe, in his *Christs Teares over Jerusalem*, 1593, severely criticises the English ladies of his day, thus : " Their heads, with their top and top-gallant lawn baby caps, and snowresembled silvery curlings, they make a plain puppet stage of. Their breasts they embusk up on high, and their round roseate buds immodestly lay forth, to shew at their hands there is fruit to be hoped. In their curious antic-woven garments, they imitate and mock the worms and adders that must eat them. They shew the swellings of their mind, in the swellings and plumpings of their apparel. . . ."

That decolletage was a pronounced fashion of the evening dress during the Victorian era, in spite of the prudery which distinguished the day costume, is evidence that exposure of a sex-attractive feature in the appropriate circumstances is compatible with the strictest conventions. It illustrates the singular power so many possess of being able to exercise an instinct while disapproving of its existence. We may contrast the degree of exposure permitted in that great age of prudery with the modern practice when the natural shape is so familiar that the evening dress has no surprises.

The decolletage practised ever since the fifteenth century has varied both in degree and type. We distinguish between the " square cut " opening, the " V " and the *corsage en cœur* in which the sides of the opening are covered to produce a heart shape. Very occasionally, as may be seen in some brasses of the fifteenth century, this last outline may be reversed, the central point looking upwards (e.g. in the brass, *Plate 4b*, of Elizabeth Clere at Stokesby church, Norfolk, date 1488).[1] The square opening, which is familiar in Holbein's portraits was a Renaissance mode of the first half of the sixteenth century, borrowed from Italy ; its somewhat hard horizontal line imparts a severity to the costume and, as it appears to add to the breadth of the upper part of the chest, it seldom suits the English type. Consequently it has not been a popular mode in this

[1] The absence of erotic symbols in mediæval costume is striking ; perhaps the early marriage age and the absence of choice of husband made furtive allusions of the sort unnecessary. The very low decolletage of the fifteenth century may be seen in the effigies round the tomb of the Earl of Warwick at Warwick (1460) ; in that of the Countess of Westmoreland at Brancepeth church, Durham (1485) ; and in that of the Countess of Arundel (*Plate* 3) at Arundel (1487).

country.[1] Its effect, however, is entirely altered when the transverse line is drawn right across below the shoulders as seen in the fashion of the bertha in the period of Charles the Second and its Victorian revival between 1840 and 1860.

Then the head and shoulders seemed to be emerging from a dress which was about to slip down off the chest altogether, and we may suppose that gave the fashion an attraction of its own. The line of the Victorian bertha was " as low as possible " so as to reveal those champagne-bottle shoulders which were so much admired ; but the cut of the bodice was definitely distracting.

The " V " opening, which can be detected as a tentative experiment in the last half of the fifteenth century, was then the initial stage towards becoming the " open robe " of the sixteenth, in which the bodice was open to the waist over a stomacher or under-robe. Since that time the " V " has frequently been used as a pointer towards the small waist, notably in the Gothic designs of the Early Victorian period, varied by the opening *en cœur* imitating the natural curves of the breasts. Innumerable variations and modifications of these types have been used, perhaps the most singular being the deep U-shaped opening of the Jacobean period.

Here, then, is—or has been—a fashion which illustrates on what flimsy foundations our standards of " decency " stand, a fashion which would be highly indelicate in one epoch and perfectly respectable in another, which would be shocking to propriety in the day costume but which becomes correct at nightfall, exposing an area of skin which the modern girl would

---

[1]The square opening of woman's dress began to appear before the Tudors. It may be seen in the effigy of Lady Crosby (see Chap. I) and also in the effigy of Joan of Navarre, the second wife of Henry IV, in Canterbury cathedral, the date of which is about 1420.

consider indecent but which her grandmother would have thought ladylike.

Allied to the art of exposure by decolletage is the art of displaying the shape of the bosom by the moulding of the dress over it. This modification has been practised from the fourteenth century and is perhaps even more sex-attractive than decolletage. The emphasis which the Art of Costume has always devoted to that region reflects the importance which men have attached to it.

That admiration, whether expressed in the plainer language of Pepys or Smollett or in the more genteel Victorian phrases—" he thought he had never seen such a beauty—such a bust—such an arm—such a waist " (from *Ask Mamma*, by Surtees, 1858), has never been wanting.

Although the bosom—that is, the shape of the breasts or in modern phraseology " the figure," has very naturally provided the principal region except the face in which the art of sex-attraction could be practised, other regions too have often been exploited for that purpose.

These, by the simple device of partial or complete concealment except from the favoured few, are thereby given a power of sex-appeal which they do not intrinsically possess. Under such circumstances the Art of Costume will devote inordinate attention to those regions for the time being and then allow them to lapse into comparative neglect. Conversely such regions may have a reign of varying duration as areas to be exposed, either bare of covering or but thinly veiled.

We may now consider some of these, always bearing in mind that areas bereft of covering do not necessarily imply sex-appeal. Bare legs may merely mean—no stockings available.

The head is naturally the most important region and presents a curious paradox ; part, the face, is always bare and part is always covered, by the hair, with in addition some form of headgear. Up to the middle of last century, to be more precise, a woman of any social standing was seldom without some kind of head covering except during most of the seventeenth century.

Indoors a cap by day and in the evening some sort of headdress was the rule, as though the head without any covering would be too intimate a spectacle to reveal. And yet between 1620 and 1690 women were bareheaded even out of doors quite in the modern fashion. Under such circumstances elaborate attention is paid to hairdressing to make the hair as attractive as any headgear could be.

The device of veiling the face in order to accentuate the privilege of exposing it to the favoured few has often been practised for special occasions, as at the masked ball, but the Victorian era introduced the notion of wearing a veil out of doors by day : this, however, rapidly became more of a class distinction than a sex-attractive device.

In a still greater measure the principle of veiling a region has been applied to the neck, especially behind. Even when in evening dress the front of the neck might be bare the back of it would be shielded, perhaps only symbolically, by a neck ruff, a Medici collar, a border of lace or frilling, by a large bow or even by the hair itself arranged to protect that region with its erotic associations.

On the other hand attempts to break down this particular form of reticence have never been very successful, and the notorious " backless dress " fashion which followed the first Great War, surviving nearly to the Second, had the disadvantage, obvious to all except the wearer, that its effect on the spectator could not be gauged by the woman practising it. It had been preceded towards the close of the Napoleonic wars by a similar fashion ; thus in 1813 it was reported " that old-fashioned article a shoulder strap is entirely exploded and the fullest style of dress is to be nearly naked."

But three years later the truth was admitted with refreshing candour : " The disgusting and frightful fashion of showing the backbones is disappearing. Have not many men declared that they are tired of looking at naked women ? " The same sort of comment was audible fifteen years ago.

The arm bare to the shoulder has only once been a fashion—that is, during the period of the " backless dress " when any form of nudity was acceptable. For the first time also the arm was seen bare to the shoulder in the day dress.

But we have to distinguish between exposures for the purpose of sex-attraction and those for some other reason ; thus, the elbow sleeve in the day dress may have an elaborate lace ruffle, as in the eighteenth century (*Plate* 17) ; we deduce a form of attraction. Or it may be perfectly plain, as in the day dress of to-day. We deduce this is for convenience in work.

Reference has already been made in a previous chapter to the significance of the small hand and glove. The attraction exerted by the covering of the hand has often been rivalled by the covering of the foot and ankle. As features of attraction these do not seem to have been considered until the knitted stocking of Elizabethan times replaced the clumsy cloth covering ; the knitted stocking allowed the shape of the foot and ankle to be shown, discreetly, in a graceful way, and the ornamental " clock " at the ankle—originally a utilitarian device for concealing the seam—is itself presumptive evidence that this was meant to be shown at appropriate moments. When, for example, we find such " clocks " drawn on sepulchral brasses (such as on that to Martha Knapp, St. Peter's church, Ipswich, dated 1604), we can hardly suppose it was accidental.

The shortening of the skirt about 1610 heralded an

era of elaborately decorated stockings, and also those poetic outbursts such as Suckling's familiar line, " Her feet beneath her petticoat like little mice stole in and out," and Herrick's " tempestuous petticoat," which, with similar sweet disorders, he admits, " do more bewitch me than when art is too precise in every part."

The foot exposure led at the Restoration to the high-heeled shoe which has ever since recurred from time to time as a fashion, though perhaps not necessarily as a sex-attractive device. Thus, it emphasises the arch of the foot, and a Victorian lady was heard to declare that a high arched foot was evidence of good family. " The Lower Orders all have flat feet." But the high heel also fore-shortens the foot and so appears to make it look small—that is, more attractive because it is less like a man's foot.

We have to note that clocks tended to disappear from stockings as soon as the ankles became constantly visible, and as the leg up to the knee is now habitually seen it has lost its former magic in spite of efforts to sustain it by painted toenails and artificial tanning. The game of croquet in the '60's provided opportunities for a happy blend of " exposure " and " concealment," a writer in '67 remarking : " One of the chief reasons of the pleasure men take in the game is the sight of a neatly turned ankle and pretty boots." The sentiment is repeated, in Disraelian phraseology, in the pages of *Lothair* : " The players themselves, the prettiest of all the spectacle, with their coquettish hats, and their half-veiled and half-revealed under-raiment, scarlet and silver, or blue and gold, made up a sparkling and modish scene." (1870.)

Enough has been said to indicate how exposure and concealment have been, as it were, played off one against the other, region bidding against region for attention until presently both are eclipsed by a rival attraction brought to the surface by a turn of Fashion's wheel.

If the fashions of some past epoch are studied it is possible to determine wherein lay their power of attraction, what region was temporarily in the ascendant and whether the method was exposure or concealment. We can hardly do justice to the Art of Costume unless we first establish its purpose and methods of obtaining it.[1]

The third form which sex-attraction can adopt, in addition to exposure and concealment, is the method of allusion. This likewise may be localised or general ; some particular sex feature may be recalled either in the design of the dress or in its pattern. Not infrequently modern dress materials display breast and buttock patterns and even phallic symbols though naturally they are not recognised as such.

A less debatable form of local allusion is the kind of artifice which draws the eye towards a particular region such as the small waist or the configuration of the hips. For this purpose lines of trimming and the like may serve as pointers ; indeed it may be said that all noticeable lines in a dress are usually of this nature. Similarly brilliant patches of colour serve the same purpose so that whenever a costume exhibits these sorts of signals it is not difficult to detect their meaning. In short, they aim at first catching the eye and then leading it towards the most captivating region.

More interesting because less crude are allusions of a general nature and of these there have been many. Thus, a century ago feminine fashions aimed at imparting an air of helpless prettiness which no doubt appealed to the man of that day. Fashions of the present time are stamped with the spirit of youth, health and vigour, and the costume of the modern girl alludes to these features in unmistakable ways.

Not by any means have feminine fashions invariably

---

[1] The buttoned sleeve from elbow to wrist, so commonly seen in brasses of the fourteenth and fifteenth centuries, could hardly have been for use but rather to catch the eye and draw attention to the shape of the forearm in its close-fitting sleeve (*Plates* 1, 2, 4*a*).

favoured youth. The Edwardian styles were essentially to suit the mature configuration, and the same might be said of the bustle era. The large trained skirt (*Plate* 33) seems to require a woman of a certain age, and there have often been modes which we find difficult to associate with immaturity. If we attempt to analyse that impression we shall, I think, instinctively think of the typical Regency dress as belonging to a much more youthful generation than do, let us say, the dresses of the late Victorian period.

Yet the charm of the former is not æsthetic ; the Regency dress with its narrow skirt and its fantastically high waist breaks the laws of proportion ; its outline is hard and its shape ungraceful. But when worn by an appropriate model it always excites admiration, though it may not win much when hung in a museum case. It is evident that its attraction is in its emphasis on the youth of the wearer.

To come to more recent times, if we look at the dresses, especially those worn by day, of the period 1925-30, we can hardly fail to recognise the marked accent on youthfulness. The knee-length skirt, the " schoolboy " build of figure to say nothing of the bobbed hair, supplied a very suitable setting for a rising generation in a new world, but it was a mode which was attractive only when the wearer was immature.

Show such costumes to the girl of to-day and they will be taken for schoolgirls' dresses.

The fact that the fashions of an epoch seem designed to suit best women of a particular age—from the proverbial " seventeen to thirty-seven "—implies that that was the age of greatest attraction in that epoch ; in other words, masculine inclination is drawn towards different ages in different epochs. For the last thirty years at least it has been very markedly towards youth, even immaturity.

But it also seems that different epochs have their ideal types of women, to judge from contemporary fiction and other sources. Those types actually face us in the pages of *Punch* from the pencil of Leech, du Maurier and their successors. As we look at them it is hard to realise that they and the modern generation are of the same race. And it is precisely those degrees of difference which indicate the variations in the prevailing sex-appeal. The difference is largely due—to the Art of Costume.

Never has this Art forgotten its primitive function, to attract Man, and, we may add, never has it failed to accomplish its purpose.

When, however, we compare its methods in the costume of the two sexes it is remarkable how much more variable has been the feminine than the masculine. The ideal man's costume has presented a more uniform picture. Though he wears different kinds of clothes his essential build persists from century to century ; Roderick Random, Rawdon Crawley and the latest film star cause the same flutter of hearts. The part of the " manly hero " is, in theatrical phrase, a straight one ; if Nature has been kind, the Art of Costume can only add superfluous charm.

But Woman has had to play a wide range of "character parts," entailing even change of physique, now divinely tall, now cosily petite ; switching from buxom to slim, from appealingly fragile to hard-boiled.

Her adaptability to such quick-change turns amounts to genius. At the present day her methods of sex-attraction are to emphasise youth, health and physical ability in a manner generalised instead of localised. The old technique of distortion and over-emphasis has been, temporarily at least, abandoned (Cf. *Plates* 19 and 48). *See Appendix B.*

But it would be rash to assume that even two great wars would suffice to cause habits and methods centuries old to be permanently discarded. Forms of expressing the fundamental instinct of sex-attraction are governed by social conditions which indeed dictate to the Art of Costume both the materials it is to use and the style of their arrangement.

Nature still dictates the theme.

APPENDIX A

FROM *A Collection of the Dresses of Different Nations Ancient and Modern particularly Old English Dresses after the Designs of Holbein, Vandyke, Hollar . . .*, by Thomas Jeffreys, 1757 :

" . . . The Europeans are so much at liberty to follow their own fancy in the Figures and Materials of their dress, that the Habit has become a kind of Index to the Mind, and the Character is in some Particulars as easily discovered by a Man's dress as by his conversation. As to the Dresses of Women they have never been military, and therefore have never been short ; for besides the Alterations that convenience or caprice have introduced into the female Habit, there are several which have had a more latent and less innocent cause.

" The Dress of Women has long been considered as a Decoration of Beauty and an incitement to Desire ; and in this view it has been the object of much Thought, Ingenuity and Solicitude ; but it does not always appear that those who intend to multiply or secure their conquests by Dress, always knew how best to exert that power which the Choice of their Dress put into their Hands.

" When the British Lady thinks fit to dress so as to discover the whole Breast, the British Gentleman soon looks upon it with as much indifference as the naked Indian looks upon all the rest ; but if she covers it with a handkerchief and contrives this covering so that it will accidentally discover what it appears intended to hide, the Glimpse that is thus casually given immediately and forcibly seizes the Imagination, and every Motion is watched in hopes that it will be repeated ; so if by any accident a Lady discover half her Leg, the Fancy is instantly alarmed, though when the Actress appears in breeches and discovers the whole, she is the Object of indifference if not of disgust ; for the same reason the Figure of a naked Venus produces less effect than that of a dressed Figure with the petticoat raised so as to discover the garter.

" It follows that if she dresses most immodestly so as most to excite licentious Desires, she does not dress most immodestly who uncovers most of her Person, but she who covers it so that it may be accidentally seen.

" And upon this Principle it was that the Grecian Legislator when he observed that many of the Youth lived unmarried, directed the women to wear long Garments which covered the whole Person from the Shoulders to the Feet, instead of discovering all the Breast and half the Leg, and ordered that the Robe should be cut in Slashes from the Hip to the Knee so that when they stood or sate still the two sides of the Opening should fall together but should, by dividing when they walked or used any other Motion, casually discover the Parts which at other Times were concealed.

" Many changes of Female Dress will be found to proceed from unskilful Attempts to allure by discovering more and more the Person, and by the Disappointment which succeeded the Exposure and at last induced a sudden Transition to a closed Dress by which the whole Person was covered."

APPENDIX B

Mrs. Otter is described in Ben Jonson's *Silent Woman*, 1609, as having : "a most vile face and yet she spends me forty pounds a year. All her teeth were made in Blackfriars, both her eyebrows in the Strand and her hair in Silver Street. She takes herself asunder still, when she goes to bed, into some twenty boxes."

Concealing signs of age is of course a form of sex-appeal.

A hundred years later, in the eighteenth century, we find a gentleman complaining of "the modern mode of artificial eyebrows. The other night at cards I observed across the room that my wife's eyebrow had loosened in the heat and begun to shift." Drawing her attention to the catastrophe in a loud voice, he says, "she immediately uttered a loud shriek and was removed from the room in a succession of fits."

This technique of sex-appeal may be contrasted with that practised towards the close of the century, as indicated in a letter from a husband writing in 1786, describing the effect of his wife's costume : "I assure you she made such a figure the other night at Ranelagh, where all the world was assembled, that her appearance actually put me to the blush, while I was in raptures at the sight of her beauty. She was without any stays and being quite free from such an encumbrance the fine play of her easy shape was exhibited in a very advantageous light. She had nothing on but a white muslin chemise, tied carelessly with celestial blue bows : white silk slippers and slight silk stockings, to the view of every impertinent coxcomb peeping under her petticoat. Her hair hung in ringlets down to the bottom of her back and even rested upon the unnatural protuberance which every fashionable female at present chuses to affix to that part of her person."

The pendulum of sex-appeal has swung to and fro from exposing bits of the body to adding artificial bits, of which false hair is one of the most remarkable. Shiploads of bought hair, carcases of dead birds and skins of animals, adorned the prudes of the 1870's and '80's. "At a recent public assembly every third woman seemed to be painted, and eyebrows and eyelashes coloured, and false hair worn."

The padded bodice of the Victorian wedding dress, the constant advertisements for " figure improvers " and artificial bosoms with hip pads, bustles and similar contrivances for improving Nature's curvatures, composed a formidable—and on the whole a very successful —technique.

INDEX

Acting, and costume, 37
Addison, Joseph, quoted, 184
Aesthetic aspects, 37 *et seq.*;
    Movement, 47, 159
Agincourt, 8
Alpaca, 173
Angel sleeve, 98
Aniline dyes, 139, 158
Anne, Queen, 212*n.*
Anne of Bohemia, 184*n.*
Armada, 8
Art, good and bad, 3
Arundel, Countess of, 223*n.*
Austen, Jane, quoted, 213
Axis of costume, 39 *et seq.*

Back-fastening dress, 124-5
Backless dress, 194, 226-7
Balance, law of, 48-9
Balzac, Honoré de, 27
Barkley (Barclay), Alexander,
    quoted, 46
Bathing costumes, 187-8, 207-8,
    222
Battledress, 214
Beauty, and fashion, 5-6, 40;
    Wilde on, 45; and sex attrac-
    tion, 196
Beaver hats, 74*n.*
Becomingness, 37, 43-4
Bentham, Jeremy, 179
Berdewell, W., 88*n.*
Bernhardt, Sarah, 97
Bicorne hats, 73
Bishop sleeve, 99
Black Death, 169
Blanchfront, Sir J., 57*n.*
Blouse and skirt style, 90, 93,
    165, 169
Bolero, 89

Boleyn, Anne, 90*n.*
Bolton, 172
Bonnets, 11, 22, 108, 111-12, 114,
    195
Boots, 185
Bowler hats, 71, 72, 73, 76, 186
Braces, 127-8, 181
Brasses, 14, 23, 32-3, 57*n.*, 88,
    90*n.*, 108-9, 113, 114*n.*, 223
Breeches, 8, 56-7, 59, 60, 64, 65,
    127-8, 155-6, 179, 182, 190, 212,
    213
Brittany, 13
Brocades, 143, 152
Brontë, Charlotte, quoted, 213
Brummel, Beau, 77
Buckram, 180
Bulver, John, quoted, 21-2, 47
Burgundy, 13
Burney, Fanny, 212
Burnouses, 198
Bustles, 47, 126
Butterfly headdress, 23, 113
Buttons, 125-8
Byron, Lord, 76

Caen, 14
Calais, 14
Calicoes, 172
Camlet, 170
Capes, 89, 121, 123, 131
Caps, 72, 74, 117, 118, 119, 186
Caracos, 123
Casawecks, 123
Cashmere, 174
Catherine, Tsarina, 20
Cavalier costume, 58, 109
Caxton, William, quoted, 137
Charles I, King, 56, 113, 127, 151,
    171, 173

Charles II, King, 8, 113, 176, 208, 224

Chaucer, Geoffrey, 147-8, 207; quoted, 10, 47, 109, 169, 170

Check patterns, 156

Chesterfield overcoat, 121, 186

Cheviots, 174

Chimney pot hat, 67, 72, 74

Chintzes, 153, 172

Church, influence of, 8-9, 10-11, 113

Classical principle, 46, 48, 84

Clere, Elizabeth, 14n., 223

Cloaks, 98, 109, 120, 121, 122, 141, 151, 177, 198

Cloche hat, 108

Closed dress, one-piece, 86-8; two-piece, 88-90

Clothing, definition of, 3-4

Coarse materials, use of, 165

Cocked hats, 71n.

Cod-piece, 207, 209

Coleman, George, quoted, 115

Collars, 11-12, 77, 164, 186

Colour, modern use of, 68-9, 145-6, 156-7, 159-60; principles of, 133 et seq.; good taste in, 133, 160-1; warm and cold, 134-5; psychological effects of, 135-6; and lighting, 138-9; methods of using, 140 et seq.; use in costume, 147 et seq.

Cony, Thomas, quoted, 214-15

Copenhagen, 36

Corduroy, 175

Corsets, 180

Costume, primitive ideas expressed by, 3; an art, 3 et seq.; and personality, 4-5, 13, 31, 43-4; modesty in, 7-9; distinction of sexes in, 9-10; factors in development of, 14-15; acme of, 15-16; symbolism in, 17 et seq.; sources of information, 31 et seq., 147, 170; painters and period, 31-2; aesthetic

aspects of, 37 et seq.; principles of form, 46 et seq.; basic formulae of, 50; form in man's, 55 et seq.; male headgear, 70 et seq.; form in woman's, 79 et seq.; descriptive terms, 84-5; woman's sleeve and glove, 94 et seq.; woman's headgear, 105 et seq.; indoor headgear and hair-dressing, 112-19; accessory garments, 120-4; fastenings, 124-8; fashion revivals, 128-32; principles of colour, 133-46; use of colour in, 147-62; texture and materials, 163-75; mobility in, 176-91; principles of sex-attraction, 192-205; sex-attraction in man's, 206-17; sex-attraction in woman's, 218-36

Cotehardie, 9n., 25, 59, 87

Cotton, 171-2, 173

Coventry, 171

Cravats, 64, 77

Crecy, battle of, 29

Crinolines, 35, 39, 83, 123, 198

Croquet dress, 188

Crosby, Lady, 14n., 224n.

Cuff links, 127

Cuffs, 61, 164, 181

Cummerbund, 179

Cut, 42-3

Cutaway coat, 185

Damask, 143

Decency, standards of, 7-8, 192-3

Decolletage, 222 et seq.

Defoe, Daniel, quoted, 153

Devonshire, Georgiana Cavendish, Duchess of, 110, 116, 126

Dickens, Charles, 67; quoted, 198

Dinner jacket, 186

Disraeli, Benjamin, 155; quoted, 228

Dolmans, 98, 122

D'Orsay, Count, 40, 65
Double dress style, 87-8
Doublets, 23, 56, 127, 169, 209
Dress shirts, 191
Dressing-gown, 157
Dyes, 139, 158

Ecclesiastical vestments, 17, 149
Echyngham, Elizabeth, 114*n.*
Edict of Nantes, Revocation of, 171
Edward II, King, 10, 148
Edward III, King, 10, 169
Edward IV, King, 143
Edward VII, King, 28
Efficiency and sex attraction, 51-2
Elephant sleeves, 99*n.*
Embroidery, 150-1
Empire dress, 32
Erotic symbols, 11, 17, 18, 19, 25-7, 220, 223*n.*, 229
Etiquette, sartorial, 27-8, 76, 124, 179-80, 185-6
Eton crop, 105
Euphemisms, 197-9
Evening dress, male, 210-11; female, 219, 223
Exhibitionism, 199 *et seq.*, 221 *et seq.*
Eyebrow plucking, 23, 106

Face, the attention paid to, 22-3, 105-7
Falding, 170
False hair, 114, 116, 236
Farthingales, 24, 53, 58, 88, 131
Fashion, and beauty, 5-6, 40; definition of, 6; plates, 33-4; journals, 35-6; evolution of, 119; revivals, 128-32; and mobility, 177 *et seq.*
Fashionable, meaning of, 38
Fastenings, types of, 124-8
Feathers, use of, 164*n.*
Fit, 43

Flannel, 174
Fontages, 115
Form, principles of, 46 *et seq.*; in man's costume, 55 *et seq.*; in woman's costume, 79 *et seq.*; other factors affecting, 120 *et seq.*; and colour, 142, 144, 162
Fourment, Hélène, 32
French hood, 114
Frieze, 170
Frock coats, 63, 67, 68, 76, 155
Frocks, 85, 86
Fuller, Thomas, quoted, 171
Fur, use of, 168
Fustian, 169

Gainsborough, Thomas, 31
Garibaldi jacket, 29
Garters, 127, 152
Genoa velvet, 171
George II, King, 77
Gilbert, Sir William, quoted, 28-9
Glasgow, 172
Gloves, 11, 19, 101 *et seq.*, 136*n.*, 152, 188, 209-10, 227
Goldsmith, Oliver, 211
Gothic principle, 46 *et seq.*, 84
Gowns, 85, 86, 87
Gray, W. de, 114*n.*
Greenland, period costumes found in, 36, 97
Grey, Sir Henry, 33

Hair-dressing, 70, 75, 105 *et seq.*; and indoor headgear, 112 *et seq.*
Harris, Lord, 28
Hardie, Keir, 186
Haweis, Mary, 47; quoted, 158
Headgear, man's, 62, 70 *et seq.*; male and female compared, 75; woman's, 105 *et seq.*, 186, 225-6
Heart-shaped headdress, 113
Heather mixture, 140
Hennin, 13-14
Henry IV, King, 224*n.*

Henry VI, King, 148
Henry VII, King, 130
Henry VIII, King, 8, 56, 176
Heraldry, 148, 149
Herrick, Robert, quoted, 228
Hetherington, James, 73
High heels, 182
Hobble skirt, 82, 132, 186
Hogarth, William, 39
Holbein, Hans, 223
Holinshed, Raphael, quoted, 21
Homosexuality, 51
Hoops, 21, 126, 186
Horned headdress, 113
Houppelande, 21, 56 and n., 87, 98
Hudson, Thomas, 32
Hue, definition of, 135
Hunting costumes, 184-5, 186
Hysterical fashions, 6

Illuminated manuscripts, 32,
    147, 178, 184
Illumination, natural and
    artificial, 138-9
Indoor headgear, 112 et seq.
Inverness cloak, 121n.
Isabella, Queen, 10

James I, King, 214
Jeffreys, Joyce, 15n.
Jeffreys, Thomas, quoted, 233-5
Jersey costume, 189
Jester's costume, 141
Joan of Navarre, 224n.
Joan, Princess, 9n.
Jonson, Ben, quoted, 136, 235

Kelly, Francis, 14, 33; quoted, 49
Kemp, William, quoted, 126
Keriell, Jane, 109n.
Kerseymere, 174
Kilts, 56
Kilvert, Rev. Francis, quoted, 208
Kirtle, 87
Knapp, Martha, 227
Knickerbockers, 188

Lace collars, 11
Lacing, 125
Langtry, Lily, 189
Laver, James, 53
Leg of mutton sleeve, 99, 100, 130
Legs, emancipation of male, 56
    et seq., 119
Lidgate (Lydgate), John, quoted,
    137
Line, 38 et seq.
Linen, 172
Linsey-woolsey, 170
Livery, 148
Lounge suit, 61, 67, 68, 74, 190
Lytton, Lord, 65

Manchester, 171
Mantles, 98, 122, 123, 198
Mantlets, 123, 157
Marie Stuart cap, 114, 131
Mary, Queen, 21
Masculinity, display of, 7-8, 21-2,
    47, 58-9, 200-1; see also Sex
    attraction
Materials and texture, 163-75
Mauntell, Sir W., 109n.
Mercer, John, 172n.
Military uniforms, and mobility,
    183-4
Mobility in costume, 176 et seq.
Monochrome costume, 140, 143-4
Morality, and exhibitionism, 201
More, Hannah, quoted, 115
Morning gown, 156
Morris, William, 131, 205
Mortimer, Roger de, first Earl
    of March, 10
Mourning, 18, 135-6
Mummers, 148
Muslin, 172, 173
Musterdevilis, 170

Nashe, Thomas, quoted, 222-3
Neck, coverings for, 76-8, 114,
    226
Neckbands, 77

Neckties, 25, 167
Nevinson, J. L., quoted, 150-1
New Look, 131-2
Newmarket overcoat, 121
Norfolk jacket, 185, 186
Norwich, 169, 171
Norwich, W., 90n.

O'Brien, Lady Susan, quoted, 197
Occupation shown by costume, 3, 11-12, 17
Open dress principle, 90-2
Ornaments on hair, 116, 236
Overcoats, 120-1, 186
Oxford mixture, 174

Padded shoulders, 22
Painters, and period costumes, 31-2; and colour, 147
Paisley, 172
Paletot, 67
Pantaloons, 156
Paradin, —, quoted, 21
Par-dessus, 120, 121, 123
Paston, Margaret, 147
Pediment headdress, 114
Pelerines, 123
Pelisse, 85, 92, 123
Pepys, Samuel, 136n., 211, 225; quoted, 57, 115, 152
Peryent, Joan, 109n.
Petticoat-breeches, 57, 209
Petticoats, multiple, 126
Photographs, 35
Picture hat, 110
Piebald colouring, 145, 148
Planché, J. R., 130
Platinum blondes, 115
Plumpton, Sir W., 136
Polkas, 123
Polonaise dress, 130-1
Polychrome costume, 140-2, 143-4
Postmen, uniform of, 19
Primitive man and costume, 3
Prince of Wales' feathers, 29

Prudery, 196 et seq., 223
Prynne, William, quoted, 116
Pyjamas, 156

Radiance, definition of, 163
Raglan overcoat, 121, 186
Raleigh, Sir Walter, 214
Ramsay, Allan, 32
Redingcote, 85, 92
Religion, influence of, 8-9, 10-11
Revival of costume forms, 128-32
Reynolds, Sir Joshua, 31
Rhinegrave, 57
Ribbons, 173
Richard II, King, 184
Riding habit, 9n., 184-5, 186
Robes, 90-2, 156, 224
Romantic Movement, 130, 131
Rubens dress, 31-2
Ruffles, 11, 164, 181
Ruffs, 23-4, 58, 76, 77, 179
Russells, 170
Russet, 170

Sad colours, 151-2
St. Leger, R., 23n.
Samite, 170
Satin, use of, 167
Saxony, 174
Scent, male use of, 209-10
Scholastic costume, 17, 20, 21, 28, 70
Scott, Sir Walter, 131
Sex attraction, 3, 4, 7-8, 49 et seq., 58-9, 64, 79, 80, 87, 94, 95, 102, 103, 118-19, 125, 157, 161-2, 187, 189; in fourteenth century, 9-10; principles of, 192-205; in man's costume, 206-17; in woman's costume, 218-36
Shade, definition of, 135
Shawls, 123, 157, 198
Shoes, 19, 21-2, 28, 64, 152, 179, 182, 191, 210, 211
Side-saddles, 184
Signet rings, 210

Silk, hats, 73-4; use of, 170-1, 173
Single dress style, 86-7
Skating costume, 189
Skirts, 12, 20, 25, 31, 53, 80, 83, 86, 158-9, 183, 186, 189, 198, 230
Sleeves, 21, 39, 49, 60-2, 94 *et seq.*, 180-1, 182, 189, 227, 229*n.*
Slippers, 156
Smartness, definition of, 38, 41, 42, 43
Smock frock, 177
Smollett, Tobias, 225
Social rank expressed by costume 3, 11-12, 17, 28-9, 80-1, 102-3, 161
Sock-suspenders, 128*n.*
Spencer, Hon. John, 211
Spencer jacket, 123
Spitalfields, 171
Sports costumes, 15, 184 *et seq.*
Stapleton, Sir Miles, 90*n.*
Starched collars, 11-12, 76, 77
Steele, Sir Richard, 211
Steeple headdress, 13-14, 113
Stockings, 64, 127, 155, 189, 227-8
Stocks, 77
Straw hats, 72, 110
Strutt, Joseph, quoted, 116-17
Stubs, Philip, quoted, 47
Stylish, meaning of, 37, 38
Suckling, Sir John, quoted, 228
Sugar-loaf hats, 109*n.*
Sumptuary laws, 11, 28, 207
Sunday best, 11
Surcoat, 57*n.*, 97
Surtout, 67, 155
Swift, Jonathan, quoted, 110
Swiss belt, 89
Symbolism, 17 *et seq.*, 135-6, 203

Tailor-mades, 15, 82, 140, 166
Tapestries, 32, 33
Teagown, 91
Tennis costume, 7, 188, 189, 215
Terry velvet, 171
Texture and materials, 163-75

Thackeray, W. M., 193
Thread, gold and silver, 172
Tilt of hats, 74-5, 107-8
Tint, definition of, 135
Tippets, 97
Tone, definition of, 135
Top hats, 185, 186
Toques, 109
Tricorne hats, 73
Trophy symbols, 29
Trousers, 59, 60, 66, 128, 155, 156, 165, 169, 174
Trunks, 169
Tubular dress, 82
Tunics, 87-8
Tweeds, 174

Ugliness in costume, 5
Underclothing, amount of woman's, 92-3; display of, 195, 202
Urswyk, Sir Thomas, 14*n.*

Valois collars, 131
Van Meteren, —, quoted, 109
Veils, 20, 22, 226
Velvet, 171, 173
Vergil, Polydore, quoted, 14
Victoria, Queen, 44
Vicuna, 174
Visites, 123

Waistcoats, 25, 27, 63, 64, 65, 67, 127, 155, 156, 167, 174, 177, 191, 212
Waistline, 49-50, 65, 81-2, 154
Wall-paintings, 147
Walking dress, 15, 187
Walpole, Horace, quoted, 126
Walsingham, Thomas, quoted, 14
War, effects of, 155
Warwick, Richard Neville, Earl of, 148
Waterloo, battle of, 29, 74*n.*
Watteau sacque, 85

Wealth, display of, 18 *and n.*, 211, 214

Weddings, symbolism at, 20, 136

Westmoreland, Countess of, 14*n.*, 223*n*

Wigs, 20, 22, 70, 77, 117, 181

Wilde, Oscar, quoted, 45

Wimple, 22

Wool, use of, 169-70, 173

Worsteds, 169, 174

Wrist watches, 128*n*.

Wycherley, William, quoted, 57

Yelverton, Julia, 33